The Collected Poems of
Amy Carmichael

Mountain Breezes

The Collected Poems of Amy Carmichael

CHRISTIAN • LITERATURE • CRUSADE
FORT WASHINGTON, PENNSYLVANIA 19034

CHRISTIAN LITERATURE CRUSADE
U.S.A.
P.O. Box 1449, Fort Washington, PA 19034

with publishing programs also in:
GREAT BRITAIN
51 The Dean, Alresford, Hants., SO24 9BJ

AUSTRALIA
P.O. Box 419M, Manunda, QLD 4879

NEW ZEALAND
10 MacArthur Street, Feilding

hardcover edition: ISBN 0-87508-790-6
paperback edition: ISBN 0-87508-789-2

Body text set in *Gilde*

This Printing 1999

Printed in the United States of America

Contents

Introduction

Amy Carmichael was born on December 16, 1867 in a gray stone house in the village of Millisle on the north coast of Ireland. Below the Carmichael house, close by the seashore, stands to this day a row of old stone cottages with low doors, thick walls, and small paned windows. In the street that runs along by those cottages are the water pumps and the iron rings set into the stones to which horses were tied. It is not hard for a visitor at the end of the twentieth century to imagine a little girl, wrapped in a woolen shawl, trying to hurry along the street with her little brother while carrying a pot of soup sent by their mother for one of the poor cottagers. The child of a loving family, she was learning to reach out in love to others.

The love which formed the climate of the Carmichael home was a sinewy one, without the least trace of sentimentality, holding the *conviction* of her father's side of the family (David Carmichael was a descendant of the Scottish Covenanters) and the *courage* of her mother's side (Catherine Jane Filson was the great-granddaughter of one whose name in Gaelic meant "I dare").

The Carmichael children were far from pampered, accustomed as they were to an ordered home and rugged winters on that cold sea. Amy, eldest of the seven, learned early that love and obedience are inseparable, as Jesus taught His disciples: "*If you love me, you will obey what I command.*" No-nonsense principles of discipline included a flat ebony ruler called a pandy, administered as needed to small posteriors. Even worse was a dose of Gregory powder, to swallow which a child had to stand still, hold out his hand at once and not pull it away, to make no fuss, and finally to say politely, "Thank you, Mother." Such treatment put iron into the Carmichael souls.

Amy gave herself unconditionally to Christ, longing to do whatever He might appoint. She went first to Japan but suffered from something called "Japan head," and was told that she could not withstand the climate. Following a short term in Ceylon, she landed at last in India in November of 1895. She studied Tamil, then organized a band of deeply dedicated Christian Indian women called "The Starry Cluster," who traveled from village to village by bullock cart to carry the gospel to women who knew nothing of Christ.

Amy was aghast when she learned of the hideous underground traffic in little children who were given or sold to Hindu temples for the purpose of prostitution, from which there was never the possibility of escape. One day, however, a little girl appeared as Amy was having her "tiffin" (early-morning tea) on the veranda. The child was led, it seems, by an angel. There was no other explanation. The child verified the terrible truth about temple servitude, and Amy began what became known as the Dohnavur Fellowship of South India. Here children, through prayer and sacrifice, were saved one by one from a life of terrible wickedness and suffering. The work continues to this day with more than four hundred children, cared for by single Indian women.

"Amma," as she was called (a term of respect for a woman), wrote a great variety of poems, but their contents clearly reveal a stout-hearted soul: "From silken self, O Captain, free Thy soldier who would follow Thee"; a willingness to take up the Cross: "From all that dims Thy Calvary, O Lamb of God, deliver me"; and an uncompromising determination to be consumed on the altar of sacrificial love: "Make me Thy fuel, Flame of God."

Amy Carmichael remained in Dohnavur without a single furlough until she died on January 18, 1951. She was buried in what is called "God's Garden." A bird table is the only marker.

"This is love: that we walk in obedience to His commands. As you have heard from the beginning, His command is that you walk in love" (2 John 6).

When asked what it was that drew them to Amy Carmichael, the answer given by those who knew her best was nearly always "It was love. Amma loved us."

*Elisabeth Elliot**

* *Author of the Amy Carmichael biography* A Chance to Die, *published in 1987 by Revell.*

Preface

It is a sad fact that many of Amy Carmichael's most moving poems are now found only in volumes long out of print. To remedy this situation is one of the goals of this publication. To make more accessible the many bits of poetry—usually untitled *in situ*—scattered throughout her various works of prose is another. But above all, we the editors wish to more adequately display both the depth and breadth of her saintly insights. For though they span nearly 55 years of her remarkable life, they are timeless.

Some of these 568 poems may strike the careful reader as (to use Amy's words) "not perfected"—but we are convinced they are a mere minority. (Can every sentiment of even the greatest muse be graded above average?) Most of her verses we find to be not only mature but truly discerning and stirring to the spirit. Some we regard as genuine masterpieces, both as to form and content—and we trust you will come to the same conclusion.

Much effort has been taken to title the poems and to group them by theme, so as to increase their helpfulness to the heart yearning for a closer walk with Christ. Accordingly, we have divided them under seven major heads: Worship, Petition, Surrender, Ministry, Wartime, Encouragement, and Youthful Thoughts. Many of the poems, of course, overflow the bounds of their designated category—for who can contain the zephyrs which sweep refreshingly across a mountainous terrain? And such are these "mountain breezes."

It is our desire and hope that the same Spirit who moved the heart of His servant to express herself in these vibrant stanzas will captivate your heart and mind also as you enter into the cascade of these inspiring words.

Robert Delancy
Elinor Rogers
Joann Longton

Reference Abbreviations and Book Titles

ACD .... Amy Carmichael of Dohnavur
BT .... Buds and Teddies
CD .... Candles in the Dark
DS .... Dohnavur Songs
EHW .... Edges of His Ways
FF .... From the Forest
FSL .... From Sunrise Land
FT .... Figures of the True
FTR .... Fragments That Remain
GBM .... Gold by Moonlight
GC .... Gold Cord
GM .... God's Missionary
K .... Kohila
LB .... Lotus Buds
MB .... Meal in a Barrel
MP .... Made in the Pans
NS .... Nor Scrip
P .... Pans
PVV .... Pools and the Valley of Vision
PU .... Ploughed Under
RFB .... Rose From Brier
RSP .... Ragland, Spiritual Pioneer
TG .... Thou Givest . . . They Gather
TJ .... Toward Jerusalem
TMS .... Though the Mountains Shake
Unp .... Unpublished
WHP .... Whispers of His Power
Wd .... Windows
Wg[1] .... Wings, Part 1
Wg[2] .... Wings, Part 2

Take This Book

Take this book in Thy wounded hand,
    Jesus, Lord of Calvary;
Let it go forth at Thy command;
    Use it as it pleaseth Thee.

Dust of the earth, but Thy dust, Lord;
    Blade of grass, in Thy hand a sword—
Nothing, nothing unless it be
    Purged and quickened, O Lord, by Thee.

ACD, GC

1 Poems of Worship

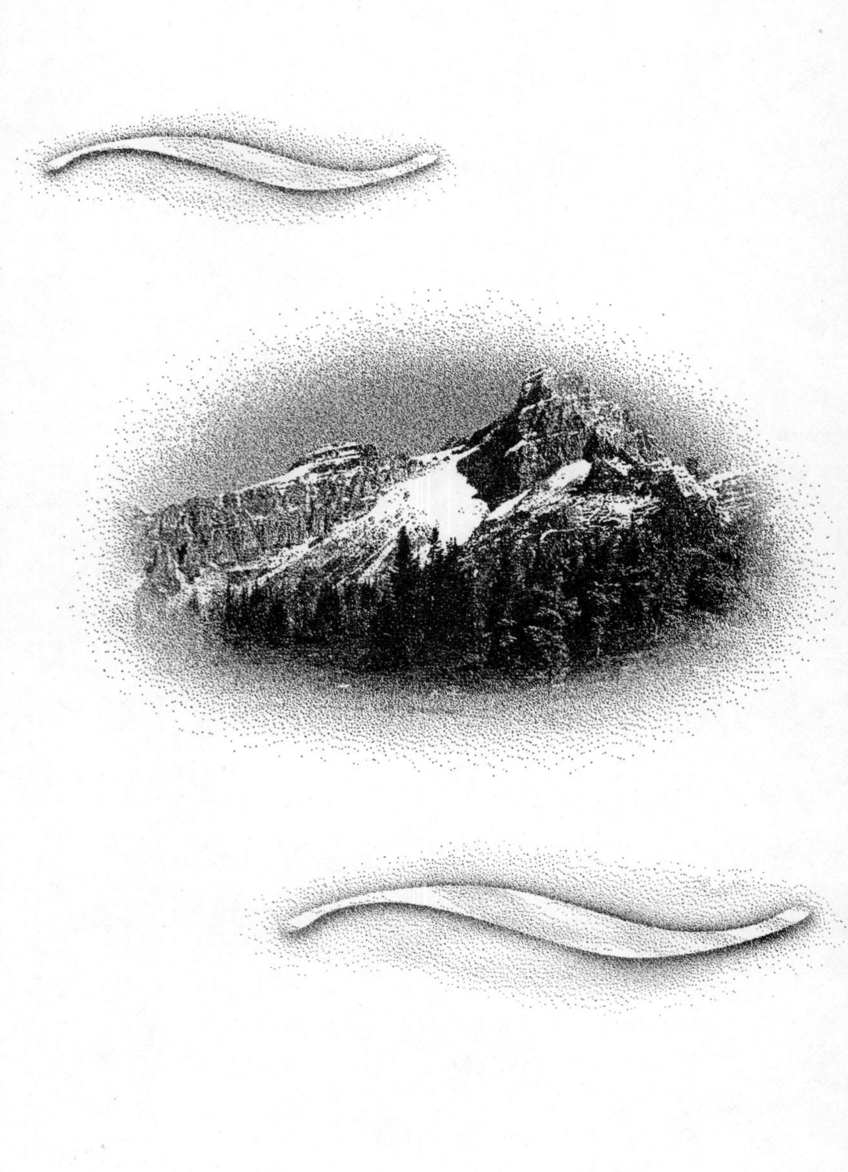

God of the Stars

I am the God of the stars.
They do not lose their way;
Not one do I mislay.
Their times are in My Hand;
They move at My command.

I am the God of the stars,
Today, as yesterday,
The God of thee and thine,
Less thine they are than Mine;
And shall Mine go astray?

I am the God of the stars.
Lift up thine eyes and see
As far as mortal may
Into Eternity;
And stay thy heart on Me.

ACD, TMS, Wg[1]

So Near

Below, above, around thee everywhere—
So is My love, like clearness of blue air.

To find the air so high and yet so low,
Tell Me, belovèd, hast thou far to go?

• • • • •

So high, so low—but I had thought Thee far,
Remote, aloof, like glory of a star.

And is the way of love so near to me?
Then by that way I come; I come to Thee.

GBM

Not Far to Go

It is not far to go,
For Thou art near;
It is not far to go,
For Thou art here;
And not by traveling, Lord,
Men come to Thee,
But by the way of love;
And we love Thee.

EHW, GC

God of the Nebulae

Lover of all, I hold me fast by Thee,
Ruler of time, King of eternity.
There is no great with Thee; there is no small,
For Thou art all, and fillest all in all.

The new-born world swings forth at Thy command;
The falling dewdrop falls into Thy hand.
God of the firmament's mysterious powers,
I see Thee thread the minutes of my hours.

I see Thee guide the frail, the fading moon
That walks alone through empty skies at noon.
Was ever way-worn, lonely traveler
But had Thee by him, blessèd Comforter?

Out of my vision swims the untracked star;
Thy counsels, too, are high and very far.
Only I know, God of the nebulae,
It is enough to hold me fast by Thee.

P, PVV, TJ, Wg[1]

Brooding Blue

Lord of the brooding blue
Of pleasant summer skies,
Lord of each little bird
That through the clear air flies,
'Tis wonderful to me
That I am loved by Thee.

Lord of the blinding heat,
Of mighty wind and rain,
The city's crowded street,
Desert and peopled plain,
'Tis wonderful to me
That I am loved by Thee.

Lord of night's jeweled roof,
Day's various tapestry,
Lord of the warp and woof
Of all that yet shall be,
'Tis wonderful to me
That I am loved by Thee.

Lord of my merry cheers,
My grey that turns to gold,
And my most private tears
And comforts manifold,
'Tis wonderful to me
That I am loved by Thee.

ACD, DS, TJ

Surprising Love

How often, Lord, our grateful eyes
    Have seen what Thou hast done;
How often does Thy love surprise
    From dawn to set of sun.

How often has a gracious rain
    On Thine inheritance
When it was weary, wrought again
    An inward radiance.

Thou who upon the heavens dost ride,
    What miracle of love
Brings Thee more swiftly to our side
    Than even thought can move?

Our love is like a little pool;
    Thy love is like the sea;
O beautiful, O wonderful,
    How noble Love can be.

EHW, Wg[1]

Immanence

Have we not seen Thy shining garment's hem
Floating at dawn across the golden skies;
Through thin blue veils at noon, bright majesties;
Seen starry hosts delight to gem
The splendor that shall be Thy diadem?

O Immanence, that knows no far nor near,
But as the air we breathe is with us here,
Our Breath of Life, O Lord, we worship Thee.

Worship and laud and praise Thee evermore;
Look up in wonder, and behold a door
Opened in heaven, and One set on a throne:
Stretch out a hand, and touch Thine own,
O Christ, our King, our Lord whom we adore.

P, RFB, TJ

Expectancy

The mountains hold their breath;
The dark plain whispereth,
"Hush, O thou singing rivulet,
The sun hath not come yet."

The dawn-wind bloweth cold,
On fen and fell and wold,
And heavy dews the lowlands wet—
But he hath not come yet.

And now the silver star
That far can see, doth far
And farther call, "The time is set,
And he will not forget."

• • • • •

Lord of the morning star,
  Lord of the singing brook,
Lord of the peaks that to a far
  And clear horizon look—

Lord of the delicate
  Faint flush in lighted air,
I with all these would watch and wait,
  Rejoicing and aware.

MP, P, TJ

Greater Joy

It was a great full moon
 That hung low in the west,
But the dear little birds sang everywhere,
 And the unborn dayspring blest.

Not one singing bird could be seen,
 But every bush and brier
Was astir with the sound of the music they made,
 That sweet invisible choir.

The hills in the wonderful light
 Sat listening, grave and mild,
And they folded the plains in their gentle arms
 As a mother might her child.

And high in the still, white air,
 All in the soft moonshine,
They rose and rose to a pearly peak
 Like a faraway holy shrine.

If this can be with the world
 In the setting of the moon,
With what riot of joy will it welcome Thee back,
 O Sun that art coming soon!

ACD, MP, P, TJ

Sunrise Hope

For sunrise hope and sunset calm,
And all that lies between,
For all the sweetness and the balm
That is and that has been,
For comradeship, for peace in strife,
And light on darkened days,
For work to do, and strength for life—
We sing our hymn of praise.

But oh, we press beyond, above
These gifts of pure delight,
And find in Thee and in Thy love
Contentment infinite.
O Lord beloved, in whom are found
All joys of time or place,
What will it be when joy is crowned
By vision of Thy face?

MP, P, Wg[1]

Face to Face

O Love Divine, if we can see
In our beloved so dear a grace,
When Love unveils, what will it be
To see Thee face to face?

GBM

Fair Is the Sunrise

Fair is the sunrise;
Fair is the sunset
Breaking in fire upon the sea.
Jesus is fairer—Jesus, Thou Fire of love;
All praise to Thee, Lord, praise to Thee.

Fair is the blue light
Brooding on the ocean,
Fair the bright wonder of the sea.
Jesus is fairer; Jesus is brighter;
All praise to Thee, Lord, praise to Thee.

Fair is the racing wave;
Fair is the flying foam,
And the pure glory of the sea.
Jesus is fairer, His glory purer;
All praise to Thee, Lord, praise to Thee.

Fair is the ocean
Dreaming in the moonlight,
Peaceful, the quiet, shining sea.
Jesus is fairer, Jesus more peaceful;
All praise to Thee, Lord, praise to Thee.

So, we Thy children,
Offer Thee our praises,
Join with the music of the sea,
Own Thee the fairest, own Thee the dearest,
Sing and give glory, Lord, to Thee.

P

Commander of the Waters

Is He not here, Commander of the waters?
Lo, the light spray leaps up aware to meet Him.
Hark how the joyful water voices greet Him—
Hail, O Commander!

He sits as King: the boulders are His footstool;
Foam-pure the lovely pageant of His gowning;
Fresh with the freshness of young leaves, His crowning—
Hail, O Commander!

Hush, there's a silence in the shadowy forest;
Hush, through the white of thund'ring avalanches
Passes a whisper: 'tis the budding branches—
Hail, O Commander!

Yea, He is here; oh, mark the falls' abandon:
What do they know of measured love or meager?
"Let Him take all," and all in all's flung eager—
Hail, O Commander!

DS

God of the Deeps

God of the deeps, how near Thou art;
  Here are Thy garments: sea and shore.
Beauty of all things show in part
  Thee whom, unseen, we love, adore.
Thine are the good salt winds that blow;
  Thine is the magic of the sea;
Glories of color from Thee flow—
  We worship Thee, we worship Thee.

God of the tempest and the calm,
  God of the tireless, patient tides,
God of the water's healing balm,
  And gentle sounds where stillness bides,
God of the stainless fields of blue,
  God of the grandeur of the sea,
Swifter than ever spindrift flew,
  Like homing birds, we fly to Thee.

God of the waves that roll and swell
  And break in tossing clouds of foam,
Thy handiwork the painted shell;
  For fragile life how safe a home.
God of the great, and of the small,
  God of the glory of the sea,
Here in the quiet evenfall
  We worship Thee, we worship Thee.

P

Lord of Lilies

God, whose glory fills the sky,
  God, whose glory fills the sea,
God, whose name is very high,
  Lifted up in majesty,

Here among the hills afar,
  By Thee planted, by Thee fed,
Lonely under moon and star
  Lo, a shining lily bed.

How didst Thou take thought to plant
  Such a garden in the wild?
Say to it, "Thou shalt not want,"
  Just as to Thy human child?

Dressed like queens in white and gold,
  Through all weather here they be,
Singing, singing as of old,
  Lord of lilies, unto Thee.

ACD, P

Grasses

Who can daunt the valiant grasses?
Everywhere the great wind passes
Bearing rain upon his edges,
There upon the utmost ledges
Of creation, drear and lonely.
Be there earth—a little only
Will content the grateful grasses—
They salute him as he passes.

Grasses, beautiful, courageous,
Through a thousand thousand ages
To all desolate places giving
Of the bare, bright joy of living,
The world's corners decorating
Without thought of fuss or feting—
I salute you, O courageous
Grasses of a thousand ages.

DS

Too High for Me

(Ecclesiasticus 2:18)

I have no word;
But neither hath the bird,
And it is heard.
My heart is singing, singing all day long
In quiet joy to Thee who art my Song.

For as Thy majesty
So is Thy mercy,
So is Thy mercy,
My Lord and my God.

(Continued)

How intimate
Thy ways with those who wait
About Thy gate;
But who could show the fashion of such ways
In human words, and hymn them to Thy praise?

Too high for me,
Far shining mystery,
Too high to see;
But not too high to know, though out of reach
Of words to sing its gladness into speech.

ACD, MP, P, TJ, TMS

Thy Love and Glory

The Preacher found him words of pure delight,
And I have sought, O Lord,
But have not ever found the golden word
To sing Thy glory right.

The Singer found a Song of Loves, and set
That love to melody.
A Song of Loves I wish to offer Thee,
But have not found it yet.

Is it that far and far, like sea, like air,
Thy love and glory flow?
How can we sing what we can never know
Till we are Otherwhere?

TMS

O for a Song

O for song of songs to sing Thee,
Who art altogether lovely;
Poor the song that we can bring Thee,
Who than dearest art more dear.

Winter was; 'tis past and over;
Every morning doth enchant us,
Bringing gifts from our great Lover
In whose garden flowers appear.

Can the birds refrain from singing
When Thou walkest in Thy garden?
Love constraineth; we are bringing
Hearts' delight to sing Thee here.

Wg[1]

Fine-Spun Gold

I cannot bring Thee praise like golden noon-light
Shining on earth's green floor.
My song is more like silver of the moonlight,
But I adore.

I cannot bring Thee, O Belovèd, ever
Pure song of woodland bird;
And yet I know the song of Thy least lover
In love is heard.

O blessèd be the Love that nothing spurneth:
We sing—Love doth enfold
Our little song in love. Our silver turneth
To fine-spun gold.

GBM, TJ, Wg[1]

After Rain

Clear shining after rain,
    And green, upspringing grass,
And light that comes again,
    Shadows that pass,

And hills and rocks and trees,
    Music of water's flow,
And wild birds' melodies,
    And winds that blow,

And buds all drenched in dew,
    Flower faces, brave and clear,
And skies of sunny blue
    Bring my Lord near—

Bring my Lord near, and say
    As though with one glad voice,
"O child of God, today
    Rejoice, rejoice!"

BT, P

Rabboni

Oh, the beauty of a garden
In the dawn, after rain;
Unto it doth appertain
Something more than loveliness,
As it were a sanctuary,
Made for Thee, Rabboni.

Oh, the rapture of the music
Of the birds in their trees;
Who can sing Thee like to these
With their pure hearts' passion flung
Far upon the living air?
As to Thee, Rabboni.

Oh, bring forth thy bud, fair garden;
Sing, ye birds, jubilantly.
Lord of gardens—it is He
Walketh these green leafy ways—
Lord of buds and singing birds,
Even He, Rabboni.

Oh, to turn me round like Mary,
See His eyes looking through
This new day's rain-washen blue.
But what needeth it to see?
Whom I worship—He is here,
Here with me, Rabboni.

DS

Christ, The All Fair

Oh, the wealth of beauty granted. Were it singular,
How much poorer life; but see it from a-near, afar;
Look up from the budding blossom, flash from star.
From the carpet of creation to her roof, through air,
On the waters as in earth-ways, tracks of feet declare
One among us whom we know not, the All Fair.
Can the land above be lovelier? "If it were not so,
I," saith He, "would have told you." Ah, the roses blow
In that garden, passing roses that we know.

And we wonder, and we worship
Very God of very God.
Say, each one of us apart,
In the depths of his heart:
Very God of very God;
My Lord and my God.

DS

God of Stars and Flowers

O God of stars and flowers, forgive our blindness;
No dream of night had dared what Thou hast wrought!
New every morning is Thy loving kindness,
Far, far above what we had asked or thought.

So, under every sky, our "Alleluia,"
With flowers of morning and with stars of night,
Shall praise Thee, O Lord Jesus—Alleluia—
Till Thou shalt fold all shadows up in light.

FTR, GC, P, Wg[1]

God of the Little Things

God of the golden dust of stars
Scattered in space,
God of the starry blessings that light
Our happy place,
God of the little things,
We adore Thee,
Come before Thee
Grateful, in loving thanksgiving.

God of the blue of glancing wing,
Song of the bird,
God of the friendly comfort of smiles,
Cheer of a word,
God of the little things,
We adore Thee,
Come before Thee
Grateful, in loving thanksgiving.

God of the fairy pollen ball,
Frail flow'ry bell,
Touches of tenderness that would seem
Nothing to tell,
God of the little things,
We adore Thee,
Come before Thee
Grateful, in loving thanksgiving.

(Continued)

God of the sparkle on our day,
Gift of the sun,
Laughter that lifts, all lovely and gay,
Ripples of fun,
God of the little things,
We adore Thee,
Come before Thee
Grateful, in loving thanksgiving.

GC, P, PU

Help Me to Adore

God showeth me
His goodness plenteously;
Come, all creation,
Help me to adore.

Ye mountain steeps,
Ye valleys and all deeps,
And cool ravine
Set in your forest green,
And sky that through
The branches showeth blue,
And boulders grey
That strew the river's way,
And streams that flow
To music as you go—
Help me, oh, help me; help me to adore.

Ye flying things
On darting, painted wings,
And joyful bird,
And creature mailed or furred,
And fugitive
Pale shadows, lights that live
On grass and flower,
And splendor of the power
Of hurricane,
And mist and quickening rain—
Help me, oh, help me; help me to adore.

MP, P

Jubilate Deo

Climbing Dawn upon the mountains:
Drifting gold and amethyst,
Fleeting wonder of the mist,
Floating wonder of the cloud—
Gazing on you, breaketh from us
Jubilate Deo!

Shining Noon upon the mountains:
Spinner that from blue to red,
Spinning seven-colored thread,
Weaves one wide, fair web of white—
Gazing on you, breaketh from us
Jubilate Deo!

(Continued)

Golden Evening on the mountains:
Spirit of enchantment yours,
Spirit of the heathery moors,
Spirit of the bluebell woods—
Gazing on you, breaketh from us
Jubilate Deo!

Gentle Moonlight on the mountains:
Did the angels weave the pale
Shimm'ring beauty of your veil
To the sound of songs in heaven?
Gazing on you, breaketh from us
Jubilate Deo!

DS

A Valley Song

(Psalm 84:6)

Oh, who that has not known it
Can tell the joy of the valley?
When the water fills the pools,
And a wind from the great sea cools
The wearisome heat of the day;
And the standing corn lands say,
"Come feed, come feed,
This is life indeed:
Seed corn for the sower,
Pressed down, running over.
This valley is the private way
By which the King will pass today;
All glory to the valley's King!"
Thus the valleys laugh and sing.

MP

In the Greenwood

Oh, the greenwood's full of music; dost thou hear it?
Is it merely water falling
Or the little wild bird calling
To his mate? It sounds to me
Something holier, something sweeter,
   Even *Benedicite*.

Oh, the greenwood's full of color; dost thou see it?
More is here than play or capture
Of the sunbeam, or the rapture
Of the leaf on living tree.
Without sound or language, hear it—
   "*Deo Benedicite!*"

Oh, the wood's full of a Presence; walk thou softly.
Feel the hush about thee; rather
Feel at heart of it thy Father
Moving through the wood to thee.
With the spirit of the greenwood,
   Sing thy *Benedicite*.

DS

Roses

Roses, roses all the year,
   Passionflowers and lilies dear,
Oleanders always here—
   Thank you, our kind Lord Jesus.

Buds and blossoms, jewels blue,
   Balls and bells all golden, too,
Fill our gardens; so we do
   Thank you, our kind Lord Jesus.

(Continued)

See, beyond that leafy bough,
Someone walks the garden now,
Thorns, not roses on His brow—
Bitter, sharp thorns, not roses.

Bitter thorns? Then it must be
Our dear Lord; for who but He
Wears that crown of infamy,
Giving us joy of roses.

O my Savior, who hast borne
Pain for me and grief and scorn,
From that crown I'd pluck the thorn,
Comfort Thy heart with roses.

FTR, P

A Dawn Song

Ye great enchantments of the changeful skies,
All loveliness of mystic pageantries,
All splendors set in light's transparent shell,
Hail my Lord, the King Emmanuel.

Ye wheeling clouds that sail the blue and trace
Wandering shadows on the mountain's face,
Or sleep in white, dream-hills of asphodel,
Hail my Lord, the King Emmanuel.

Ye foaming falls, that fling yourselves away,
Ye flying rainbows on the flying spray,
And sun-shot showers on forest and on fell,
Hail my Lord, the King Emmanuel.

And all ye green things of the flow'ry earth,
Ye birds that fill the stirring woods with mirth,
Come, let us wake the world; come let us tell:
He is here, the King Emmanuel.

DS

Hush

Hush, O hush, the moon's alight,
Pale the stars, and few and faint;
Lilies red and lilies white
Stand each like a haloed saint.
See the shadowy, dreamy trees
Bathe in pools of silver air;
Hear the whisper of the breeze
Murmur softly like a prayer.

Hush, O hush, 'tis holy ground,
Moon-washed, clean as driven snow,
Meet for Him the moonbeams crowned
In a garden long ago.
Moonbeams, crown Him once again;
Lilies, ring your sanctus bell:
King of Love and King of Pain,
Thou art here—Immanuel.

PVV, TJ

Sing Alleluia

O Lord our God, how can we fitly praise
The love that led so kindly all our days?
We bless Thee; Alleluia!

The stars that sang together at their birth
Are singing still, and singing in the earth,
A glorious "Alleluia."

Her mountains, forests, rivers and her seas
Like stars and flowers, make noble harmonies,
A joyful "Alleluia."

And we, though not as innocent as they,
Have something in our song they cannot say:
A grateful "Alleluia."

Then let us say it, sing it, for love's sake;
O song of love in me, awake! awake!
And sing thy "Alleluia."

Wg[1]

God of Our Praise

God of our praise and God of our delight,
Thy lovingkindness lasteth all the day.
Thy song like starshine filleth all the night,
And lighteneth our way.

All loveliness of flower and fern and grass,
All noble trees and singing birds therein,
All gallant things that bless us as they pass—
These praise Thee without sin.

So would we praise Thee, Lord, in whom we live,
But with a passion they can never know;
Let not our praise be faint and fugitive,
But like a fountain flow.

Wg[1]

Praise to Our Sovereign Lord

Praise, praise to Thee, our Sovereign Lord;
Praise, praise to Thee, beloved, adored;
With all Thine unseen family
We love and laud and worship Thee.

For the clear shining of Thy face
That lightens this our dwelling place;
And for the flowing of Thy grace,
Alleluia.

For Thy great glory do we praise;
Thine is the Kingdom, Ancient of Days;
And our hearts' melody we raise,
Alleluia.

TMS, Wg[1]

The King's Melody

Melody is not of earth;
   She is a flower of heaven.
Garden of God gave her birth,
   And to the spirit shriven,
A blossom of heavenly mirth.

Timbrel and harp, with the lute,
   Hither bring, merrily sing;
Sing to thy Lord, and Him flute
   Who of thy heart is the King;
His beautiful will salute.

Wg[1]

Take Wings and Soar

Consider how great things
   The Lord has done for you;
O let your soul take wings
   And praise His love anew.
Resist the downward pull and soar,
   And sing whom you adore.

Look up, look up, arise
   Above the clinging earth;
He waiteth to surprise
   The quickened heart with mirth.
Resist the downward pull and soar,
   And sing whom you adore.

Wg[1]

For Simple Things

God of my praise, to Thee be praise
For children and their loving ways;

For all the things that lighten earth,
For quiet peace, and merry mirth;

For every friendly bird that sings,
For little, lovely, simple things;

For loyal comradeship that grows
The stronger for each wind that blows;

But most of all because Thou art
The sunshine of my happy heart.

God of my praise, to Thee be praise,
Today and through my length of days.

WHP

In Little Things

O noble love, most noble love of God,
Who shall Thy tenderness in little things declare?
Tell me to what I may Thy gentle grace compare?
I search through land and sea,
All jewel mines, the kingdoms of the air,
The flowery hills of Thine own Galilee—
Find nothing anywhere.

TMS

His Surprises

The day is drenched in Thee:
In little, exquisite surprises
Bubbling deliciousness of Thee arises
From sudden places,
Under the common traces
Of my most lethargied and 'customed paces.

NS

Heaven's Wonder

(Zephaniah 3:17)

Heaven's wonder do I find in Love's rejoicing
Over a thing of nought;
It passeth words—angelic songs outvoicing;
It passeth thought.
He will be silent in His love—Heaven's wonder;
Deep in that love I rest.
I will be silent; silence cannot sunder
Bird from her nest.

Heaven's wonder do I find when glad love singeth
And, as if unaware
Of earthiness in thing belovèd, wingeth
Me otherwhere.
In joy and stillness, song and pure love longing,
Love's holiest mysteries meet.
All that is in me, come adoring, thronging
About Love's feet.

Wg[1]

Mary's Kiss

(Luke 7:44–45)

And may we all be Thine own Marys, Lord?
Dear worthy Lord, how courteous Love's reward:
For all the little that I give to Thee,
Thou gavest first to me.

Rich is Thy harvest, O Thou Corn of Wheat:
A cloud of lovers gather round Thy feet.
What miracle of love that Thou shouldst miss
Low on Thy feet, one kiss.

GBM, TJ

Better Thy Love

Better Thy love, Lord, better than wine;
Dust of the earth, yet, Lord, we are Thine.
King of our hearts, Lord Jesus adored,
Glory, O Lord, to Thee.

Jesus belovèd, Jesus adored,
Jesus our only Master and Lord,
Worship we now, Redeemer adored;
Glory, O Lord, to Thee.

Wg[1]

Love's Small Lights

A fretted fringe of gold
Upon the quiet grey,
A mist of golden, fold on fold,
The birth robes of the day.
The splendor rose, the plain
Like softest opal shone;
The valley opened her domain
Like a pavilion.

Great skirts of glory swept
The mountains where we stood;
Hushed lay the whole bright world, except
For music from the wood.
And as the colors woke
In separate ecstasy
We worshiped, till a faint fear broke
Our *benedicite*.

Vast spaces lay around;
As dust we seemed, or less,
Blown up to these pure heights, and found
Alone in littleness.
We turned abashed, but near,
A rock new-cleft was lit
As though a very hemisphere
Of star dust spangled it.

Each crystal kindled, flashed
    Lovely and several;
None hid its little face abashed
    Because it was so small.
God of these depths and heights,
    Thy kindness will not ban
The flash of love, Father of Lights,
    From Thy poor dust of man.

DS

Each Known to Him

O praise the Lord, for it is good
    And pleasant and a joyful thing
To lift the heart, as all men should,
    Who have so dear a Lord to sing.

The number of the stars He tells,
    And calls each star by his own name;
No two of all His flow'ry bells
    Or leaves or grasses are the same.

So individual is His thought
    For all of us, did one let go
The hand of Joy and, sore distraught,
    Forget to sing, His heart would know.

From rainbow did a color float,
    Or did a shining sun burn dim,
That were far less for Him to note
    Than dumbness of a child to Him.

(Continued)

O save from that! Let grateful song
And jubilance of melody,
And loving merry-makings, throng
The road that leads us home to Thee.

EHW

So Sweet His Smile

For ah, the Master is so fair,
His smile so sweet to banished men,
That they who see Him unaware
Can never rest on earth again.
And they who see Him risen afar
On God's right hand to welcome them,
Forgetful stand of home and land—
Desiring fair Jerusalem.

PU

Rhapsody

(Isaiah 62:4)

"Thou shalt be called My Pleasure"—who hath dreamed
Of such a name for desert land redeemed?
And His desire is toward me—O my Lord,
This is indeed a Heavenly wonder-word.
What hast Thou found to be desired in me
In whom is nothing, nor could ever be?

Like sap of life, that, flowing through the bough,
Doth nourish leaf and bud and flower, art Thou.
And as the tree desireth life, so I
Desire my Lord of Life, exceedingly.
But that the Sap should so desire the tree
Is, O Beloved, a wonder unto me.

TG

The Bread of Heaven

Lord Jesus, when beside the sea
Thou spakest of the multitude
Who had not with them any food,
Thy word was even unto me.

"They have no need to go away."
Why should they go to seek elsewhere
When Thou, the Bread of Heaven, wert there,
As Thou art here, my Lord, today?

My love to Thee, my thanks to Thee,
For now Thy child is comforted.
Thou art my Home, who art my Bread,
And every place is Galilee.

TMS

The Glory in the Midst

(Zechariah 2:5)

The Glory in the midst art Thou,
The Sunlight in the air;
The crown of crowns is on Thy brow,
Thy touch is everywhere.

And lowly gath'ring round Thy feet
In this Thine own abode,
O Love Divine, our love would greet
Thy love on every road.

Thine, Lord, the fruit on laden bough,
And Thine the treasure store;
The Glory in the midst art Thou;
We worship and adore.

Wg[1]

If It Were Not So

(John 14:2)

I thought I heard my Savior say to me:
"My love will never weary, child, of thee."
Then in me, whispering doubtfully and low:
  How can that be?
  He answered me,
"*But if it were not so,*
I would have told thee."

I thought I heard my Savior say to me:
"My strength encamps on weakness—so on thee."
And when a wind of fear did through me blow—
  How can that be?
  He answered me,
"*But if it were not so,*
I would have told thee."

O most fine Gold
That naught in me can dim,
Eternal Love, that has her home in Him
Whom, seeing not, I love,
I worship Thee!

GC, P, RFB, TJ

I Will Sing to Thee

In the shadow of Thy wings
  I will sing for joy;
What a God, who out of shade
  Nest for singing bird hath made!
Lord, my Might and Melody,
  I will sing to Thee.

If the shadow of Thy wings
 Be so full of song,
What must be the lighted place
 Where Thy bird can see Thy face?
Lord, my Might and Melody,
 I will sing to Thee.

GC, RFB

His Faithfulness

O wind of God, blow through the trees;
 O birds of God, come sing your song;
For now I know the joy that frees,
 The joy that makes the weakest strong.

The vapors march in shining crowds,
 High in the trackless roads of air;
I look, and lo, unto the clouds,
 His faithfulness is even there!

Pass foolish fears; the fresh winds blow;
 O birds of God, come sing with me.
My God is faithful, this I know;
 My Father, I have all in Thee.

Wg[1]

Sunset

For the great red rose of sunset,
Dropping petals on the way
For the tired feet of day—
Thanks to Thee, our Father.

For the violet of twilight
Singing, "Hush, ye children, hush";
For the afterglow's fair flush—
Thanks to Thee, our Father.

For the softly sliding darkness
Wherein many jewels are
Kindly-eyed, familiar—
Thanks to Thee, our Father.

For the comfort of forgiveness
Taking from us our offence,
Steeping us in innocence—
Thanks to Thee, our Father.

For the viewless, tall white angels
Bidden to ward off from us
All things foul, calamitous—
Thanks to Thee, our Father

That Thy love sets not with sunset,
Nor with starset, nor with moon,
But is ever one high noon—
Thanks to Thee, our Father.

DS, TJ

Love Traveling

Love, traveling in the greatness of His strength,
Found me alone,
Wearied a little by the journey's length,
Though I had known,
All the long way, many a kindly air,
And flowers had blossomed for me everywhere.

And yet Love found me fearful, and He stayed;
Love stayed by me.
"Let not thy heart be troubled or dismayed,
My child," said He.
Slipped from me then all troubles, all alarms;
For Love had gathered me into His arms.

GBM, TJ

The Little Running Rills

O God of the moonlight and stillness and peace,
And silver mist folding the soft, sleeping hills,
In Thee is renewal, in Thee is release,
O God of the valleys
And the little moonlit, running rills.

O God of the sunlight and man's busy day,
Of close crowding cares and the clashing of wills,
In Thee is renewal—oh, let us be gay,
Refreshed and refreshing,
Like the little sunlit, running rills.

P

Shall Never Thirst

Faint is the famished forest-green
And parched the pools of the ravine;
The burning winds have blown away
The soft, blue mist of yesterday.

The furry creatures of the wood
Have fled and left a solitude.
No song of merry, singing bird
Or laughter of the stream is heard.

So, Lord my God, Thy child would be,
If for one hour bereft of Thee.
But Thy great fountains from afar
Flow down to where Thy valleys are;

And for the least is nourishment,
Verdure and song and heart-content.
For where Thou art, there all is well,
Our Life of life, Immanuel.

TJ

River of God

(Isaiah 41:18)

River of God, Thy quick'ning streams
  Cause me to bud again;
My winter past, as one who dreams,
  I see my summer reign.
For my bare height fresh pasture yields,
  Where never grass did grow;
And in the borders of my fields
  I see fair lilies blow.

My glowing sand becomes a pool,
And all around is green;
All here is restful, quiet, cool,
As in a deep ravine.
O for a worthy song to sing
Thy goodness unto me.
O Christ, my one Eternal Spring,
All glory be to Thee.

MP, P, TMS, Wg[1]

A Song of Lovely Things

I sing a song of lovely things,
Too lovely to discover;
We only catch a hint of them,
Like flashing wings—
The wings of our great Lover.

On wings of wind He rode and flew,
Made darkness His pavilion,
But at His brightness, vapors passed;
The day was blue—
For light is His dominion.

He was acquainted with my grief,
Drew me from many waters;
For thus it is He leads His own,
Commands relief—
To loving sons and daughters.

He put a new song in my mouth;
His love is ever bringing
Cool leaves of healing from His Tree;
And though in drouth—
How can I keep from singing?

Wg[1]

Thy Comfortable Word

Lover of souls, Thee have I heard,
Thee will I sing, for sing I must;
Thy good and comfortable word
Hath raised my spirit from the dust.

In dusty ways my feet had strayed,
And foolish fears laid hold on me,
Until what time I was afraid
I suddenly remembered Thee.

Remembering Thee, I straight forgot
What otherwise had troubled me;
It was as if it all were not;
I only was aware of Thee.

Of Thee, of Thee alone, aware,
I rested me, I held me still;
The blessèd thought of Thee, most Fair,
Dispelled the brooding sense of ill.

Then quietness around me fell,
And Thou didst speak; my spirit heard.
I worshiped and rejoiced, for well
I knew Thy comfortable word.

Whoso hath known that comforting,
The inward touch that maketh whole,
How can he ever choose but sing
To Thee, O Lover of his soul?

EHW, MP, P, RFB, TJ

Daily Blessings

For the love that like a screen
Sheltered from the might-have-been;
For that fire could never burn us,
Deeps could never drown or turn us;
For our daily blessings, Lord,
Be Thy name adored.

For the gentle joys that pass
Like the dew upon the grass,
New each morning, lighting duty
With a radiance and a beauty;
For our daily blessings, Lord,
Be Thy name adored.

Many a storm has threatened loud,
And then melted like a cloud,
Seeking to distress, confound us,
Met Thy great wings folded round us;
For our daily blessings, Lord,
Be Thy name adored.

GC

O What a Love!

(Psalm 97:11)

Fire cannot burn, nor can the waters drown us;
They can but call Thy gracious help again.
And lovingkindness, tender mercies crown us,
Though we be least of all the sons of men.

O what a Love that patiently empowereth;
O what a Love that blesseth common days,
In earthly garden soweth seed that flowereth
In light and gladness; Lord, Thy love we praise!

Wg[1]

Praise, Praise Jehovah

Praise, praise Jehovah, God of our salvation;
Praise, praise to Thee, on whom we cast our care.
We offer Thee our loving adoration;
Praise, praise to Thee, the God who answers prayer.

For when we brought Thee him whose eyes were darkened,
Then, then was wrought the miracle of sight.
Thine ear attentive, bent to us and harkened;
"Let there be light," Thou saidst, and there was light.

We came to Thee for clear and heavenly vision,
That with Thy will our will be in accord.
We came in need of Thy divine provision,
And Thou didst hear and answer, blessèd Lord.

Wg[1]

For Child Redeemed

For child redeemed and given to us to cherish,
For Spoiler spoiled, and foeman overcome,
Praise, praise to Thee who willest none should perish
But all be sought and found and gathered home.

Praise, praise to Thee that tenderness enfoldeth
Each little child, and others not found yet.
Praise, praise that Love in little child beholdeth
Small starry jewel for Thy coronet.

TMS

We Praise Thee

For the glory of Thy majesty,
We praise Thee.
For Thy pitiful compassion,
Lord, we praise Thee.
For the Holy Spirit of Judgment,
We praise Thee.
For the love that passeth knowledge,
We praise Thee.
Lifting up our hearts and voices,
Lord, we praise Thee.

Wg[2]

Lord, Our Redeemer

Lord, our Redeemer, well hast Thou guarded us;
We had plunged blindly, mercy retarded us;
Were we misled, Thy hand directed;
Were we in trouble, Thy power protected.

Never protector ever so motherly,
Never companion ever so brotherly;
In all our way Thou wert beside us,
And through confusion, Thy hand did guide us.

Were secret perils?—praise for their vanishing;
Were secret foemen?—praise for their banishing;
Strong to uphold, Love faileth never;
Thine be the majesty now and forever.

Wg[1]

Thou Art . . .

Thou art my Stony Rock
Thou standest very high,
And yet Thou art accessible,
My God, yea very nigh:
A thought, a wish, an infant's cry,
And I, in Thee, am set on high.

Thou art my Castle too,
Set firm upon the rock;
And never blast of hurricane
Nor fearful earthquake shock
Can shake my bastion, or unlock
My castle door, set on that Rock.

Thou art my spacious Room,
My very pleasant place;
And even I, who heretofore
Cramped in a narrow space
Was strait shut up, do by Thy grace
Walk free in this, my pleasant place.

Thou art—oh, what art Thou?
What thing on earth, in air,
Can fitly set Thee forth, my Lord,
Who art beyond compare?
Oh, nothing, nothing anywhere
Can set Thee forth, my only Fair.

MP, P

Great Is Our God

Great is our God and great is His power,
He is our Fortress, He is our Tower;
The Lord is righteous in all His ways,
Unto His name be glory and praise.

Wg[2]

Opening Our Windows

Opening our windows toward Jerusalem,
And looking thitherward, we see
First Bethlehem
Then Nazareth and Galilee,
And afterwards, Gethsemane;
And then the little hill called Calvary.

TJ

Rock and Fortress Tower

Rock of my heart and my Fortress Tower,
Dear are Thy thoughts to me;
Like the unfolding of some fair flower,
Opening silently.
And on the edge of these Thy ways,
Standing in awe as heretofore,
Thee do I worship, Thee do I praise
And adore.

(Continued)

Rock of my heart and my Fortress Tower,
Dear is Thy love to me;
Search I the world for a word of power,
Find it at Calvary.
O deeps of love that rise and flow
Round about me and all things mine,
Love of all loves, in Thee I know
Love Divine.

ACD, EHW, GC

From Sin Set Free

The shadows of the underworld
Compassed about my guilty soul;
And thunderbolts were on me hurled,
And lightnings flashed. And on a scroll
Was written down, without, within,
The secret of my hidden sin.

Without, within, I saw it stand,
In clearest words accusing me,
Till, as it were, a wounded hand
Annulled its record, set me free.
With that the stormy wind did cease.
A voice commanded: there was peace.

O Savior stricken for my sin,
O God who gavest Him to grief,
O Spirit who didst woo and win
My troubled soul to seek relief,
O Love revealed at Calvary,
Thy glory lights eternity!

MP, P

On Calvary's Cross

I have a Savior; though I sought
Through earth and air and sea
I could not find a word, a thought,
To show Him worthily.
But planted here in rock and moss
I see the Sign of utmost loss;
I hear a word—"*On Calvary's Cross*
Love gave Himself for thee."

GBM

Thou Didst Die for Me

O my belovèd Lord,
Thou Bread of Life adored,
Thou who didst die for me,
I worship Thee.

O my belovèd Lord,
Thou Wine of Life outpoured,
Thou who didst die for me,
I worship Thee.

O my belovèd Lord,
Risen, returning Lord,
Jesus Beloved, Adored,
I worship Thee.

Wg[1]

Cleanse Us

As we consider
Thy Cross and Passion,
Burial, Rising,
Ascension and Returning,
May Thy most precious Blood
Cleanse us, O Savior.

Now we, adoring,
Offer our worship,
Trusting Thy merits
As incense pure commingling;
Uplifting heart and voice,
Sing we Thy glory.

Wg[1]

Lord of Love And Pain

O Lord of love and Lord of pain,
Who, by the bitter Cross,
Dost teach us how to measure gain,
And how to measure loss—
Whom, seeing not, our hearts adore,
We bring our love to Thee;
And where Thou art, Lord, evermore
Would we Thy servants be.

GC, RFB, Wg[1]

A Carol

There are two Bethlehems in the land,
Two little Bethlehems there.
O wise men, do you understand
To seek Him everywhere?
The heavenly Child lies holily,
The heavenly Child lies lowlily,
No crown on His soft hair.

There are three crosses on the hill,
Three dreadful crosses there,
And very dark and very chill
The heavy, shuddering air.
Is there a sign to show my Lord,
The sinner's Savior, Heaven's Adored?
'Tis He with thorn-crowned hair.

For in His lovely baby days
Heaven's door was set ajar,
And angels flew through glimmering ways
And lit a silver star.
No need for halo or for crown
To show the King of Love come down
To dwell where sinners are.

But when He died upon the Rood,
The King of Glory, He,
There was no star, there was no good,
Nor any majesty.
For diadem was only scorn,
A twisted, torturing crown of thorn—
And it was all for me.

RFB, TJ

Love's Stripes

Lest dead in sins I languish,
  Know not my need of purging,
Thou didst endure sore anguish
  And crown of thorns and scourging.
So dearly hast Thou bought me,
Who never even sought Thee.

To keep my feet from falling,
  My hands for Thine own using,
Thy feet to hurt appalling,
  Thy hands to man's abusing
Thou willingly didst offer;
For love, didst all things suffer.

The men Thou madest felled Thee;
  The cords of death did bind Thee;
The pains of Sheol held Thee;
  The dews of death did blind Thee—
O Love, to such a Splendor
Of Love, what can I render?

O Love, than gold more golden,
  Not fully yet beholden,
O Love, whose only token
  Is heart by loving broken,
I worship Thee, I sing Thee,
And love's whole treasure bring Thee.

Wg[1]

Love Lavished

O deeps unfathomed as the sea,
    O heights that reach beyond the high,
O Love that lavished all on me,
    I know Thee now, I know Thee nigh.
O Love that is not here or there,
    But like Thine own eternity
Is here, is there, is everywhere,
    I yield, I love, I worship Thee.

Wd, Wg[1]

The Rescue

Oh, praise the Lord, oh, praise the Lord,
    Ye children of His heritage;
Rejoice in Him with one accord,
    For He a furious fight did wage
To save you from the terrible one.
The Lord your God great things hath done.

For on a blessèd, blessèd day
    From Heaven's high place, with pity, He
Perceived the little, helpless prey
    (Prey of the terrible were ye);
He tracked the lion to his lair;
He fought him and He conquered there.

But in the fight, His head, His side,
    His hands, His feet were wounded sore;
No mind can think, no word describe
    The sharp and dreadful pain He bore;
Alone, He braved the lion's rage
To make of you His heritage.

(Continued)

Safe to His fold He brought you in,
   Oh, tenderly He loves you all;
And now to guard what He did win
   He makes Himself a fiery wall,
And stands unwearied round about
To keep the ravening lion out.

We praise the Lord; we praise the Lord,
   Glad children of His heritage;
We do rejoice with one accord
   That He to save us did engage.
The Lord our God great things hath done:
He saved us from the terrible one.

DS

To Love We Sing

O Thou whose dearest name is Love,
   We worship, we adore;
Life's long confusions only prove
   Love known and loved before.

Now, in the church Thou hast redeemed,
   To Love, great Love, we sing;
For who of mortal man has dreamed
   Love's final triumphing?

How tender is Thy touch, O Love,
   And yet how sure, how strong.
Though all our trusted things remove,
   To Love we sing our song.

We sing, and as we sing we know
That miracle of grace,
Love's sudden, quick'ning overflow,
The shining of Thy face.

Wg[1]

A New Focus

He who has felt that Face of beauty,
Which wakes the world's great hymn,
For one unutterable moment
Bent in love o'er him,
In that look finds earth, heaven, men and angels
Grow nearer through Him.

GC

Worshiping the Lord

Glory and honor are in His Presence;
Strength and gladness are in His place;
Worshiping the Lord in the beauty of holiness,
I will continually seek His Face.
Seeking the Lord and His glorious strength,
I will be mindful of His ways;
I will give thanks to His holy Name,
And glory in His praise.

I will give thanks, for the Lord is good;
And His mercy endureth forever.
My heart shall rejoice as I seek the Lord,
And His marvelous works remember.
Glory and honor are in His Presence;
Strength and gladness are in His place.
"The Lord reigneth," I will say among the nations,
That they may turn and seek His Face.

Wg[1]

I Follow Thee

Shadow and coolness, Lord,
  Art Thou to me;
Cloud of my soul, lead on,
  I follow Thee.
What though the hot winds blow,
Fierce heat beats up below?
Fountains of water flow—
  Praise, praise to Thee.

Clearness and glory, Lord,
  Art Thou to me;
Light of my soul, lead on,
  I follow Thee.
All through the moonless night,
Making its darkness bright,
Thou art my heavenly Light—
  Praise, praise to Thee.

Shadow and shine art Thou,
  Dear Lord, to me;
Pillar of cloud and fire,
  I follow Thee.
What though the way be long,
In Thee my heart is strong,
Thou art my joy, my song—
  Praise, praise to Thee.

EHW, MP, P, RFB, Wg[1]

The Ways of the Lord

Thy ways by quiet waters
   And pleasant pasture land
Lead on across the levels
   Of tawny wastes of sand,
Through perilous mountain passes,
   In beating wind and rain,
Through valleys set with fountains,
   And out and on again—
And I sing, yea, I sing in the ways of the Lord,
That great is the glory of the Lord.

How often when outwearied,
   My force and courage spent,
I apprehend a Presence—
   Belovèd, immanent;
Then colors wake about me,
   And living waters flow,
The world moves on to music,
   The night is all aglow—
And I sing, yea, I sing in the ways of the Lord,
That great is the glory of the Lord.

No mortal ear has heard it,
   No mortal eye perceived,
No swift imagination
   Has ever yet conceived
How singular the beauty,
   How bountiful the grace
Prepared for him who presses
   To Thy fair dwelling place—
And I sing, yea, I sing in the ways of the Lord,
That great is the glory of the Lord.

MP, P

Perfect Leader

(2 Samuel 22:31,33)

As for God, His way is perfect;
    This is my song.
When I called on Him He heard me,
For the battle did He gird me,
In my weakness made me strong.
    This is my joyful song.

And my way He maketh perfect;
    This is my song.
Uphill, downhill, though it windeth,
Often through a mist that blindeth—
All day long and all night long,
    This is my joyful song.

Perfect Leader of Thy people,
    Thou art our song.
Thine the love that never faileth,
Thine the power that all prevaileth;
Lord, in Thee our hearts are strong.
    Thou art our joyful song.

Wg[1]

Our True Guide

Thou hast performed the thing that Thou hast spoken,
Guided our steps and shown us what to do;
Never, O Lord, hath word of Thine been broken;
Thou art the Truth, and we have proved Thee true.

WHP

One Thing Have I Desired

(Psalm 27:4)

One thing have I desired, my God, of Thee,
That will I seek: Thine house be home to me.

I would not breathe an alien, other air;
I would be with Thee, O Thou fairest Fair.

For I would see the beauty of my Lord,
And hear Him speak, who is my heart's Adored.

O Love of loves, and can such wonder dwell
In Thy great Name of names—Immanuel?

Thou with Thy child; Thy child at home with Thee—
O Love of loves, I love, I worship Thee.

EHW, PU, TJ, Wg[1]

Home to Heaven

What will it be, when, like the wind-blown spray,
Our spirits rise and fly away, away?
Oh, lighter than the silvery, airy foam,
We shall float free. All winds will blow us home.
We shall forget the garments that we wore;
We shall not need them anymore.
We shall put on our immortality,
And we shall see Thy face, and be like Thee,
And serve Thee, Lord, who hast so much forgiven,
Serve Thee in holiness—and this is heaven!

K

A Foretaste of Thy Country

For the loveliness of dawn
　Upon the sleeping sea,
For the vapors spun of mist of pearl
　Where great lights be,
　　Alleluia.

For the winding roads that lead
　Up through the fields of air,
Whither angels that have kept their watches
　Homeward fare,
　　Alleluia.

For the wonder of the waking world,
　Her silences;
For the magic of her moving colors'
　Gentleness,
　　Alleluia.

For the love that, lest our faith and hope
　Wax faint and cold,
Opens morn and eve a vision
　Of the City of Gold,
　　Alleluia.

Of what sort must be Thy country?
　Oh, to think that we
Have a portion in a beauty
　Passing earth, air, sea;
　　Alleluia.

DS

Glory, Glory, Glory to God

Glory, glory, glory to God—
This is the song of the sea.
All the earth shall be filled, shall be filled,
With His majesty.

Glory, glory, glory to God—
What though we do not see
All things under our kingly Christ,
Crowned in truth is He.

Glory, glory, glory to God—
And we believe to see
All the earth that He ransomed, filled
With His majesty.

P

We Conquer by His Song

We see not yet all things put under Thee.
We see not yet the glory that shall be;
We see not yet, and yet by faith we see;
Alleluia, Alleluia.

We see the shadows gathering for flight,
The powers of dawn dispel the brooding night,
The steadfast march of the triumphant light;
Alleluia.

Be we in East or West, in North or South,
By wells of water or in land of drouth,
Lo, Thou hast put a new song in our mouth;
Alleluia.

(Continued)

Therefore we triumph; therefore we are strong,
Though vision tarry and the night be long;
For lifted up, we conquer by Thy song;
Alleluia.

ACD, TJ

Even I Will Sing

(Judges 5:3)

I, even I, will sing unto the Lord,
Forever and forever the Adored.
I, even I, though I be dust, will sing
To Him who even now is triumphing.

Where darkness was, He said, "Let there be light"—
I saw the blind receiving heavenly sight.
His miracles are with us once again;
O worthy is the Lamb that has been slain!

Shepherd of Israel, what can baffle love,
Or cause divine compassion to remove?
Out of a fall, love makes a steppingstone,
And quite reverses all the foe has done.

Love, only love, these mighty things can do;
What love has purposed, love will carry through.
I, even I, will sing unto the Lord,
Forever and forever the Adored.

Wg[1]

Easter Praise

O Christ of Easter, Jesus Christ our Lord,
Forever be Thy Name beloved, adored,
From everlasting the eternal Word—
Alleluia! Alleluia!

Not with the pomp of trumpet, drum and fife,
But with the quiet power of endless life,
Conqueror of conquerors, in that awful strife
Thou didst triumph—Alleluia!

Ancient of days, King of eternity,
Who broughtest light and immortality,
Where Thou art, there shall Thy servants be,
And shall serve Thee. Alleluia!

To Thee be the glory and dominion,
To Thee, the Father's well-beloved Son,
To Thee, the Risen and the Coming One.
Alleluia! Alleluia!

FTR

A Glad Doxology

Let the hosts of darkness shout;
Let them rage and roar;
Christ will put them all to rout
As He did before.
Praise Him,
Praise Him,
Praise Him heartily;
Sing your glad doxology.

(Continued)

See you shall, for He is God;
Praise prepares His way.
Feet that on the sea have trod
Tread the waves today.
Praise Him,
Praise Him,
Praise Him joyously;
Sing your glad doxology.

FTR

Our Conquering Christ

Art Thou not marching to music,
Conquering Christ?
Hark to the trumpets and bugles sounding afar.
Welcome the glow in the east that declareth
The Morning Star.

All souls are Thine, not the foeman's,
Conquering Christ.
Passeth, like dream of a sleeper, dark heathendom.
Hasteth the jubilant hour when Thy Kingdom,
O Lord, shall come.

Praise waiteth for Thee in Zion,
Conquering Christ.
Crowned shalt Thou be, beloved and reverenced then.
Thine is the Kingdom, the power, the glory
Forever. Amen.

GC, P

The Seventh Song

(Revelation 11:15)

And there will come a day
  (The other songs all sung)
When suddenly is flung
  Upon the aerial way
By the angelic throng,
  The music of the Seventh Song.

For our Redeemer comes;
  Though King of kings He be,
Yet His bright majesty
  Demands not beat of drums,
Nor trumpets loud and long,
  But only an adoring song.

O Lord of common men,
  We sing, and in our heart
Wonder, have we a part
  In that supreme "Amen,"
That pure, adoring word,
  The lover's song to his Adored?

Lover—the burning name
  Would seem too great to use,
Did not Thy dear love choose
  To fan the flax to flame.
Love gave that glorious word,
  The song of songs, to love's Adored.

Wg[2]

Sevenfold Adoration

Before e'er the kingdoms
Of this world are vanquished
And have become the Kingdoms of the Lord,
Sevenfold, triumphant adoration riseth . . .

And though there be darkness
Like the smoke of furnace,
Sound of trumpets, sword and famine, death,
Ceaseless the golden, shining song ascendeth . . .

Through great voices, thunderings,
Lightnings and an earthquake,
Tranquil the steadfast music of that song—
Pure words of glory, confident, ascending . . .

O come, let us adore Him,
The Christ, the Royal Rider,
The Conqueror of conquerors,
Lord of lords.

Wg[2]

The Seventh Vial

(Psalm 56:4)

In God will I praise His word;
In God have I put my trust.
The towers of the foeman of the Lord
Shall crumble into dust.

Yes, our eyes shall see them fall,
And our ears shall hear them crash;
And they shall be no more at all
When His keen lightnings flash.

When the Vial is poured in the air,
And a Voice says, "It is done,"
Then all the world, at last aware,
Hails our Belovèd One.

Wg[2]

Denouement

(Revelation 11:15)

Though sun and moon and stars be not,
The heavens a vanished scroll,
The pillars of the earth are His;
Be fixed in God, my soul.
The waves may roar, the nations rage,
And yet at His command,
At the four corners of the earth
The four great angels stand.
And swiftly hasteneth the day
Foretold in His sure word:
"The kingdoms of the earth shall be
The kingdoms of the Lord."

K

Enthroned

We worship Thee,
Who art the First,
Who art the Last;
We worship Thee.

We worship Thee,
O King of kings,
And Lord of lords;
We worship Thee.

We worship Thee,
The Lamb of God
Upon the Throne;
We worship Thee.

Wg[1]

Be Glory Forever

The crimson rose fadeth,
The budding bough withereth,
The waxing moon waneth,
The morning star setteth;
But Thy love abideth,
All radiance surpasseth,
Thy love everlasting,
My Lord and my God.

How great is Thy goodness,
How great is Thy beauty,
Lord Jesus, Redeemer,
Most merciful Savior;
To Thee who hast loved us,
To Thee who hast washed us,
Be glory forever,
Amen and Amen.

Wg[1]

2 | Poems of Petition

Wordless Prayer

O Lord, my heart is all a prayer,
But it is silent unto Thee.
I am too tired to look for words;
I rest upon Thy sympathy
To understand when I am dumb;
And well I know Thou hearest me.

I know Thou hearest me because
A quiet peace comes down to me,
And fills the places where before
Weak thoughts were wandering wearily;
And deep within me it is calm
Though waves are tossing outwardly.

GC, MP

Lead Us in Prayer

Savior, in whom we have access with confidence,
Lead us in prayer today;
Here at Thy feet we lay
All our desires; do Thou
Direct us now.

O loving Comforter, help our infirmities;
That which we know not, teach;
Fashion our mortal speech
That we may know to pray
The Heavenly way.

EHW

Empty, We Come

O Love of loves, we have no good to bring Thee,
No single good of all our hands have wrought.
No worthy music have we found to sing Thee,
No jeweled word, no quick up-soaring thought.

And yet we come; and when our faith would falter
Show us, O Lord, the quiet place of prayer,
The golden censer and the golden altar,
And the great angel waiting for us there.

GBM

Only a Prayer

The sun has set. I have no song to bring Thee,
Yet Thou hast been a Shadow from the heat;
And out of dearth a quickened faith would sing Thee,
Who all day long hast been my cool Retreat.

I do not see my withered leaves turn golden;
Poor was the fruit that ever on me grew.
Nought but Thy love, unfathomed, unbeholden,
Would bear with me as Thou hast hitherto.

I have no song. I cannot see to gather
One songful word in this dim twilit hour.
I am a prayer, only a prayer, my Father:
Give me to give—a leaf or bud or flower.

TMS

Wandering Thoughts

Gather my thoughts, good Lord; they fitful roam
Like children bent on foolish wandering,
Or vanity of fruitless wayfaring—
O call them home.

See them—they drift like the wind-scattered foam;
Like wild sea birds, they hither, thither fly,
And some sink low, and others soar too high—
O call them home.

Wherever, Lord, beneath the wide blue dome
They wander, in Thy patience find them there:
That, undistracted, I may go to prayer—
O call them home.

EHW, TJ, WHP

Unperturbed Prayer

Lord Jesus, Intercessor,
Oh, teach us how to pray:
Not wave-like, rising, falling,
In fitful clouds of spray.
The mighty tides of ocean
A deeper secret know;
Their currents undefeated move
Whatever winds may blow.

Lord Jesus, Intercessor,
Creator of the sea,
Teach us the tides' great secret
Of quiet urgency.
Spindrift of words we ask not,
But, Lord, we seek to know
The conquering patience of the tides
Whatever winds may blow.

GC

Not Weighing, but Pardoning

(Job 28:7)

There is a path which no fowl knoweth,
Nor vulture's eye hath seen,
A path beside a viewless river
Whose banks are always green—
For it is the way of prayer.
Holy Spirit, lead us there.

Oh, lead us on; weigh not our merits,
For we have none to weigh;
But, Savior, pardon our offenses.
Lead even us today
Further in the way of prayer.
Holy Spirit, lead us there.

ACD, TJ

Teach Me

Teach me to pray Thy prayer;
Out of the depths I pray,
Teach me to climb Thy stair,
Teach me to think Thy way.

TMS

We Would See Beyond

(Lamentations 3:44)

Lord, art Thou wrapped in cloud,
That prayer should not pass through?
But heart that knows Thee sings aloud,
Beyond the grey, the blue;
Look up, look up to the hills afar,
And see in clearness the evening star.

Should misty weather try
The temper of the soul,
Come, Lord, and purge and fortify,
And let Thy hands make whole;
As we look up to the hills afar,
And see in clearness the evening star.

For never twilight dim
But candles bright are lit,
And then the heavenly vesper hymn—
The peace of God in it;
As we look up to the hills afar,
And see in clearness the evening star.

ACD, GC, P, RFB, TJ

Communing in Prayer

Jesus our Lord, the thought of Thee
Unlooses prayer and song;
Oh, by the blessèd thought of Thee,
We would be borne along.

Bear us along to realms of prayer,
To regions yet undreamed;
Oh, let us meet and commune there—
Redeemer and redeemed.

Wg[2]

Let Hindering Flesh Retire

Lead us, lead us, blessèd Spirit,
    To the open land of prayer;
Trusting in the Savior's merit,
    We would meet our Father there.
Burn, oh, burn,
    Holy Fire;
        Let the hindering flesh retire.

Wg[2]

Open Thy Windows

Open Thy windows, Lord, we pray;
Thou art as Thou wert yesterday.

Thou hast not brought us, Lord, so far
To leave us without pilot star.

Teach us to pray: our faith renew,
O do as Thou art wont to do.

That we may work Thy will today,
Open Thy windows, Lord, we pray.

Under Thine opened heavens may we
Worship, adore, rejoice in Thee,

And dwelling in that shining place
Hear our Lord's voice and see His face.

Wd

Soaring Prayer

Lord, teach our prayers to soar; O let them rise.
Let me be occupied with highest gain;
Rumor of earth, let it not anywise
Pull down our prayers to some poor, lower plane.
Thy purposes are far above our sight;
What of eternal ends can mortals know?
Great Spirit, guide us that we pray aright;
Deep thoughts of God, our shallows overflow.

Thy name, O Lord, Thy name exalted be;
Thy purposes fulfilled, Thy will be done,
That all the world in all her corners see
The glory of Thy Well-belovèd Son,
That all the world in all her corners own
The Prince of Life, for sinners crucified,
The Prince of Peace, the Lamb upon the Throne,
The travail of His soul now satisfied.

Wg²

Two Gardens

There were two gardens in the land,
And both lay on a hill;
And one was called Gethsemane,
The other was near Calvary;
And both are with us still.

Lord, when we climb our Olivet,
Show us the garden there;
And teach us how to kneel with Thee
Beneath some ancient olive tree
And learn to pray Thy prayer.

(Continued)

And when we climb the farther hill,
Where once the mighty powers
Of hell defied Thee, lift our eyes
To where the peaceful garden lies
That welcomed Thee with flowers.
K

Do Thou for Me
(Psalm 109:21)

Do Thou for me, O God the Lord;
Do Thou for me.
I need not toil to find the word
That carefully
Unfolds my prayer and offers it,
My God, to Thee.

It is enough that Thou wilt do,
And wilt not tire;
Wilt lead by cloud, all the night through
By light of fire,
Till Thou hast perfected in me
Thy heart's desire.

For my beloved I will not fear;
Love knows to do
For him, for her, from year to year,
As hitherto.
Whom my heart cherishes are dear
To Thy heart too.

O blessèd be the love that bears
  The burden now,
The love that frames our very prayers,
  Well knowing how
To coin our gold! O God the Lord,
  Do Thou, do Thou.

RFB, TJ

O Splendor of God's Will

O splendor of God's will,
  Clear shining mystery,
I worship and am still,
  Hushed by the thought of Thee.
Thy great and noble ways
  Lowland and mountain know;
Fair flower-bells chime their praise,
  And to Thee waters flow.

O Will most lovable,
  Young budding trees aflame
And all things beautiful
  Illuminate Thy name.
Far hast Thou passed my prayer;
  Good hast Thou been to me;
Thy lover everywhere,
  Blessed Will, make me to Thee.

GC, Wg[1]

Where Dwellest Thou?

O what is it that wanders in the wind?
And what is it that whispers in the wood?
What is the river singing to the sun?
Why this vague pain in every charmèd sense,
   This yearning, keen suspense?

Often I've seen a garment floating by,
Fringe of it only; golden brown it lay
On the ripe grasses, fern-green on the ferns,
And in the wood, like bluebells' misty blue
   Whitened with mountain dew.

I laid me low among the mountain grass;
I laid me low among the river fern;
I hid me in the wood and tried to hold
The lovely wonder of it as it passed,
   And tried to hold it fast.

It slipped like sunshine through my eager hands;
See, they are dusted as with pollen dust,
Soft dust of gold, and soft the sense of touch,
Soft as the south wind's sea-blown evening kiss;
   But I have only this . . .

This dust of vanished gold upon my hands,
This breath of wind blowing upon my hair,
Stirring of something near, so near, but far,
Glimm'ring through color's fleeting preciousness—
   The fringes of a dress.

O Wearer of that garment, if its hem,
Hardly perceived, can thrill us, what must Thou,
Its Weaver and its Wearer, be to see?
Master, where dwellest Thou? O tell me now,
 Where dwellest Thou?

The grasses turned their golden heads away,
And shyer and more wistful stood the ferns;
The little flowers looked up with puzzled eyes;
Only the river, who is all my own,
 Left me not quite alone . . .

But mixed his music with my human cry,
Till somewhere from the half-withdrawing wood
Sound of familiar footsteps: Is it Thou?
Master, where dwellest Thou? O speak to me.
 And He said, "*Come and see.*"

PVV, TJ

God's Footsteps

O hush of dawn, breathe through the air
 And fill the heart in me.
Still is this mountain land, as where
 God's footsteps be.

And can it be He walks these woods,
 These paths that we have swept?
Then may my heart with all her moods
 Be holier kept.

For not to this dear place belongs
 Aught but the good and gay.
Be all my thoughts like wild birds' songs
 On this Thy day.

ACD, DS, K

Fulfill Thy Will

(Psalm 42:5)

"O my soul, why art thou vexed
And disquieted in me?"
Why cast down and sore perplexed,
Goest thou so heavily?
Hath the Lord thy God forgot?
Can it be He careth not?

Nay, He careth. Clouds of sadness
Quick dissolve in gracious rain.
God of all my joy and gladness,
I will tune my harp again:
I will sing Thy love long tried,
And Thy comforts multiplied.

I have proved the heavenly treasure
Sustenance in desert land;
I have tasted of the pleasure
Stored for us at Thy right hand.
Now right joyously I praise
Thee, the Succor of my days.

Surely peace, like some fair river,
Reacheth even unto me;
And my leaf need never wither
For my root is hid in Thee.
Ever let Thy love fulfill
In me, Lord, Thy welcome will.

MP, P

Teach Thou Me

That which I know not teach Thou me.
Who, blessèd Lord, teacheth like Thee?
Lead my desires that they may be
According to Thy will.

Kindle my thoughts that they may glow,
And lift them up where they are low;
And freshen them, that they may flow
According to Thy will.

GC

O Lord, Our Strength and Confidence

O Lord, our strength and confidence,
Our eyes are unto Thee;
Thou art the rock of our defence,
Our song of victory,
Thou who dost still the violence
Of any raging sea.

Thou at the flood didst sit as King;
What are our floods to Thee,
To whom it is a little thing
To walk upon the sea?
We wait to hail Thee conquering,
King of eternity.

Only, O Lord our God, we pray,
Teach us to do Thy will,
Through windy hours and flying spray
Thy purposes fulfill,
Until the word of yesterday
Thou speakest—"Peace, be still."

P

Peace, Be Still

(Mark 4:39)

Master, speak Thy "Peace, be still"
To the tumult of the will;
Walking on the restless wave,
Come and save.

Wind and wave obey Thee, Lord;
Speak, O speak the calming word;
O command the tossing will:
"Peace, be still."

Wg[1]

Help Us to Follow

O Lord of Calvary, suffering, slain,
We worship low before Thy Cross.
O Lord of death and Lord of pain—
To us the gain, to Thee, the loss.

O Lord of comfort, love and life,
Although we fail, Thou art the same.
O Lord of strength in days of strife,
We glorify Thy Holy Name.

O Lord of calm, above the sea
We hear the whisper of Thy call;
Help us to rise and follow Thee,
Obedient, joyful, giving all.

Wg[2]

As One Forgiven

My Lord, my Love, came down from heaven;
With sharp wild thorn they hurt His brow,
Before e'er He could say, "Forgiven,
From Egypt, even until now."

My Lord, my Love, was sorely riven;
His pure soul He to death did bow
That He might say to me: "Forgiven,
From Egypt, even until now."

O Love, that Thy poor child hath shriven
I know not why, I know not how;
Help me to live as one forgiven—
From Egypt, even until now.

K

God of Hope

Great God of Hope, how green Thy trees,
How calm each several star.
Renew us; make us fresh as these,
Calm as those are.

For what can dim his hope who sees,
Though faintly and afar,
The power that kindles green in trees
And light in star?

TJ

What Fear?

O Thou in whose right hand were seven stars,
And whose right hand was on Thy servant laid,
How tender was Thy touch, Thy word, "Be not afraid."
Thou who didst say, "O man greatly beloved,
Fear not," and "Peace be unto thee, be strong,"
What wealth of grace and mercy doth to Thee belong!

Thy touch, Thy word, and lo, like to a cloud
That was, but is not, in the fields of air,
So is the fear we feared; we look—it is not there:
Dissolved, departed, banished by Thy touch.
Oh, as we pray, purge us from every fear,
Thou who dost hold the stars—our Lord, art Thou not here?

TG

More Than a Conqueror

(Romans 8:37)

Lover Divine, whose love has sought and found me,
Thou dost not leave me when the night is round me;
Cause me to be, held fast by Love Eternal,
More than a conqueror.

Open my eyes to see the stars above me;
Quicken my heart that I may feel Thee love me;
Make me, and keep me through Thy love eternal,
More than a conqueror.

What storm can shatter, gloom of darkness frighten
One whom the Lord doth shelter, cherish, lighten?
O let me be, through powers of love eternal,
More than a conqueror.

RFB, Wg[1]

For Us and These

Christ our Captain, hear our prayer:
Warriors we ask of Thee,
Comrades who shall everywhere
Stand for love and loyalty;
Servants who with souls aflame,
Kindled from Thine altar fire,
Live to magnify Thy name,
Live to meet Thy least desire;
Lovers who in love abide
In the Secret Place of rest,
Yielded to be crucified
That Thy life be manifest;
Laborers who joyfully
Choose rewards unseen today.
Cause us, O our Lord, to be
Like to these for whom we pray.

ACD

Until the Stars Appear

(Nehemiah 4:21)

Make us Thy laborers.
Let us not dream of ever looking back;
Let not our knees be feeble, hands be slack;
O make us strong to labor, strong to bear,
From the rising of the morning until the stars appear.

Make us Thy warriors,
On whom Thou canst depend to stand the brunt
Of any perilous charge on any front;
Give to us the skill to handle sword and spear,
From the rising of the morning until the stars appear.

(Continued)

Not far from us, those stars—
Unseen as angels, and yet looking through
The quiet air, the day's transparent blue.
What shall we know, and feel, and see, and hear
When the sunset colors kindle and evening stars appear?

TG, TJ

The Last Defile

Make us Thy mountaineers—
We would not linger on the lower slope.
Fill us afresh with hope, O God of Hope,
That undefeated we may climb the hill
As seeing Him who is invisible.

Let us die climbing. When this little while
Lies far behind us, and the last defile
Is all alight, and in that light we see
Our Leader and our Lord—what will it be?

ACD, TJ

Though

Let spirit conquer, though the flesh
Be strong to prison and enmesh.

And though the Shining Summit be
Far, far from me, Lord, far from me,

And though black precipices frown,
"*O let me climbe when I lye down.*"*

*Vaughan (1622-1695)

TJ

Thy Way Is Perfect

(2 Samuel 22:31)

Long is the way, and very steep the slope;
Strengthen me once again, O God of Hope.

Far, very far, the summit doth appear;
But Thou art near, my God, but Thou art near.

And Thou wilt give me with my daily food,
Powers of endurance, courage, fortitude.

Thy way is perfect; only let that way
Be clear before my feet from day to day.

Thou art my Portion, saith my soul to Thee,
Oh, what a Portion is my God to me!

TJ

Teach Me to Climb

Let the stern array
Of the forbidding be a constant call
To fling into the climb my will, my all.
Teach me to climb.

TMS

Grant Us . . .

Grant us inward fortitude:
Will to choose the highest good,
Eyes to see the jewel set
In plain duty's coronet;
Spirits sensitive and pure,
Disciplined to serve, endure—
And fulfilled with sweet content,
All their powers to please Thee bent.

K

Dawn

Beauty of Dawn, I come to Thee;
Pour through my cold and dark ravine,
Lighten the leaves of this my tree;
Cause them to shine in living green.

Light of my heart, I come to Thee;
Oh, let me see Thy conquering might.
Powers of the darkness compass me—
Stronger art Thou, O Lord of Light.

What is their power, my Lord, to Thee?
Shadows of fear, oh, flee away;
I hear my Captain calling me—
Where is the night? 'Tis dawn, 'tis day.

Wg[2]

Thy Peter's Word

(Luke 22:32)

Lest I should faint before the race be run,
Lest I should quail before the fight be won,
O heavenly Intercessor and my Lord,
Fulfill to me Thy comfortable word—
Thy Peter's word. How can I be afraid
If Thou dost say to me, "But I have prayed"?

TMS

Security

When stormy winds against us break,
    Stablish and reinforce our will;
O hear us for Thine own Name's sake;
    Hold us in strength, and hold us still.

Still as the faithful mountains stand
    Through the long, silent years of stress,
So would we wait at Thy right hand,
    In quietness and steadfastness.

But not of us this strength, O Lord,
    And not of us this constancy;
Our trust is Thine eternal word,
    Thy presence our security.

TMS

Make Us Calm

Jesus, our Risen Lord,
King of the grave,
Ruler of threatening powers,
Fierce wind and wave;
Courage and peace and song,
To Thee, dear Lord, belong;
O make us calm and strong,
Peaceful and brave.

Wg²

Tranquility

Lord of all tranquility,
O incline to us Thine ear;
Hide us very privily
When our cruel foe draws near.
Steady Thou the wills that stray;
Purify our penitence;
Move in us that we may pray
And rejoice with reverence.

Fold our souls in silence deep;
Grant us from ourselves to pass;
Lead, Good Shepherd, us Thy sheep
To the fields of tender grass,
Where Thy hush is in the air
And Thy flowers the hedges dress;
Cause for us to flow forth there
Waters of Thy quietness.

MP, P, TJ

Too Hard for Me

Jesus, mighty Savior,
  Lover of the soul,
Who but Thee can quicken,
  Who but Thee make whole?
This that I have brought Thee
  Is too hard for me,
But is anything too hard,
  My Lord, for Thee?
By Thy Cross and Passion,
  Precious blood outpoured—
Plead I now: Command deliverance,
  Blessèd Lord.

K

Turmoil

Lord, Thou knowest, Thou beholdest
Shame of Christendom;
Cloudy is the night and stormy;
Star of Morning, come, O come.

All the air is full of turmoil,
Trumpet, beat of drum,
Nations rising against nation;
Conqueror of conquerors, come.

Heavy-laden are the peoples,
Wand'ring blind and dumb,
Yet their very need is calling:
Even so, Lord Jesus, come.

(Continued)

Blessèd be the Love that gave us
This of prayers, the sum:
Shine, O shine forth, Prince of Glory;
King of kings, Thy Kingdom come.

Wg[2]

Renew Our Force

(Matthew 14:27)

Renew our force, O Lord, that waging
A tireless war against the foe,
We may together forward go,
Undaunted by his angry raging.

O Spirit of Power and Love, enfold us;
O valiant Spirit of Discipline,
Turn Thy bright face on us and shine;
And shame our dullness, and uphold us.

Thou hast not given a spirit of fear.
The word is strong: "Be of good cheer!"
And Thou art here.

GC

Teach Us, O Captain

Mighty, mighty is the Lord;
 Mighty is the piercing sword.
Teach us how to use our weapons;
 Teach our fingers how to fight.
O unconquerable Captain,
 Put the enemy to flight.

Patient, patient is the Lord;
 Long delayed is Love's reward.
God of hope and God of patience,
 Tender and compassionate—
O unconquerable Captain,
 Teach us how to watch and wait.

Wg[2]

I Would Be Steadfast

What though I stand with the winners,
 Or perish with those that fall?
Only the cowards are sinners;
 Fighting the fight is all.

Strong is my foe who advances;
 Snapped is my blade, O Lord.
See their proud banners and lances—
 But spare me the stub of a sword.

GC

Perseverance

Sing, heart within me, though no shout ascendeth,
No trumpet soundeth on this battlefield.
Yet sing, my heart, O sing the Grace that lendeth
Courage to stand thy ground and not to yield.

Not in me, Lord, Thou knowest, was there ever
Strength to endure, or any fortitude.
Now in the silence, come—for I would never
Miss Thy bright Presence, walk in solitude.

Broken my sword—what use a weapon broken?
Yet with that broken blade till set of sun
I fain would fight. O blessed be the token—
The secret token saith: Fight on! Fight on!

TMS

Provision in Battle

Arouse in our hearts, O Christ,
The faith that welcometh battle:
  Strange defeats may sore distress,
  Crippling wounds afflict, oppress;
  Never let our weariness
  Weaken faith within.

Create in our hearts, O Christ,
The peace that halloweth battle:
  Battle cries assault the ear,
  Cries of triumph or of fear;
  Never let them domineer
  Over peace within.

Maintain in our hearts, O Christ,
The joy that lighteneth battle:
Bitter in persistency
Though the grief of battle be,
Never let despondency
Dull the joy within.

Awake, lute and harp, and play
The mystic music of battle:
Make us strong, O Christ, make strong;
Grant that nothing stifle song;
The song of the Lord prolong—
Be our Song within!

MP, P

Come, Victorious Warrior

Stir up Thy warrior strength
And come to our help, O God.
Right are Thy judgments, King of saints,
And the place Thy feet have trod—
Be it mountain, plain, or the utmost sea—
Is strewn with the spoils of victory.
Alleluia, Amen.

Vain is the help of man;
The prince is a thing of nought;
Dust in the balance, vanity,
And the sum of all they wrought,
Like a withered leaf from a fallen tree
Has perished away from memory.
Alleluia, Amen.

(Continued)

Oh, whet Thy glitt'ring sword,
  Lay hold upon battle bow;
Arrows as lightnings Thou dost send
  To make all the nations know
That the shields of the earth belong to Thee
With whom is the power and victory.
  Alleluia, Amen.

MP, P

Yield? . . . Oh, Never!

"My wells run over;
Grace shall not fail—
Ever and ever
In Me prevail.
Stand stiffly in the fight;
Stand stiffly for the right;
Yield to the hosts of night?
Never, oh, never!

"I am thy refuge,
Readily found;
Ever and ever
Stand, stand thy ground.
Go forth in this thy might,
Stand strong, advance and smite;
Yield to the hosts of night?
Never, oh, never!"

Oh, my Redeemer,
Leader and Friend,
Ever and ever,
On to the end,
Keep Thou my hope alight;
Let nought my faith affright;
Yield to the hosts of night?
Never, oh, never!

DS

Strengthen the Brave

(Psalm 93:4)

Lord God Omnipotent, King of the Ages,
Mighty the waves, like the waves of the sea,
Flood after flood lifts his billows and rages.
What is the noise of those waters to Thee?

Father, we rest in Thee; O let us never
Dream of defeat, for defeat cannot be.
Comfort and strengthen the brave, wheresoever
They toil and suffer that souls may be free.

Spirit of Discipline, hold our wills steady,
Faithful and peaceful through pleasure and pain;
Weld us together in comradeship, ready
For the great Day of Thy coming again.

FTR

Thy Kingdom Come

"Thy Kingdom come, King of Eternity";
We bring this prayer of Dew and Fire to Thee.

The hearts of men are failing them for fear;
But we lift up our heads, for Thou art near.

Though lamps of earth are darkened one by one,
Thy stars abide. Thy holy will be done.

Though smoke of earth becloudeth blue of skies,
Like tongue of flame, this prayer of prayers shall rise;

And as it riseth, life's confusions pass;
Down falleth peace, like dew upon the grass.

And yet our prayer still burneth up to Thee:
"Thy Kingdom come, King of Eternity."

TMS

Strengthen Us to Carry Through

Trumpets, bugles of the Lord,
Sound the mighty battle word;
Sound it till our flagging spirits
Rise and answer, "Hitherto,
God of battles, Thou hast led us;
Strengthen us to carry through."

Trumpets, bugles of the Lord,
You have sounded, we have heard.
"Captain of our souls," we answer,
"Work in us to will and do;
Though the hosts of hell oppose us,
Strengthen us to carry through."

Trumpets, bugles of the Lord,
Sound again the glorious word;
Sound it if the flesh would falter,
Seek to smother and subdue;
Hold us fast and hold us faithful;
Strengthen us to carry through.

Wg[2]

A Warrior Soul

O Lord, this Gideon make
  A warrior soul;
And when for Thy Name's sake
  He pays the toll
And goes without the camp,
Let nought his spirit damp.
  Not solitary he
  Who follows Thee.

O perish coward fears;
  Are battles won
Without shed blood or tears?
  Let not Thy son
Count any pain too sore
That Christ his Captain bore.
  Would he choose ease who knows
  What his Lord chose?

No, never, by Thy grace,
  Shall that choice be!
O reinforce and brace
  Thy son that he
Shall be Thy warrior,
And more than conqueror.
  So fortify each hour,
  For Thine's the power.

Wg[1]

Warfare Won

Jehovah Nissi, disappoint
  Thine ancient enemy.
Because Thy throne he hath defied,
By virtue of the Crucified
  We claim the victory.

The Terrible would hold his prey;
  O Lamb of God, command
The shining legions of the light
To put this Amalek to flight;
  The Cause is in Thy hand.

Our hands be steady, then, until
  The setting of the sun;
Then sudden, through the cloudy skies
The dawn shall break, the song shall rise,
  The song of warfare won.

EHW

Beauty and Battle

Beauty and battle—both are of Thee.
Lighten mine eyes till I joyfully see
Beauty in all that Thou givest to me,
  Lord of the light.

Battle and beauty—both must there be.
Grant me Thy courage that, fearless and free,
Facing the odds, I may conquer with Thee,
  Lord of the fight.

Unp

Thy Great Cathedral

(A Song of the Open Air)

Lord, here Thy great Cathedral stands,
A house of God not made with hands;
High overhead the splendid roof—
From trivial thoughts how far aloof—
And underfoot the lovely floor
Call us to wonder and adore.

Thy hand piled up these mighty walls,
Made for sweet music, streams and falls,
Filled it with bird song, dressed with flowers,
With ferns and moss, and made it ours.
Oh, purify our praise that we
Who love Thee, Lord, may worship Thee.

We see no holy table spread,
But art Thou not our Living Bread?
O Bread of Life, O one True Vine,
Grant unto us the Bread and Wine,
Till in communion mystical
We apprehend things spiritual.

MP, P

Things Not Seen

Great Son of Man, who walked our dust,
    Thy love will not forget
The power the temporal has to thrust
    And overset.

O let Thy touch make things we see
    Transparent to our eyes,
That secrets of Eternity
    We may surprise.

And let the things which are not seen
    Shine like the stars at night
Till all the space that lies between
    Be filled with light.

EHW, FT

To Higher Things

O Radiant Lord, as morning dew,
    Thy freshness meets us everywhere.
A faith that never dares the new,
    Unhazardous and wavering prayer—
Oh, do we choose this dust, that we
    So often offer it to Thee?

Oh, lift our souls to higher things,
    And lift our thoughts to Thy desire;
Give us the faith that mounts on wings;
    Give us the love that burns like fire,
The love that leads to Calvary;
    Not less than this, we ask of Thee.

GC

For Burning Love

O for a love, for burning love
 Like fervent flame of fire;
O for a love, for yearning love,
 Love that will never tire;
Lord, in my need I appeal to Thee,
 Grant me now my heart's desire.

TMS, Wg[1]

The Prince's Love

The Prince of Life was crucified;
He hung upon the bitter tree,
For love of all—for love of me.

The Prince of Life, He rose again;
He triumphed in great majesty,
That I and all might be set free.

The Prince of Life is Heaven's King;
I am the least of things that be;
And yet He says He cares for me.

O Prince of Life, give me Thy love,
The thirst of love that was in Thee
From Bethlehem to Calvary.

K, Wg[1]

Ask . . . But Give

Deep unto deep, O Lord,
Crieth in me;
Gathering strength I come,
Lord, unto Thee.
Jesus of Calvary,
Smitten for me,
Ask what Thou wilt, but give
Love to me.

GBM, Wg[1]

Uplifting Power

And can it be what I have sought:
This quick, uplifting power,
This quiet peace that passes thought,
This bud that breaks in flower;

This sense of wings, of flashing wings,
This light where all was dim?
Lord Jesus, how the dumb man sings
When Thou dost come to him.

Oh, it was Thou for whom I longed;
And Thou hast longed for me.
Oh, pardon that I ever wronged
The deep, deep love in Thee.

Wg[1]

The Heavenly Power of Love

Whatever wind may blow,
 Whatever rain may chill,
O keep the fire of love aglow,
 Mine eyes on Calvary's hill.

There, there I apprehend,
 For there alone I see
The love that loveth to the end;
 O give that love to me.

Renew it day by day
 As Thou dost, Lord, renew
The water in the waterway,
 The sky's eternal blue.

O let me never fail,
 But ever live to prove,
The heavenly power that doth prevail,
 The heavenly power of love.

Wg[1]

Thou Lovest Me!

Thou knewest me before I was;
 I am all open unto Thee;
And yet Thou lovest me, because—
 Thou, my Lord, lovest me.

No other reason can I find;
 No other reason can there be;
No human love, were it not blind,
 Could ever care for me.

(Continued)

But Thy pure eyes do read me through;
    My soul is naked unto Thee;
And yet—oh wonder ever new—
    Thou, my Lord, lovest me.

And Thou wilt love. If good of mine
    Had caused Thy glorious love to be,
Then surely would Thy love decline
    And weary, Lord, of me.

I may not fear, for to the end
    Thou lovest. Who save only Thee,
The sinner's Savior and his Friend,
    Would set his love on me?

And on Thee now my heart is set;
    Thy name is music unto me.
O help me never to forget
    That I am loved by Thee.

EHW, MP, P

Father of Lights

(James 1:17; Ecclesiasticus 25:11)

Father of Lights,
No faintest variation
Was ever shown by Thee.
"Love passeth all things for illumination";
I worship Thee.

Father of Lights,
No shadow cast by turning
Was ever cast by Thee.
O Flame of love, so steadfast, so discerning,
I worship Thee.

Father of Lights,
Thy very name Love giveth
To son reborn in Thee.
Grant me to walk as one who ever liveth,
O Light, in Thee.

Wg[1]

Love's Eternal Wonder

Lord belovèd, I would ponder
    Breadth and length and depth and height
Of Thy love's eternal wonder—
    All embracing, infinite.

Never, never have I brought Thee
    Gold and frankincense and myrrh;
In the hands that, groping, sought Thee,
    Precious treasures never were.

What was that to Thee? The measure
    Of Thy love was Calvary.
Stooping low, Love found a treasure
    In the least of things that be.

Oh, the passion of Thy loving;
    Oh, the flame of Thy desire!
Melt my heart with Thy great loving;
    Set me all aglow, afire!

TJ, Wg[1]

Endurance

(Isaiah 41:10; John 14:3)

God of patience and endurance,
    Steadfast as the steadfast stars
Stands Thy promise, Thine assurance
    Unto Thine ambassadors:
"I, thy God, will strengthen thee . . .
Where I am, there thou shalt be."

Lord, we would endure; O sift us
    Clear of weakness; make us strong.
Lord, we would endure; O lift us
    Into joy and conquering song.
Cause us in Thy peace to dwell,
Seeing the invisible.

Let us welcome all life's weather,
    Whatsoever it may be;
And, or singly or together,
    Find our heart's delight in Thee,
Our Redeemer, our Adored,
Lover and belovèd Lord.

EHW

Ministry of Song

For joy of song that Thou hast given us, Lord,
Brave battle song, like flashing of a sword,
Love's jewel song, alight with golden word—
        Our adoring alleluia.

For sweet and mystic power of melody
That wings the soul so swiftly up to Thee,
Harpers of God—for their great ministry—
We adore Thee. Alleluia!

Forgive us, Lord, that ever we have failed
When, had we sung, we should have far out-sailed
Mist of the earth, and risen and prevailed,
And adored Thee. Alleluia!

O let us live and breathe no otherwhere
Than in the clearness of that upper air,
Fulfilled with song to Thee who reignest there.
Alleluia! Alleluia!

TMS, Wg[1]

Foundations

Set our foundations on the holy hills;
Our city found
Firm on the bedrock of the Truth; our wills
Settle and ground.
Cause us to stand to our own conscience clear;
Cause us to be the thing that we appear.

Water our city with the river of God
Whose streams are full;
Make Thou the glowing sand, the barren sod
To be a pool.
Source of all beauty, may our city be,
By Thy good grace, a pleasance, Lord, for Thee.

(Continued)

Hallow, O Lord, our city's day, the while
We work in joy,
So that our common deeds may cast a smile,
And life's annoy
Be all forgotten, as Thy servants meet
About Thy business in our city street.

MP, P, TJ

Builders' Needs

(2 Chronicles 24:9–12)

O King of kings, once Thou didst make decree,
Forthwith expenses should be given to them
Who built Thy temple in Jerusalem.

We are Thy builders, Lord; we come to Thee:
Let the expenses for Thy work be given;
Open once more the windows of high heaven.

Wd

Life's Street

As when in some fair mountain place
Beneath an open roof of sky,
Where almost see we face to face,
All but perceive Thy host sweep by,
We feel our sin and folly fade—
Intrusive things that cannot be—
Smitten by glory and afraid,
Condemned by such high company . . .

So let it be, Lord, when we know
 The pressures of life's crowded street,
The ceaseless murmur of its flow,
 The mud that lies about our feet.
O lift our souls; from star to star
 We would ascend, until we be
In heavenly places still, afar—
 The while we walk life's street with Thee.

TJ , Wg[1]

Moonlight

Moonlight's tranquility:
A shimm'ring ocean, like a silver band
Between the misty sky and misty land,
And dreaming mountains sweeping to the sea.

The forest slowly heaves
And murmurs as the low night wind awakes;
The moon rides through her filmy vapors, takes
Handfuls of moonbeams, strews them on its leaves.

The shining grasses light
The fells with flow'ry arrows silver-tipped,
And their long spears are bright as though they dipped
In dews of silver through the silver night.

Lord, when we take our part
Tomorrow in life's duty, feel the rush
Of hurrying hours, let not their passing brush
The sense of moonlit quiet from our hearts.

DS

Evensong

The world is still. Sunlight and moonlight meeting
Lay long, soft shadows on the dusty road;
The sheep are folded, not a lamb is bleating.
Fold me, O God.

The feverish hours have cooled, and ceased the wrestling
For place and power; hushed is the last loud word;
Only a mother calls her wayward nestling,
"Come, little bird."

Never a stir but 'tis Thy hand that settles
Tired flowers' affairs and piles a starry heap
Of night lights on the jasmine. Touch my petals;
Put me to sleep.

DS, RFB, TJ

The Silver Song

Day unto day, Lord speaketh in light,
And in the darkness, night unto night;
Never a dark but somewhere a song
Singeth the whole night long.

Oh, precious things put forth by the moon—
Let not the heat and hurry of noon
Silence the silver song that I heard,
Stifle the low, sweet word.

GC

Thou Be . . .

"Thou be my loving, that I Thy love sing";*
Thou be my longing, that I to Thee cling;
Thou be my thinking, that I Thy will know;
Thou be my willing, that I Thy will do.

Me to redeem, Thou didst die on the Tree;
Dearworthy, dearworthy art Thou to me.

* Richard Rolle, fourteenth century

K

Today

O God, renew us in Thy love today;
For our tomorrow we have not a care;
Who blessed us yesterday
Will meet us there.

But our today is all athirst for Thee.
Come in Thy stillness, O Thou heavenly Dew;
Come Thou to us—to me—
Revive, renew.

TJ

Give Us . . .

Oh, give us heavenly wisdom, Lord,
That all the windings of the way
And all the questions of the day
Shall find us loyal to Thy word.

Oh, give us courage, patience, song—
The song that sings and does not quail,
The love that loves and does not fail,
The heart that suffers and is strong.

Wg[2]

Love's Repose

O Love in whom alone is love's repose,
Give me to welcome thorn as well as rose.

Thy way is perfect; only let that way
Be clear before my feet from day to day.

Thou art my Portion, saith my soul to Thee;
Oh, what a Portion is my God to me.

Wg[2]

Strange Ashes

But these strange ashes, Lord? this nothingness,
This baffling sense of loss?
"Son, was the anguish of My stripping less
Upon the torturing Cross?

"Was I not brought into the dust of death,
A worm, and no man, I?
Yea, turned to ashes by the vehement breath
Of fire—on Calvary?

"O son beloved, this is thy heart's desire:
This and no other thing
Follows the fall of the Consuming Fire
On the burnt offering.

"Go now and taste the joy set high, afar—
No joy like that for thee—
See how it lights thy way like some great star.
Come now and follow Me."

MB

Unconvinced

Is to rack souls joy?
Does turn of screw make songs? or hammering
Of most unkindly fortune waken music?
Such hammers fall too heavily for that.

GBM, PVV

Not Only . . . But Also

(Philippians 1:29)

Not only love but also loneliness—
Yea, even so.
What though the nearest may not ever know
All that in this must be,
That being a secret between Thee and me,
Thou knowest. And it cannot work me ill,
Being Thy will;
And by and by
Thou wilt satisfy.

But unknown years stand up and stare at me.
The sun beats hot;
I look around for shelter, find it not.
Companion me;
Be shelter, Lord, to me!
O let Thy shadow be
As the cool starlit night—in noonday—unto me.

MP

Thy Healing Word

(John 14:27)

Jesus, blessèd Lord,
Jesus, heart's adored,
Speak, O speak Thy healing word
Even to me.

Jesus, blessèd Lord,
Jesus, heart's adored,
Now for this Thy loving word
Praise, praise to Thee!

Wg[1]

Bluebells

Once in a granite hill
God carved a hollow place,
Called the blue air, and said, "Now fill
This emptiness of space."

Or was it angels came,
And set among the fells
A crystal bowl, and filled the same
With handfuls of bluebells?

Hot hours walked overhead;
Our valley grew more sweet,
Though elsewhere gentle colors fled
Fearing those burning feet.

Those burning feet—the fells
Are withered where they go,
But still the misty blue bluebells
Only the bluer blow.

O God, who made the bowl
  And filled it full of blue,
Canst Thou not make of this, my soul,
  A vase of flowers, too?

Let not the hot hours make
  Thy child as withered fells,
But fill me full, for love's dear sake,
  With blue as of bluebells.

MP, P

Show Me the Shining of Thy Face

As when on mountain, wood and stream,
  A chilly mist doth sudden fall,
And passeth as a shining dream
  The glory that did lighten all,

So is it, Savior, when a chill
  As if of mist oppresseth me;
Where is the garden, where the hill,
  Gethsemane and Calvary?

My joyous colors faint and fade
  In cloudiness of dim distress;
And whispering doubts assail; afraid,
  I walk as in a wilderness.

In such an hour, send forth Thy wind
  That it may purge my heavy air;
The base affections of my mind—
  Let them be sought out, dealt with there.

(Continued)

O sweetness, move in me, renew;
    Look down from heaven, Thy dwelling place;
And do as Thou art wont to do.
    Show me the shining of Thy face.

DS, MP, P

Obedience

Father, not for vision do I seek Thy presence—
Vision Thou hast granted long, long ago—
But for obedience to the heavenly vision,
Though fogs be smothering, drifting to and fro,
        And daylight be declining.

Love to love unfoldeth loveliness of loving,
Peace to peace revealeth the pearl that we call peace.
O Love of God, fulfill me, overflow me;
O Peace of God, within me still increase
        Thy pure, soft shining.

TMS

Darkened Glasses

As a young child—who looks from mountain land
    In early dawn
On kindling sky, and sea whose silver band
    Curves as if drawn
By shining fingers round the world—is fain,
Though dazzled, still to gaze and gaze again;

So do Thine older children, Lord, forget
    That naked eyes
May hardly bear the Greater Glory set
    In other skies;
And finite, pressing on the infinite,
Know but the wounding of excess of light.

Then, as the child's companion gives a glass
    Darkened to him,
And he, unhurt, sees shapes of wonder pass
    The ocean's rim—
Curled flames afloat in sky of daffodil,
Colors of joy, before invisible—

So, dear Companion of our mountain climb,
    So doest Thou.
Life's darkened glasses we have many a time
    Miscalled, but now
It is not so. Oh, pass before us, pass,
Till we are where they need no darkened glass.

DS

The Heap of Leaves

A pool near a swift water-race:
On its smooth floor a heap of leaves—
Brown, orange, crimson, olive, yellow—
Each lying close beside his fellow,
All gathered very carefully
By the wise water in that place.

(Continued)

I took a handful of dry leaves;
I tossed them out above the heap.
Perceiving my small stratagem,
The eddy caught them, played with them,
Then swept them downstream casually,
Not worth his while to keep.

They danced off like bright shells, unbroken,
Their pretty outlines curled and crisped.
Those in the pool were sodden, wetted
By many a mile of water, fretted
By strange experience. And to me
The thing was a token.

O God, that my poor, battered hopes,
Soaked through and through in baths of tears,
Might yet be gathered, dealt with so
That—from their perishing—plants should grow
To bring forth pleasant fruit to Thee
Through the far distant years!

MP

No Footprint

There is no footprint on the sand
    Where India meets her sapphire sea;
But, Lord of all this ancient land,
    Dost Thou not walk the shore with me?

And yet the goddess holds her state
    Along the frontiers of the sea,
And keeps the road, and bars the gate
    Against Thy tender Majesty.

O Purer than the flying spray,
O Brighter than the sapphire sea—
When will the goddess flee away,
And India walk her shore with Thee?

GC, P, TJ

White Falls

White falls, white falls,
Leaping down the grey rocks,
Gay in the sunshine,
Grave in the shade,
I hear your music,
Hear the words you're singing:
"On and on and on, nor be afraid."

Doth aught bar you?
Gentleness prevaileth;
Open gates before you
Turn to ways your walls—
Till your ravine
Is altogether lovely,
Carven to the music of his falls.

Thou whose voice is
Like to many waters,
Be our ravine,
The lovelier for our flow;
Teach us the words,
And teach us the music
These Thy waters had so long ago.

DS

Soar, Run, Walk

(Isaiah 40:31)

Bear us on eagles' wings,
Lord, lest we faint,
Far, far from groveling things;
Purge from their taint.

Jesus of Calvary,
Draw us to run after Thee;
Hold us to walk with Thee,
Walk, and not faint.

EHW

Gather Us, Lord

Gather us into Thy love, O Lord.
Seeing no glimmer of sun or star,
Exceedingly tossed with tempest we be,
And the land so far—
Gather us into Thy love.

TMS

Give Me a Quiet Mind

When winds are blowing, waves are rising, falling,
And all the air is full of dust and spray;
When voices, like to sea birds' plaintive calling,
Confuse my day;

Then, then I know Thee, Lord of highest heaven,
In newborn need discover Thee, and find
Nought can discomfort him to whom is given
A quiet mind.

When hopes have failed, and heavy sadness crusheth,
And doubt and fear would weave their deadly spell,
Then thought of Thee my troubled spirit husheth;
And all is well.

In midnight hours when weariness ignoreth
Heaven's starry host, and battle wounds are mine,
Then Thy right hand uplifteth and outpoureth
Love's oil and wine.

O blessèd Lord, beyond the moment's sorrow
I see above, beneath, before, behind—
Eternal Love. Give me today, tomorrow,
A quiet mind.

TMS, Wg[2]

To Serve Him Still

I've never seen Him shining through the air;
I've never heard His footsteps anywhere;
And yet, where'er I've gone, I've met Him there.

How often in a busy nursery,
Or kitchen, schoolroom, office—there did He
Meet me with lovingkindness, welcome me.

And now when that is past, and still I wait,
Forbid that dullness clog and dominate,
And I become a cumberer at Thy gate.

TMS

Quicken Again

Pardon, Lord, my deadly dullness.
Like clear shining after rain
Is Thy bright perpetual presence;
Father, quicken me again!
Thou hast done it hitherto;
Do as Thou art wont to do.

Grant instead of deadly dullness
Power, and love, and discipline.
Shine, O bright perpetual Presence,
Father, lighten me within!
Thou hast done it hitherto;
Do as Thou art wont to do.

Wg[2]

Hear and Forgive

(1 Kings 8:30)

"Hear Thou in heaven, Thy dwelling place;
    And when Thou hearest, Lord, forgive";
Our light is Thine unclouded Face;
    In Thine ungrievèd love we live.

And purge us as we seek Thy face,
    Purge fitful faith and fugitive;
"Hear Thou in heaven, Thy dwelling place;
    And when Thou hearest, Lord, forgive."

Wg[2]

Let Us Look Up

Great God of strength and quietness,
Of heights undreamed, of depths profound,
Our poor endeavors shame us less
Than thoughts that often hedge us round:

Our noisy, vain imaginings,
Our busy fears, when we might rise
Serene as on an eagle's wings,
And taste the bliss of heavenly skies.

Thine angels swift, obedient,
Who do Thy pleasure joyfully,
Are round about us, well content
To succor one beloved by Thee.

And Thou our God dost on us wait,
Attentive to our lightest call;
Thy gentleness would make us great
Were we not set on being small.

Forgive us, Lord; in us renew
A faith that cannot fear mischance;
Let us look up and see the blue,
The love light on Thy countenance.

Oh, never, never let us be
As those who have not heard the voice
That calls to us perpetually:
Rejoice; again I say, Rejoice!

MP, P, Wg[1]

My Today

All the field of my Today
Is in shadow, passes from me;
No more can I sow in it;
No more can I grow in it
Anything of joy or sorrow;
It has passed away, away.
Lies before me my Tomorrow.

In me I hear voices say
As my field recedes in shadow:
"What seed didst thou sow in it?
What plants didst thou grow in it?
Will it bring forth joy or sorrow?"
O thou field of my Today,
How wilt thou appear Tomorrow?

Holy Lord, my poor Today
Cries aloud to Thee for pardon;
Take my new field, sow in it
What Thou wilt should grow in it;
Let me not sow seeds of sorrow.
Holy Husbandman, I pray
Keep the field of my Today.

DS

Hallow My Days

(Ecclesiasticus 33:7–9)

"Why doth one day excel another, when the light
Of each is Thee?" O Lord, I do not know.
But since, Lord, it is so,
I come to Thee
Who didst create both these my days and me.

Our exalted days require Thee, lest our thought
Escaping downward by some secret door
Grovel as heretofore.
Hallow, O Lord, our holy days, that nought
May turn Thee from us through those blessed hours
When all our walks and gardens offer flowers.

Our ordinary days without Thy touch
Die double deaths. The Usual cries to Thee
To quicken speedily
Its sometimes barrenness; for life has much
Of sandy levels. Do Thou, Lord, inspire
Our ordinary: be our dull days' fire.

Creator of my individual days
All variously distinguished, each is good,
Distributed by Thee; my gratitude
Bestir; awaken praise.
Look back I dare not, knowing what I know;
O great Forgiver, flow
Over my yesterday; and my today—
Let it be clear and precious. I commit
Its outgoings to Thee: Lord, hallow it.

MP

Let It Blossom

Goodly my heritage, fair is my lot;
Wonderful, Master, art Thou.
I who am least of the things that are not,
Sing with the bird on his bough—
Sing of the love that unfathomed, untracked,
Led me, will lead evermore.
True is Thy word: not a good have I lacked;
Lord, I adore, I adore.

O make my fallow land soft with Thy showers,
Sunburnt and hard though it be;
Grant it a springing of corn and of flowers;
So let it blossom to Thee—
So let it blossom that Thou shalt forget,
Jesus, my Lord crucified,
Thorn that once wounded Thee, pain that beset;
Travail of love, satisfied.

Wg[2]

Lord of Times and Seasons

Lord of all our times and seasons,
    Not of vain caprice
Suns revolve. Command Thy coolness,
    Dews of peace.

When each duty crowds the other
    Through the sultry days,
Plant the little flower of patience
    By our ways.

When the slothful flesh would murmur,
    Ease would cast her spell,
Set our face as flint till twilight's
    Vesper bell.

On Thy brow we see a thorn-crown,
    Blood-drops in Thy track;
O forbid that we should ever
    Turn us back.

ACD, DS, TJ

Before Sleep

My Lord, my Love, my heart's eternal Light,
Shine on Thy lover through the hours of night.
Shine on my thoughts, my very dreams be found
About Thy business on some holy ground.

Should friendly angel come to meet me there,
Let me not miss him, deaf and unaware.
And if I may, one other prayer I bring:
O Lord my God, make no long tarrying.

TJ

The Glory of That Light
(Acts 22:11)

"I could not see
    For the glory of that light"—
Let the shining of that glory
    Illumine our sight.

Things temporal
    Are transparent in that air;
But the things that are eternal
    Are manifest there.

Jesus our Lord,
    By the virtue of Thy grace,
In the shining of Thy glory
    Let us see Thy face.

GC, RFB, TJ

Save the Children

O save our children. Lord, we come to Thee,
Nor can we rest till they are gathered in.
O save them lest they wander carelessly;
Save them and keep them from the power of sin.

Grant they may hear Thy love's persuasive call,
Good Shepherd, who for our dear children died.
We seek them with Thee, till Thou find them all,
And Thy long travail has been satisfied.

Wg

Teach the Children

The children, Lord, the children—
Our thronging prayers find word
In one deep heart petition:
Do Thou for them, O Lord;
Do Thou for them and teach them
To use their Shield and Sword;
Thy gallant lovers, make them.
Do Thou for them, O Lord,

That disciplined and fearless,
They fight the fight and win,
Do Thou for them, we pray Thee,
O Spirit of Discipline.
With heavenly power endue them;
With heavenly love fulfill.
Perform in them Thy pleasure;
Teach them to do Thy will.

Wg[2]

Equip The Children

O Father, for our children hear
  Our deepest heart's desire:
Give love eternal, crystal clear,
    The perfect love that casts out fear,
      Thy love's consuming fire.

Burn out the dross, refine the gold;
  Complete the work begun,
And prove Thy power, as of old,
  In human character to mold
    The likeness of Thy Son.

(Continued)

Give courage equal to the strain,
And hope that will not yield
But marches fearless in the train
Of warrior souls who welcome pain
On Thy great battlefield.

Wg[2]

Protect the Children

Protect the little ones who see
A sweetness in each story told,
Who hear in every song of Thee
More than the old.

Thou knowest many a child who heard
Of Bethlehem and Calvary
And sought like some small, eager bird
To fly to Thee,

And then was hindered. Hear our cry,
O loving Lord, for these your things,
Lest held from Thee, they fall and lie
With broken wings.

These whom Thy lovingkindness charms,
The children here and everywhere,
Dear Lord, take up into Thy arms,
And keep them there.

Wg[2]

Recall the Wandering Children

As little birds that far have flown
  Across an untracked sea,
All unawares, by winds unknown,
  Are swept from where they fain would be—
  So these are swept from Thee.

Recall Thy lost young birds, O Love,
  Before the sun has set
And all is dark below, above;
  O let them turn and not forget
  That they may find Thee yet.

For once Thou wert their only home,
  Their heart's abiding nest;
Oh, better that than drifting foam,
  And wistful wandering, unblest—
  O call them back to rest.

Wg[2]

For Our Children

Father, hear us, we are praying,
Hear the words our hearts are saying;
We are praying for our children.

Keep them from the powers of evil,
From the secret, hidden peril;
Father, hear us for our children.

(Continued)

From the whirlpool that would suck them,
From the treacherous quicksand, pluck them;
Father, hear us for our children.

From the worldling's hollow gladness,
From the sting of faithless sadness,
Father, Father, keep our children.

Through life's troubled waters steer them;
Through life's bitter battle cheer them;
Father, Father, be Thou near them.

Read the language of our longing,
Read the wordless pleadings thronging,
Holy Father, for our children.

And wherever they may bide,
Lead them Home at eventide.

ACD, BT, DS, GC, TJ

For Daily Needs

Father, we come to Thee for bread,
  For all who hungry be;
That little children may be fed,
The sick and sorrowing comforted,
  We come, O God, to Thee.

We thank Thee for the loving word
  That bids us cast our care;
O Lord of lily and of bird,
We come to Thee; our prayer is heard,
  And Thou dost answer prayer.

Wd

Evening Prayer

Hallow our meal, dear Lord.
 This eventide,
Master beloved, adored,
 With us abide;
So from Thy plenitude
 Shall we be fed,
And all our common food
 Be Presence Bread.

EHW

Come, Lord Jesus

Because of little children soiled,
And disinherited, despoiled,

Because of hurt things, feathered, furred,
Tormented beast, imprisoned bird,

Because of many-folded grief,
Beyond redress, beyond belief,

Because the word is true that saith
The whole creation travaileth—

Of all our prayers this is the sum:
"O come, Lord Jesus, come!"

TJ

Console

For troubled hearts we pray.
 The grievousness of war
Has driven joy away,
 And sun and moon and star.

Console the sore distressed,
 The wounded bound in pain,
The broken, for whom rest
 May never be again.

Like bells at evening time
 Let words of healing come,
Till, led by that clear chime,
 They find themselves at Home.

TMS

Hope

Our human hope, it waxeth but to wane,
Hope faileth not that of Thy love is born;
Make hope our habit; blessèd love constrain,
Till flowers shall bloom where now is only thorn.

Wd

The Unexplained

Teach us in silence of the unexplained
 To see Love's dearest, Love's most secret sign,
Like the White Stone, a precious thing unstained—
 And as at Bethany, the glory Thine.

TMS

Nothing in the House

Thy servant, Lord, hath nothing in the house,
Not even one small pot of common oil;
For he who never cometh but to spoil
Hath raided my poor house again, again—
That ruthless strong man, armed, whom men call Pain.

I thought that I had courage in the house,
And patience to be quiet and endure,
And sometimes happy songs. Now I am sure
Thy servant truly hath not anything;
And see, my song-bird hath a broken wing.

• • • • •

My servant, I have come into the house—
I who know Pain's extremity so well
That there can never be the need to tell
His power to make the flesh and spirit quail:
Have I not felt the scourge, the thorn, the nail?

And I, his Conqueror, am in the house,
Let not your heart be troubled—do not fear:
Why shouldst thou, child of Mine, if I am here?
My touch will heal thy song-bird's broken wing,
And he shall have a braver song to sing.

RFB, TJ

For All in Pain

Dear Lord, for all in pain
We come to Thee;
Oh, come and smite again
Thine enemy.

Give to Thy servants skill
To soothe and bless;
And to the tired and ill
Give quietness.

And, Lord, to those who know
Pain may not cease,
Come near, that even so
They may have peace.

Wg[2]

For the Ill

Lord, from the depths, to Thee we come,
For Thy beloved is ill.
O Thou who art our one true home,
Recall the wandering will.

Will in the soul to will and do
The thing it once did vow;
O cleanse, forgive, restore, renew—
Love only knoweth how.

Out of the depths we cry to Thee
In fellowship of pain,
That all Thy travail, Lord, may see
Love's triumph once again.

Wg[2]

She Whom Thou Lovest

She whom Thou lovest, blessèd Lord, is ill.
With Thee is counsel; give Thy servants skill.
O Great Physician, touch her and restore,
As Thou hast done before.

We would not press Thee, for Thou knowest well
Our need of her that word could never tell.
We would not press Thee, as if all unproved,
Thy love for Thy beloved.

But as in eventide in Galilee
They brought their sick, we bring her unto Thee;
And from the depths we pray: do Thou fulfill
For us, for her, Thy will.

TMS

He Whom Thou Lovest

He whom Thou lovest, blessèd Lord, is ill.
With Thee is counsel; give Thy servants skill.
O Great Physician, come again, restore,
As Thou hast done before.

We would not press Thee, for Thou knowest, Lord,
Our need of him, a need that passes word.
We would not press Thee, as if all unproved,
Thy love for Thy beloved.

As in Judea and in Galilee
They brought their sick and suffering unto Thee,
So we bring ours and pray Thee to fulfill
Thy good and perfect will.

Wg[2]

Come, Mighty Vanquisher

Lord, Thou hast suffered; Thou dost know
The thrust of pain, the piercing dart,
How wearily the wind can blow
Upon the tired heart.

He whom Thou lovest, Lord, is ill.
O come, Thou mighty Vanquisher
Of wind and wave; say "Peace, be still,"
Eternal Comforter.

RFB

In Mercy, Heal

Deal Thou with them, O God the Lord;
 Deal Thou with them.
According to Thy Name of Love,
 Deal Thou with them.
The floods that else would overflow,
 Rebuke and stem.

Sweet is Thy mercy, God the Lord,
 And we have proved
That mercy sweet. O God of Love,
 Thy well-beloved
Are ill and need Thee. Deal with them,
 Thine own beloved.

WHP

Indraneela

Dear little feet, so eager to be walking—
    But never walked in any grieving way;
Dear little mouth, so eager to be talking—
    But never hurt with words it learned to say;
Dear little hands, outstretched in eager welcome,
    Dear little head, that close against me lay—
Father, to Thee I give my Indraneela;
    Thou wilt take care of her until That Day.

ACD

Lent to Thee

Dear Master, all the flowers are Thine,
And false the whisper, "ours" and "mine."
We lift our hearts to Thee and say:
"Lord, it was Thine to take away."

And yet, though we would have it so,
Lord, it is very good to know
That Thou art feeling for our pain;
And we shall have our flower again.

So help us now to be content
To take the sorrow Thou hast sent.
Dear Lord, how fair Thy house must be
With all the flowers we've lent to Thee!

FTR

Toward Jerusalem

O Father, help, lest our poor love refuse
For our beloved the life that they would choose,
And in our fear of loss for them, or pain,
    Forget eternal gain.

Show us the gain, the golden harvest There
For corn of wheat that they have buried here.
Lest human love defraud them, and betray,
    Teach us, O God, to pray.

Teach us to pray remembering Calvary,
For as the Master must the servant be.
We see their face set toward Jerusalem;
    Let us not hinder them.

Teach us to pray. O Thou who didst not spare
Thine Own Belovèd, lead us on in prayer;
Purge from the earthly; give us love divine,
    Father, like Thine, like Thine.

ACD, GBM, GC, TJ

For Souls Renewed

Lord, who didst wear humanity,
We come for souls renewed by Thee:
Give them the triumph of Thy constancy.

Keep them sincere in deed and word,
Obedient to their Royal Lord,
Ready-to-hand for Thee—like provèd sword.

Make them prayer warriors; let them be
Enrolled in ranks that stand by Thee,
Strong in the triumph of Thy constancy.

Wg[1]

Guard Your Own

O God, in whom we live and move,
Without whom life were death—
We bring Thee those in whom Thy love
Has breathed the living Breath.

O make them, keep them sensitive
In pure obedience;
In all they do, in all they give,
Be loving reverence.

Their weakness do Thou garrison;
Cause all their fears to cease.
O guard what Thou hast dearly won,
In Thine eternal peace.

Wg[1]

Be Thou Their Vision

O Lord, we bring Thee these for whom we pray—
Be Thou their strength, their courage and their stay;
And should their faith flag as they run the race,
Show them again the vision of Thy face.

Be Thou their vision, Lord of Calvary.
Hold them to follow; hold them fast by Thee.
O Thou who art more near to us than air,
Let them not miss Thee ever, anywhere.

FTR

For Them That Love Thee

(Judges 5:31)

"Let them that love Thee be as the sun
When he goeth forth in his might,"
Till the stars of evening kindle one by one;
So let them run in light.

Let them that love Thee breathe heavenly air,
And so, refreshed in peace, be strong,
Till the bells of evening, joyful and aware,
Call them to evensong.

K, Wg[1]

For Comrades

Giver of strong desire that bringeth
Comrades to Thee in faithful prayer,
Praise we the love that far out-wingeth
All that our utmost thought could dare.
Now unto Thee do we commit them,
Comrades beloved, everywhere.

Do Thou for them, O Lord, well-knowing
All that their tongue could never tell—
Rivers of sorrow overflowing,
Shadows that gathered, hopes that fell.
Do Thou for them; through all confusion,
Lord, let Thy peace be sentinel.

O let the melting fire that burneth
Burn in their hearts, and let them stand
Fearless as one who ever learneth
More of the power of Thy right hand.
Love of Thy Cross—let that inspire them,
Steadfast to live at Thy command.

Wg[2]

As One Company

Our Sovereign Leader and Belovèd Lord,
Make strong the threads of this, Thy golden cord;
Make fast the knot that binds us one in Thee,
In loyalty.

Let holy fealty be our bond sincere;
Let us be each to other crystal-clear—
Clear as the jasper in Thy City wall.
So keep us all.

O keep us facing toward Jerusalem.
Steep are the hills; let us not turn from them.
Let us go forward as one company,
Rejoicingly.

Wd

Rescue, Lord

Dearworthy Lord, full preciously
Thou dost defend Thine own.
In this assault we clearly see
A hand against the Throne.

And so our hands are lifted up
Lest there be bitter loss—
Refusal, Savior, of Thy Cup,
Denial of Thy Cross.

O turn the Powers of Calvary
On this imperiled soul;
Let him who is sore wounded be,
By piercèd Hands, made whole.

Wg[1]

Help Thy Warriors

(Matthew 13:28)

Savior of men, compassionate,
  We come to Thee; on Thee we wait.
We know not all the need, but Thou
  Dost know it all, dost know it now.

"An enemy hath done this"—Lord,
  Long, long ago it was Thy word.
O help Thy warriors valiantly
  To put to flight that enemy.

MB, Wg[1]

Our Traveler

Great Traveler, whose pure footsteps fell
On earth and air and on the sea,
Oh, guard our traveler, Lord; for well
They journey who are kept by Thee.

Be home to him, be joy and song,
Be peace in midst of noise of words;
Oh, let his heart be calm and strong,
And carefree as the woodland birds.

And keep his windows stainless too,
That on the road where wanderers be,
The lamp of joy, clear shining through,
May show the way, dear Lord, to Thee.

Wg[2]

Show the Way

Order his steps, O Savior, lest he stray;
For all is new—he does not know the way.
Thy word is light; no other lantern, Lord,
Need we, nor ask we, but Thine own clear word.

Lord, give him grace, that he obey his light;
Courage and faith, lest he should fail in fight.
O knit his heart to Thee, that he be found
Steadfast in Thee, and in Thy statutes sound.

Wg[1]

By Cloud or Fire

Great Leader, guide him by cloud or fire;
Let him be loyal to Thy heart's desire.
Be Thou his shelter from the wind and rain;
Cleanse from the dust and tedious travel stain.

Great Captain, gird him; the foe is near;
Be Thou his vision, valor, patience, cheer;
And lest he falter if the fight be long,
O let Thy joy be strength to him and song!

Wg[1]

For the Wanderer

Thou who makest intercession,
    Give to us to share
In that holy intercession;
    Deepen prayer.

Some have chosen dust and ashes,
    Fruit of poison tree;
Let them have nor peace nor pleasure,
    Wanting Thee.

Let Thy fiery Law arrest them;
    Let Thy love constrain,
Till they turn, repentant, humbly,
    Home again.

Keep Thine own alert, courageous;
    Strengthen them to stand
Till Thou comest, or we meet them,
    In Thy land.

Wg[2]

Wounded Hearts

O Love eternal, Love divine,
In wounded hearts pour oil and wine.
Where darkness broods like moonless night,
O Light of Life, let there be light.
And Thine the praise, the glory be,
When Thy beloved come home to Thee.

WHP

The Unconcerned

Jesus my Savior, whom to know
Is life and liberty,
We pray for these who come and go
Without a thought of Thee.

Eternal Lover, Thou hast skills
To draw men's hearts to Thee;
O lead them to Thy holy hill,
The hill of Calvary.

Wg[2]

The Heavenly Chart

Jesus, Lord of Love and Light,
  As a boat upon the sea
In the dark and cloudy night,
  Is the soul that knows not Thee.
But to many in their need
  We have given Thy heavenly chart;
As they ponder, as they read,
  O illuminate their heart.

Lost are they, deceived, undone;
  In their sky there is no star.
Jesus Savior, Holy One,
  Near art Thou where seekers are.
As the star of Bethlehem
  Led the wise men long ago,
Let Thy word reveal to them
  Him whom it is life to know.

Wg[1]

Blinded Eyes

For those who have Thy holy Word
That giveth light, we come to Thee:
Open their blinded eyes, O Lord;
Oh, touch their eyes that they may see!

And cause that mighty Word to shake
The very fabric of the soul
Till all its proud defenses break;
Then, Lord, renew and make them whole.

The sin-enchanted, the deceived—
Oh, shatter their security;
Be Thy true Word beloved, believed—
That they may walk at liberty.

Wg[2]

Self-Banished Ones

Lord Jesus Christ, Thou knowest all
Whom, loving still, we bring to Thee;
O Love Divine, we pray, recall
Thy banished ones to Calvary—

Self-banished ones; but Thou hast said,
"All souls are mine"; we claim that word,
What though they be among the dead?
Sting them to life, arouse them, Lord.

Thy fiery Finger, burning Fear—
Strip bare their souls until they see
Their naked need, and turn and hear
Thy word of love: "Come back to me."

Wg[2]

For Hardened Hearts

For those with hardened hearts we pray,
Who hear and heed not, nor will move
Even to turn and look Thy way,
Although Thou art all love.

Lord Jesus Christ of Calvary's Tree,
Who by Thy death wrought victory:
Renew in us a mighty faith
For them for whom we pray.

Wg[1]

Ice-Cold Hearts

And so, for ice-cold hearts we pray,
Who hear and heed not, will not move
To come to Thee, nor look Thy way—
Although Thou art all love.

O melt their snowfield, Love Divine—
What is there that Thou canst not do?
Thou who hast melted even mine:
Dear Savior, melt theirs too.

PU

God of the Impossible

God of the impossible,
Grant our hearts' desire:
Faith for the impossible,
Love that cannot tire,
Hope like love that never faileth,
Hope that shall inspire.

Wg[1]

The Drifting Ones

Lord, some who listened all but came
And touched Thy garment's hem:
The blind, the deaf, the dumb, the lame—
Thou knowest them.

But they have drifted; oh, do Thou,
Whose love is never bound
By our poor limits, follow now
Till they be found.

Wg[2]

The Faltering Ones

For those whose hearts are drawn to Thee,
  Who fain would follow at Thy word,
But falter, knowing there will be
  Not peace, but sword—

For these we pray, for these so near
  It seems a touch would draw them in;
And yet they linger, held by fear
  Or bound by sin.

Lord Jesus, who for sinners died,
  Show them the meaning of Thy Cross,
That loosed and purged and fortified
  They welcome loss!

Wg[1]

Let Us Believe

Savior, who bore the bitter Cross,
  That he for whom we come today
Might be redeemed and purged from dross—
  To Thee, triumphant Christ, we pray.
What though our faith be swept by storm?
Thou who has promised wilt perform!

Faithful art Thou to perfect those
  In whom Thy grace begins to move.
Changeful the tide of feeling flows,
  Changeless Thine everlasting love.
Not hell itself can countermand
The saving strength of Thy right hand!

Renew within us quenchless hope,
  O God of Hope, though oftentime
He slip upon the upward slope;
  Let us believe that he will climb.
O let us sing before we see;
And glory, glory be to Thee!

Wg[1]

Wake Them, Breath of God

Come from the four winds, Breath of God,
And breathe upon these slain;
Wake them from death, O Living Breath,
That they may rise again.

Come from the four winds, Voice of God;
Command their liberty;
From death's dark night lead them aright
To reign in life by Thee.

Wg[2]

Keep Me Shining

Lord, the shadow of Thy hand
  Is a refuge from the heat,
Is a rock in weary land,
  Coolness to sore-blistered feet.

In the shadow of Thy hand,
  Loving right and hating wrong,
Quick to serve at Thy command,
  Keep me shining, peaceful, strong.

Unp

3 Poems of Surrender

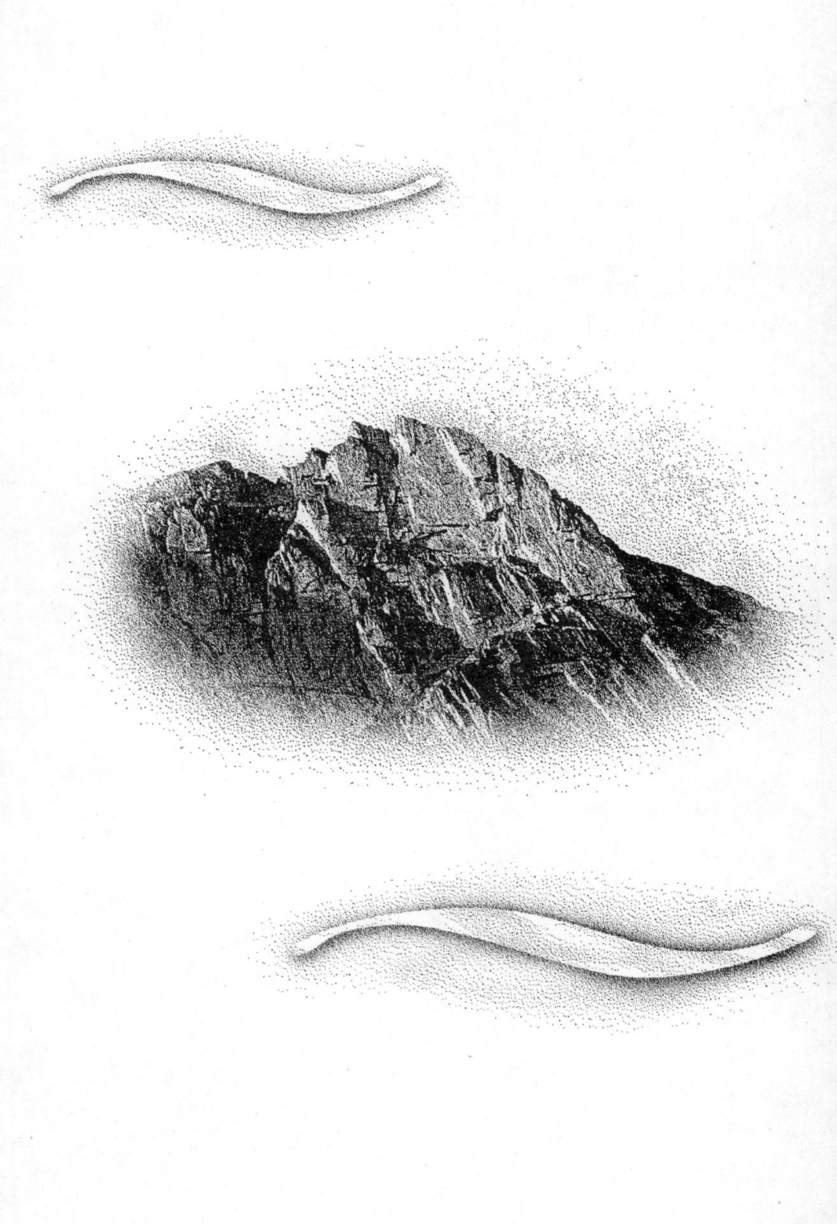

NO SCAR?

Hast thou no scar?
No hidden scar on foot, or side, or hand?
I hear thee sung as mighty in the land;
I hear them hail thy bright, ascendant star.
Hast thou no scar?

Hast thou no wound?
Yet I was wounded by the archers; spent,
Leaned Me against a tree to die; and rent
By ravening beasts that compassed Me, I swooned.
Hast *thou* no wound?

No wound? No scar?
Yet, as the Master shall the servant be,
And piercèd are the feet that follow Me.
But thine are whole; can he have followed far
Who has nor wound nor scar?

GC, TJ

ROYAL SCARS

We follow a scarred Captain;
  Should we not have scars?
Under His faultless orders
  We follow to the wars.
Lest we forget, Lord, when we meet,
  Show us Thy hands and feet.

O wounded One, most Royal,
  Who wert set at nought,
No trumpets were, no banners
  On field our Captain fought.
When we forget and seek for stars,
  Show us Thy wounds, Thy scars.

Wg[1]

Two Swords

Thy sword was bathed in heaven;
And that great sword
Bathed in clear glory, Lord,
Has conquered me—
And conquering, set me free.

Oh, bathe my sword in heaven,
Lest creeping rust
Or stain of earthly dust,
Dim the bright blade
Pledged to my Lord's crusade.

Thy sword, bathed in high heaven,
Purged ancient wrongs;
To Thee my sword belongs
For that same fight.
Bathe it, O Lord, in light.

GC

Divine Paradox

But all through life I see a cross
Where sons of God yield up their breath:
There is no gain except by loss,
There is no life except by death;
And no full vision but by faith
Nor glory but by bearing shame,
Nor justice but by taking blame.
And that Eternal Passion saith:
"Be emptied of glory and right and name."

GC, RSP

The Shell

Upon the sandy shore an empty shell,
    Beyond the shell infinity of sea;
O Savior, I am like that empty shell,
    Thou art the Sea to me.

A sweeping wave rides up the shore, and lo,
    Each dim recess the coiled shell within
Is searched, is filled, is filled to overflow
    By water crystalline.

Not to the shell is any glory then:
    All glory give we to the glorious sea.
And not to me is any glory when
    Thou overflowest me.

Sweep over me, Thy shell, as low I lie;
    I yield me to the purpose of Thy will;
Sweep up, O conquering waves, and purify,
    And with Thy fullness fill.

TJ

Forget the Shell

An empty shell lay by the sea;
    The waves rolled up, and all forgot
To think of that which mattered not;
    They only saw the sea.

So be it, Lord; let this Thy shell
    Be lost in glory of the sea;
And as the waves sweep over me,
    Let all forget the shell.

FTR

O Wave of God

O Wave of God, arise and overflow
High watermark on this our stretch of shore.
Great Wave of God, deal with us till we know
Something beyond all we have known before—
Far, far beyond all we have known before.

O Following Wave, from utmost Deeps arise;
We yield to Thy majestic urgency;
Forbid we ever or in anywise
Refuse to yield our all, lose all in Thee;
Sweep on, O Wave, we yield ourselves to Thee.

Wg[2]

How Can I Not Love Much?

O King of Love, Thy royal ways
    With thy poor vassal pass my thought.
What word can fitly frame Thy praise?
Thy love illuminates my days—
    Love to a thing of nought.

O Lord of Love, how privily
    Thou comest; and Thy finger's touch
On hidden string, known but to Thee,
Attunes to sweetness all in me.
    Loved so, how not love much?

But what is much? Rock-pool to sea,
    Faint taper to a furnace glow?
O Love, who art Infinity,
Whose secret source no man may see,
    Flow through me, overflow.

Wg[1]

All My Fountains

(Psalm 87:7)

"All my fountains are in Thee,"
Word of mountain mystery:
Higher than earth's flowers grow,
Far above the highest snow,
Lies the watershed
Whence my stream is fed.

Living fountain, now I pray:
Let no boulder block the way;
If such hindering thing there be
Lurking deep in pool, in me,
Mighty floods sweep down
And uproot that stone.

They that sing and they that dance
Bring me word of jubilance:
Never need my stream run low,
Waters never cease to flow
From the hills afar,
Where my fountains are.

Wg[1]

Fulfill Me Now With Love

Father of spirits, this my earnest plea
I bring again and yet again to Thee:
Fulfill me now with love, that I may know
A daily inflow, daily overflow.

For love—for love my Lord was crucified;
With cords of love He bound me to His side.
Pour through me now; I yield myself to Thee,
O Love that led my Lord to Calvary.

CD, EHW, TJ, Wg[1]

Pour Love Through Me

Love of God, eternal Love,
Sweep my barriers down!
Fountain of eternal love,
Let Thy power be known;
Fill me, flood me, overflow me;
Love of God, eternal Love,
Sweep my barriers down!

Love of God, eternal Love,
Pour Thy love through me!
Nothing less than Calvary love
Do I ask of Thee;
Fill me, flood me, overflow me;
Love of God, eternal Love,
Pour Thy love through me!

Wg[1]

Love's Overflow

Spirit of Wind, Spirit of Fire,
Fulfill in me Thy great desire;
Enter and purge each hidden cell—
That Christ in me may dwell.

That I be rooted fast in love,
And in that love may live and move,
O Love Eternal, let me know
Love's mighty overflow.

Wg[1]

For Love I Come

For love, brave love that ventureth,
For love that faileth not, I come;
For love that never wearieth,
Nor findeth burdens burdensome.

I come for hope that springeth green,
And burneth steadfast like a star;
For faith that pierceth through the seen
To things eternal, things that are.

O Love, that lightenest all my ways,
Within, without, below, above—
Flow through the minutes of my days;
The sum of all my life be love.

EHW, Wg[1]

All One Way

There is no fear in love, so we draw near;
Thy perfect love, O Lord, has cast out fear.

As wheat before the wind bends all one way,
So would we bow before Thy wind today.

Our several choices, Lord, we would forgo;
Breath of the living God, O great Wind, blow.

TJ

Refining

Lord, make my heart
    Pure as the gannet's wing,
That has no part
    In aught defiling.
And make my love
    Deep as the blue, blue sky,
Steadfast above
    The small clouds floating by.

Wg[1]

Our Daily Dress

Blest be the love that leadeth son and daughter
Safe to the Homeland, land of Heart's Desire;
Thy traveler's fear not overflowing water
Or blistering flame of fire.

No fire nor flood can stay us, yet a trifle
Can sometimes cause the Song in us to cease,
As though a gnat were given power to rifle
Our treasure-store of Peace.

But when we think upon Thy Cross and Passion,
Shame smiteth us for our unthankful ways.
Strip from us, Lord of Joy, the dull, the ashen;
Our daily dress be Praise.

Wg[2]

Tune Thou My Harp

Tune Thou my harp;
There is not, Lord, could never be,
The skill in me.

Tune Thou my harp,
That it may play Thy melody,
Thy harmony.

Tune Thou my harp;
O Spirit, breathe Thy thought through me,
As pleaseth Thee.

RFB

Lord of Music

Let me sing your song, ye waters;
  Bid your falls their voices lend—
Let your thousand springing daughters
  Each to me be kindly friend.
Swept up in their nobler music,
  Let my poor earth tunes have end.

What am I but dust and ashes?
  Ye alone are clear and pure;
Passing I, as passing flashes
  Light upon you; ye endure.
Take my falt'ring chords and lose them
  In your glorious overture.

Oh, ye fail me; turn I rather,
  Lord of music, unto Thee.
In the Kingdom of Thy Father,
  Tender all the judgments be.
Take my human alleluias;
  Perfect Thou the harmony.

DS

A Joy to Thee

Let me see Thy face, Lord Jesus,
  Caring not for aught beside;
Let me hear Thy voice, Lord Jesus,
  Till my soul is satisfied.

Let me walk with Thee, Lord Jesus;
  Let me walk in step with Thee.
Let me talk with Thee, Lord Jesus;
  Let Thy words be clear to me.

Heavenly music, strength and sweetness,
  Joy of joys art Thou to me;
O Belovèd, my Lord Jesus,
  Let me be a joy to Thee.

Wg[2]

To See and Know Him

My heart said unto Thee:
My face would seek Thy face;
O Lord, grant me this grace:
Shine down on me.

Myself would cloud my skies.
Let self be crucified;
Let love be fortified;
Anoint mine eyes.

Thee would I see and know;
All else would I forget.
Let Thy fair beauty set
My life aglow.

TMS, Wg[1]

The Pebble Parable

Where light and water mixed and made a glory,
  Glistened a pebble in a golden pool.
Wond'ring, we sought to read its hidden story:
  Where was it carven? Shapen by what tool?

Then from the water did we take it, craving
  A thing so lovely for our own desire.
Ah, but it dulled, missing the water's laving,
  Missing the mystic ministry of fire.

Dear Lord, how often hast Thou stooped and spoken
  By parable, without or word or sound.
Flow over me; my heart accepts the token.
  Where but in Thee are my fair colors found?

DS

No Treasures . . . But Love

I cannot ever come the priest's great way,
  With hands full of sweet incense beaten small;
I have no treasures in my hands today,
  No precious thing at all.
But wonderful art Thou to him who loves,
  I read, and I am comforted;
For he who had not even two poor doves
  Might bring to Thee instead
    A handful of fine flour—
    As I do, Lord, this hour.

TMS

The Golden Censer

(Revelation 8:3)

Eternal Love, we have no good to bring Thee,
No single good of all our hands have wrought;
No worthy music have we found to sing Thee,
No jeweled word, no quick up-soaring thought.

And yet we come. And when our faith would falter,
Show us, O Love, the quiet place of prayer,
The golden censer and the golden altar,
And the great angel waiting for us there.

TJ, Wg[1]

Directed Prayer

O God, Thy thought is far above
My utmost thought of Thee,
And yet Thy thought to me is love;
And Love comes near to me.

O Love, come near and nearer still;
Fold me in quietness
Till all the movements of my will
Thy conquering power confess,

That so, of Love alone aware,
Love flowing over me,
Thy Spirit may direct my prayer
To that which pleaseth Thee.

Wg[1]

In Silence

What do I know of listening? O my Father,
Teach me in silence of the soul to gather
Those thoughts of Thine that, deep within me flowing,
Like currents of a river, guide my going.

Light of Thy Spirit in me, fainter, clearer,
Burneth and shineth, as I further, nearer,
Stand toward that light. O steady my decision
To wait in silence for the heavenly vision.

But not for luxury of spiritual rapture
Would I thus wait; but as the bird doth capture
The purposed note, so I, obedient, bringing
The purposed work, would offer it with singing.

FTR

The Covenant

O think upon the Covenant;
Thy children in captivity,
Stained with their own works, come to Thee—
Thy Covenant their plea.

In a great, howling wilderness
They wandered many and many a day;
Thou, Seeker of the souls that stray,
Didst not cast them away.

Sweet is Thy mercy: Thou didst seek,
Didst find, didst succor. Wherefore now
Do we the things we disallow?
Walk with defeated brow?

(Continued)

O God the Lord, who showed us light,
Forever be that sin abhorred
That drew us from our Sovereign Lord.
Take sacrifice, take cord,

And bind unto the altar's horns
That which is Thine—yea, all of me—
That in a new Captivity
I may indeed go free.

Teach me to do the thing that pleaseth Thee,
For Thou art the Lord my God.
Let Thy loving Spirit lead me forth
Into the Land of Righteousness.

DS

Interruptions

I sat upon the bank of a fair river,
Reposeful, unaware
Of that which lay in it to greet my spirit;
Nor did I greatly care
To look for lessons on a day so lovely,
My thoughts being otherwhere.

But as, regardless, I regarded fondly
The manner of its flow,
The silver flash, the mazy dance, the mellow
Lights of the underglow
Where brown and amber mixed, and little fishes
In bright shoals come and go,

I marked how sunken rock that intercepted
Its swiftly ordered race
It welcomed, as it were a benediction,
Set in the appointed place—
And covered as with soft caress, the wrinkles
Of that untoward face.

Or if forbiddingly the rock uplifted
Its countenance and frowned,
The stream accepted the unkindly thwarting
With smiles that would abound
In sparkles, light-tossed spray like silver laughter,
As it slipped smoothly round.

Forgiveness, Lord! O send forth Thy swift lightnings;
Cause them to scorch and slay
That which in me to the occasion lendeth
Effectual power to fray
The edges of my patience. O grant to me
To live the river's way.

MP

The Sign

Lord crucified, O mark Thy holy Cross
On motive, preference, all fond desires;
On that which self in any form inspires
Set Thou that Sign of loss.

And when the touch of death is here and there
Laid on a thing most precious in our eyes,
Let us not wonder; let us recognize
The answer to this prayer.

TG, TJ

The Question

I hear Thee in the silence of the mountains,
The thunder of the falls,
The wind-song of the grasses, melody
Of bird upon the tree;
And all things high or lowly
Discourse of Thee to me.
What profit is it if thou be not holy?

I see Thee in the light upon the river,
The shadows of the wood;
The wildflowers on the mountainside profess
The colors of Thy dress;
As though for my joy solely
All things do Thee confess.
What profit is it if thou be not holy?

I know Thee in the sweeping of the tempest,
The smothering of the mist;
In delicate glories of the earth and air,
In changes fierce or fair,
Proceeding swift or slowly,
I am of Thee aware.
What profit is it if thou be not holy?

MP, P, TJ

Sickness

Now doth great Truth walk in with naked torch
And searcheth through to the inmost secret coil
Of our involvèd being: every strand
Of flimsy thread discovering in the web
Spread out upon the loom; the essential thing,
The nucleus of character, being known
For what it is; the Master-word of life
Interpreted by acts stripped bare of all
Health's decorative dressing—that which is
Being shown, that and no other.
Wherefore, let us set
A watch upon ourselves while yet we hold
The reins of will to guide our spirit's choices—
Lest, unawares, life's chiefest word be "self,"
All thoughts revolving round it; and self-love
Staining the substance of its central cell,
Color its very being; and inwrought,
As thread in web, a rotten selfishness
Ruin the whole.

MP

Broken

Buried in a mighty forest
    Is a valley where a mild
River moveth over burnished,
    Copper-colored rock; and wild,
Plumèd pandanus, tall tree fern,
    Wealth of climbing maidenhair—
Light flung, rioting everywhere—
    Deck the banks of this, my burn.

(Continued)

And the glen among the mountains,
  Sweet with silence, is for me
Life's ideal. Thus, my flowing
  I would choose might ever be:
Tranquil, ordered, unperturbed,
  Fair festooned, harmonious, whole—
Even as the quiet soul
  Of this river. . . . Sudden curbed,

As a living thing, my river
  Drew up, faced a black abyss
Yawning wide; as if affrighted,
  Broke forth, leaped, and vanished. This
Is thy work, blind force. Why did ye
  Break upon my river, shout—
Crashing through her peace—and flout
  All her innocent green'ry?

Through the forest, down the boulders
  Climbed I; caught a phantom gleam,
Heard a music, followed, found it—
  Found my river again. O stream
Broken thus, this sudden glory
  Crowning thee, rebuketh me
Who miscalled calamity
  That which perfecteth thy story.

All the trees of all the forest,
  Leaning over, listened. Fell
Voices of tumultuous waters,
  Visions that no tongue may tell,
Pure, perpetual, things of wonder;
  All of me was eye and ear;
Oh, to see the glory clear,
  Catch the whisper in the thunder!

And I caught it; words to utter
    Fail. I only know I knew
Not among the silver sedges
    May God's rivers linger. Few
But receive an inward token;
    And then gath'ring all their might,
Leap—and mingling with the light,
    Know the mystery of being broken.

MP

Arouse Us, Lord

O Lord our God, arouse us; we are sleeping,
    Dreaming we wake. But up the steep defile,
Shapes as of phantoms, through the black night creeping,
    Hail the vain dream that stayeth us awhile.
Only the faithful stars their watch are keeping;
    Shame on the sloth that would our strength beguile!

What aileth us, that drowsy indecision
    Holdeth us thrall? Hark, hark, the call to war!
Lord God of battles, fear we man's derision?
    Fear we the stigma of the singular?
Are we as those for whom doth shine no vision,
    Nor bloweth trumpet, flasheth scimitar?

See o'er the hills the dawn awake. Bedew us,
    O Refreshing Dew; on our long-silent lyre
Breathe, Wind of God. Forgiving Love, renew us;
    Form us and discipline to Thy desire.
O Man of War, great Son of Man, endue us;
    O mighty Spirit, kindle with Thy fire!

LB, MP, P

"Pity Thyself" . . .
"Get Thee Behind Me, Satan"

Pity thyself; no other knows thy sorrow,
Thy tender, sensitive, individual sorrow
(A private thing to thee)
Which apprehensively
Doubling today's load, forward leans to borrow
That which tomorrow
May possibly arrive, if all goes ill.
Pity thyself; hug thy delusions; still
Pile up thy griefs. Cherish thine *accidie*
And weep—for preference, apart
But copiously—that those who keep in heart
(Barbarians though they be)
A certain care for thee
May, noticing the pathos in thine eyes,
Be filled with penitence and, being wise
Henceforth to antidote thy woe,
Compassionately flow
Fluid with feeling—to prepare for thee
Sweet ministration, maudlin sympathy.

Yea, pity thy dear self. Thy soul is torn
With much emotion over that which after all
Is but the common lot; for great or small
Must suffer. What though overborne
No heart need be—unless it magnify
Its griefs and choose to fly
Its comforts—still thou art forlorn.
And thou dost mourn,
Perceiving the anticipated grief
(For which is no relief

Obtained or promised) with sharp talons tear
Thy very vitals. Rare
And precious such a prescience. Not a crumb
Of comfort can I find thee. But a jest
Intrudes itself: What if the expected guest
Though thus punctiliously met,
Should quite forget
To come?

• • • • •

O Man of Sorrows, didst Thou ever feel
Thus towards Thyself? Or didst Thou ever deal
Thus with that whisper? Nay, with scorching breath
Of indignation Thou didst blast it—death
Being in it. Shame on us cravens who,
Dallying with weakness, woo
As a fain lover, pains and fears,
Luxurious tears.
Thy tears—for whom were they? All enervate
The soul thus handled. Grant me, Lord, to hate
The fondling sin. Thou, Savior, intimate
With what Thy morrow held, didst go to meet
Its dawn with willing feet
And glorious face of uttermost content,
Accepting it as sent
By Thy good Father. So, henceforth would I,
Hardened against myself, be quick to descry
In all self-pity, selfishness; employ
Pity's great power only for others' need,
Thou granting grace, O radiant Man of Joy;
And quickened in spirit, speed
Forward, undressed from that close clinging sin,
That vile, interior sin, disguised by various names. Begin,
O Strength of my right arm, to hew

(Continued)

This Agag down. Hew him in pieces. Few
Fathom his treacheries.
Arise, I say;
Let him come delicately as he may;
Regard him not, but slay—
Away with him!

MP

Agag—Self-Pity

(1 Samuel 15:32–33)

Not for Thyself, Thy pity and Thy fears,
Not for Thyself, Thy sympathy, Thy tears—
Only for others were Thy comforts spent;
Only for others, Thy compassions lent.
This secret virtue, self-forgetfulness,
This generous power to succor and to bless
By reason of an inward liberty,
Give it to me, my Lord; give it to me!

Now, by Thy grace, I do contemn, refuse
That deadly vice, self-pity. I would use
Strength that Thou givest, pity's gracious power
For others only. Grant me from this hour
To be aware of Agag, though he be,
Like Agag, walking very delicately.
Help me to rise and smite him down and slay,
And spare him not. Away with him—away!

FTR

Certain Moods

My mind affrights me; for a mad revolt
Stirs it confusedly against the powers that be,
The decorous powers, that ever from my birth
Have fostered me
In kindliest fashion. Why
Should such things be with me, my God? I try
To fit myself into the general scheme—
The well-oiled groove—
And think along familiar ways made smooth
And comfortable to proper flesh. Yet like the child
That of far things will dream,
Turning, uncharmed by any proffered joys,
To seek something beyond—
Perplexing all the fond
Imaginings of guardians—so I
Seek something out of reach of nursery employs,
Or even wisdom of the great wise Schools.

Schools! Oh the wearisome word! Their schools of thought
Do not impress me; and I break the rules
And fraternize with any whom I find
Simple, loving Thee well and humankind—
A thing forbidden to the consistent soul
Who would preserve its tidy hedges whole.
And the dull, usual routine of the devout
Does not appeal to me; therefore, I much misdoubt
This, my unruly mind,
That will not ever do the thing it ought.

(Continued)

And then, when I would wait
And meditate,
And seek a way to free
My climbing thought from out the net that tangles
Fine threads in woven meshes over me,
Sudden, the Sabbath morning silence, wounded, flies
And grievèd dies;
And round me jangles
A clamor of bells, each individual bell
Peculiar to itself; and though one mellow chime
Beaten with hammers wrought in olden time
Be more than others musical to me,
Yet who can tell
Which peals the note supreme, imperative?

But while these things were so,
I, drawing deep into my cell,
Felt all the strife
Die down; and through the clash, not mixing in it,
A music floated; and for one long minute
I forgot all but Thee,
Thee, my Redeemer. . . . Whom else need we know?
To whom, Lord, shall we go that we may live?
Thou hast the words of everlasting life.

MP

Soul Surgery

Jesus, Redeemer and my one Inspirer,
Heat in my coldness: set my life aglow.
Break down my barriers; draw, yea, draw me nigher.
Thee would I know, whom it is life to know.

Deepen me, rid me of the superficial;
From pale delusion set my spirit free;
All my interior being quick unravel;
Pluck forth each thread of insincerity.

Thy vows are on me; oh, to serve Thee truly—
Love perfectly, in purity obey—
Burn, burn, O Fire; O Wind, now winnow throughly;
O sword, awake against the flesh and slay.

Oh, that in me
Thou, Lord, mayest see
Of the travail of Thy soul,
And be satisfied!

MP, P

Deliver Me

From dullness to a friendly word,
From deafness to the song of bird,
From blindness to the birds and flowers
That grow among the rocky hours,
From all that would ungratefully
Becloud my sky, deliver me.

From craven inner selfishness
Whatever be its outward dress,
From fainting when the goal is near,
From faltering in my song of cheer,
From all that is unsoldierly,
Captain of souls, deliver me.

• • • • •

(Continued)

From coldness to the burning woe
Mine eyes have seen, my heart must know;
  From weakness in the awful fight
  Against the demons of the night;
    From all that would dishonor Thee,
    O Christ, my Lord, deliver me.

From fearing calls to do and dare,
From insincerity in prayer,
  From dread of battle wound and scar,
  From seeing mud instead of star;
    From all that would dishonor Thee,
    O Christ, my Lord, deliver me.

WHP, Wg[1]

Kindle Our Love

Father, forgive the cold love of the years;
  Here in the silence we bow;
Perish our selfishness, perish our fears;
  Kindle us, kindle us now.

Lord, we believe, we accept, we adore,
  Less than the least though we be;
Fire of love, burn in us e'ermore—
  Till we burn out for Thee.

Wg[1]

Bonded Together

Bonded together, blessèd Lord, are we.
This is Thy doing, and we worship Thee;
And heeding not man's fitful smile or frown,
Come well, come ill, seek jewels for Thy crown.

Maintain among us honor crystal clear
And perfect love that casteth out all fear;
And loyalty that breaks not under stress,
And gentle virtues of unselfishness.

O Light of heaven, shine upon our ways—
Thy joy our strength to live laborious days.
Let Thy Wind winnow, and command Thy Fire;
Only fulfill in us Thy heart's desire.

Wg[2]

Bind Us Together

Yea, we adore, O Father, we adore Thee;
Hast Thou not guided, O Thou gentle Guide?
Make pure our praises as we wait before Thee,
Whose love embraces us on every side.

Gifts hast Thou given of sister and of brother;
O royal Giver, blessèd be Thy choice.
Thee, Thee, O Master, see we in each other,
Hear in each tone Thy well-belovèd voice.

Therefore we come with worship and with wonder;
Surely the Lord is in this quiet place.
Bind us with cords that life nor death can sunder;
Draw us together as we seek Thy face.

(Continued)

Write Thou the lines of our unfinished story;
Make us, Thy ministers, a flaming fire;
Let flesh be nought—to Thee alone be glory;
Grant unto us to meet Thy heart's desire.

Wg[2]

Like Low Green Moss

We are too high; Lord Jesus, we implore Thee,
Make of us something like the low green moss
That vaunteth not, a quiet thing before Thee,
Cool for Thy feet sore wounded on the Cross.

Like low green moss—and yet our thoughts are thronging,
Running to meet Thee, all alight, afire.
Thirsty the soul that burneth in love-longing;
Fountain and fire art Thou, and hearts' desire.

Therefore, we come, Thy righteousness our cover,
Thy precious Blood our one, our only plea.
Therefore, we come, O Savior, Master, Lover;
To whom, Lord, could we come save unto Thee?

GC, TJ, Wg[1]

Household Wounds

Yes, of a truth, there shall be hidden wounding.
Strange are the gifts Love sends:
Trample the will of flesh, seek first the kingdom,
Despise all private ends—
Then shalt thou know a bruising and a grieving,
And in the house of friends.

Thy house of friends dealt hardly with Thee, Savior;
Thorns were Thy bitter dower,
Thorns that, when given to us, quickened to budding
Break sudden into flower.
Oh, solemn joy, if I may wear the garland
And watch with Thee one hour.

Only an hour—then treasures of the darkness
Like unto jewels pure,
Shall sparkle forth in light. Tarries the vision?
Wait for it; it is sure.
Oh, blessèd then the servant who though wounded
Did still exult, endure.

Right are Thy ways, great Leader of Thy people;
Sweet are Thy comfortings!
Who companies with Thee, O Man of Sorrows,
And unoffended brings
A quiet heart, finds household wounds forgotten,
And, unawares, he sings.

MP

Our Savior's Prayer

Bathed round about by moonlit air,
Beneath the olive tree,
Our Savior knelt alone in prayer;
Sore spent was He.
And solemn through the moonlit air
The prayer of prayers arose;
But what it cost to pray that prayer
No mortal knows.

(Continued)

Only our hearts within us know
When they most broken be,
To that same garden we must go—
Gethsemane.
And only one prayer meets our need;
We learn to pray it there;
The prayer of all true prayers the seed,
Our Savior's prayer.

TMS, WHP

And Yet

"Have I been so long time with thee,
And yet hast thou not known Me?"
O my Master, I have known Thee
On the roads of Galilee.

"Have I been so long time with thee
On the roads of Galilee,
Yet, My child, hast thou not known Me
Walking on the tossing sea?"

O my Master, I have known Thee
On the roads and on the sea.
"Wherefore, then, hast thou not known Me
Broken in Gethsemane?

"I would have thee follow, know Me
Thorn-crowned, nailed upon the Tree.
Canst thou follow? Wilt thou know Me
All the way to Calvary?"

GC, P, TJ

The Fellowship of His Sufferings
(Under the Olive Trees)

A hillside garden near a city gate,
    And One alone under the olive trees;
And one outside, irresolute, who late
    Has lingered, and does now himself bewail:
    "I pray Thee, let the cup pass, for I fail
        Before such agony. I cannot drink;
        Save me, O Lord, I sink."
    Confounded by this anguish, my heart sees
Only a horror of great darkness wait
    Under the olive trees.

"I *wait*." The little leaves moved at the word;
    A cloud obscured the bright face of the moon.
The lover listened; something in him stirred—
    "Did ever Lover thus entreat before?
    I may not call me lover any more,
        For never love grieved Love as I have grieved;
        And yet I had believed
    Myself Thy lover. Soon, Belovèd, soon
Thou wilt be far from me; for I have heard
    And disobeyed Thee."

                                        But the Paschal moon
Sudden shone out, flooding the darkened air
    And all the open space between the trees.
The very garden seemed as if aware
    Of holy presences. Then to that place
    Ran in the lover, fell upon his face;
        No word he spoke; no chiding word was spoken;
        But as one smitten, broken,
    As one who cannot comfort or appease
Accusing conscience, dumb, he waited there,
    Under the olive trees.

• • • • • •

(Continued)

The night dews rose, and all the garden wept,
    As if it could not ever smile again;
The night wind woke and mourned with him, and swept
    The hillside sadly; and as in a glass,
    Darkly distinct, he saw a vision pass
        Of One who took the cup alone—alone.
        Then broke from him a moan,
    A cry to God for pain, for any pain
Save this last desolation; and he crept
    In penitence to his Lord's feet again.

Then all the garden held its breath for awe;
    A lighted silence hung among the trees.
The blessèd angels, glad because the law,
    Love's law, had wooed him, waiting near heard speech
    Not to be uttered, spiritual, out of reach
        Of earthly language. Low the lover lay,
        Adoring Him whose way
    Is to enrich with such sweet mysteries.
Never an angel told the things he saw
    Under the olive trees.

Never an angel told, but this I know,
    That he to whom that night Gethsemane
Opened its secrets, cannot help but go
    Softly thereafter, as one lately shriven,
    Passionately loving, as one much forgiven.
        And never, never can his heart forget
        That Head with hair all wet
    With the red dews of Love's extremity,
Those eyes from which fountains of love did flow,
    There in the Garden of Gethsemane.

O Love—for words to sing Thy love aright!
O Love discovered 'mid the olive trees,
Oh, to find somewhere a clear pool of light
And fill my pitcher at it, pour it out
In words of shining! Oh for words about
This theme of themes, words worthy, words of fire,
Glowing to my desire!
Not such as these, O Love, not such as these
Poor, pale endeavors to express that night
Under the olive trees.

MP, TJ

Broken Savior

(Luke 22:19)

He blessed and brake and gave:
So was it, Lord, when Thou didst come to save;
Blessed with the richest blessing of high Heaven,
Thou camest here, wert broken to be given.

He blessed and brake and gave:
Thy darling from the lions, from the grave
Could not be rescued; and Thy Garden prayer
Led to the dreadful place where lions were.

And then they broke Thee, Lord.
A broken Savior calls us to His board.
O let us not forget, would we be given:
We must be blessed by Thee and then be broken.

Wg[1]

My Priest

My great High Priest,
I thank Thee that no angel, saint, nor man
Doth come between Thee and Thy last and least,
Nor ever can—nor ever may;
For Thou who art my Priest art also, Lord, my Way.

As from Thy hand I take the Bread and Wine,
I pray Thee, flow through me; Thy life be mine.

As Thou wert broken, O my Lord, for me,
Let me be broken, Lord, for love of Thee.

And as Thy death was Wine of Life outpoured,
So be my life—for love of Thee, my Lord.

TMS

For Me?

Lord Jesus, Redeemer,
 Didst Thou die for me?
For me, Lord, a sinner—
 How could such love be?
O fairest Lord Jesus,
 Didst Thou suffer scorn?
For me, Lord, a sinner,
 Wear a crown of thorn?

And were Thy hands wounded,
 Wounded, Lord, for me?
Thy holy feet piercèd
 On the bitter Tree?
And, Lord, wast Thou thirsty,
 Thirsty, Lord, for me?
O fairest Lord Jesus,
 How could such love be?

O make my heart tender;
    Pardon, pardon me,
That ever forgetful,
    I have grievèd Thee.
I would be Thy lover,
    Taking up my cross,
Thy lover forever,
    Come there gain or loss.

EHW

Rose of My Heart

Rose of my heart, what seek I now but Thee?
And dost Thou say, "Thorns grow upon My Tree"?

Thorns tore Thee, Fairest; what if I be torn?
Where Thou dost blossom, who would stay for thorn?

I hold Thee fast; I will not let Thee go;
For me doth this dear Rose of roses blow.

And so I say, Rose of my heart, to Thee:
Close by my Rose would I, Thy lover, be.

ACD, PU

A Crown of Flowers

O Savior Christ, who could forget
    The crown of thorns—the tortured hours?
But on Thy brow there shall be set
    A crown of fadeless flowers.

And may we bring our flowers to crown
    The love that won at Calvary?
Down in the grass they grow, low down,
    The least of flowers that be.

(Continued)

Immortal Love, Thy sun and showers
  Have swept our field; O take Thine own,
Thy little flowers, Thy love's own flowers,
  Dear Lord, to make Thy crown.

GC, P, RFB

No Healing Anodyne?

O wounded feet, O famished eyes,
  Is there no healing anodyne?
No spell to make the wayworn wise?
  No hint of the Divine?
But if indeed we too might bear
  The dying of the Blessèd One—
But if indeed we too might wear
  The Life of God's dear Son—
Oh, would we, could we, choose to miss
  For loveliest bud of garden born,
One blow of reed, one stab from this,
  Our Savior's crown of thorn?

There is a touch; there is a spell;
  There is a healing anodyne.
Not far art Thou, Emmanuel,
  From troubled child of Thine,
O Master of the wounded feet,
  From whose sharp crown the red dew fell.
And would I walk mid meadowsweet
  Crowned with golden asphodel?

PVV, RFB

Like Seed Corn

As the seed corn sheddeth on the threshingfloor
That which once was precious—needed now no more—
So the nearest, dearest that would hold in thrall
Let Thy winnowing fingers loosen:
Love be Lord of all.

As the seed corn falleth in the quiet ground;
As it lieth hidden, with no stir nor sound—
So would I, Thy seed corn, deep in stillness fall,
That of me there may be nothing:
Thou be All in all.

As the seed corn springeth lowly at Thy feet—
Spear of green uplifteth, yieldeth ear of wheat—
So in tender mercy, though the seed be small,
Let it bring forth for *Thy* glory
Who art Lord of all.

FTK

Surrender Unto Death

Quickener of spirits, teach me what it means
To bear about the dying of my Lord.
On stony roads, far from the land of dreams,
Teach me to walk according to that word.
For love of Thee, Lord of the thorn-crowned brow,
Myself I would surrender unto death.
Nail to Thy Cross all Thou dost disallow;
Breathe through my being, O Thou heavenly Breath.

TMS

Discipline

"Who frames his God
As One whose love unstern
Has never wrought for man a fiery law,
Has never scourged the son whom He received,
Whose holiness does not burn
Against iniquity—
He has conceived
What is not. For no myth, God's awful Rod.
Dost doubt it? Go to Calvary.
See there what angels saw,
The sinless One made sin.
Dost doubt it still? Well, be it so,
But know,
Within
All is not well with thee."

Search me, my God;
Seek to the very ground
Of this my shifting and deceptive heart;
Probe keenly, prove me, and examine me,
O God, and see
Whether in rooms within me set apart
From casual search be found
That which requires Thy Rod.
Look well, look well, my God.

Thus pondering, I prayed
By Christ's good grace;
And in a secret place
Was made aware
Of piled-up debris, stubble of desire
Vain-glorious, foolish, fuel for the fire
That must burn where
God's righteous judgments are made known to men.
Fell swiftly then
The Rod of God.

But I, surprised,
Uncomprehending, blamed
The happenings of my day. Had they conspired
To harass me unkindly? innocent me?
Till suddenly
That bitter thing, the greatly undesired,
That smiting makes ashamed,
I saw. Thus being chastised,
God's Rod I recognized.

I saw Him whom my times
Revere, obey;
I saw Him in my day,
Now evident
To quickened conscience to which circumstance
Is no mere play of irresponsible chance,
But planned intent.
Oh, then I did my holy God adore,
Who was before
Unrecognized.

(Continued)

Thus, my kind Father, God,
Did use His Rod
Which is no myth but veriest verity.
He who of old time wrote
That He would smite, now smote.
Yet never, never has He dealt with me
After my sins, or my iniquity
Had ended me.

O Father, Thou
Before whom, in my spirit I do bow,
Stripped naked of my hideous vanity,
I own Thee just, I own Thee Fatherly.
I bless Thee that Thou didst not let me go
Undealt with, as too trivial to know
Severity of scourging. This Thy work
Continue, Father, for I would not lurk
An unregarded child, undisciplined;
But, knowing I have sinned,
Oh, let me know I am forgiven. Art
To palliate sin flies from me; Father, right
Are these Thy judgments; therefore smite.
O Love, made manifest in this Thy Rod,
My God, my God.

MP

Consume Our Dross

Lord, Thou hast said, "Seek ye my face."
O Lord of love, and Lord of grace,
We cannot lift our hearts to Thee
Till Thou hast cleansed us thoroughly.

O turn Thy hand upon us, Lord,
And search us with Thy powerful word.
And by the virtue of Thy Cross
Consume and cleanse away our dross.

Wg[2]

Refining Fire

(Isaiah 1:25)

O Lord our God, to Thee is known
  Our inmost heart's desire;
Thy love is fire, Thy love alone;
  O bathe our souls in fire.

And purely purge away our dross,
  And take away our tin;
And by the virtue of Thy Cross
  Renew us, Lord, within.

O turn Thy hand, Thy wounded hand,
  On us who love Thy name,
And make of us a holy band,
  A single, burning flame.

Wg[1]

Forest Fire

O high and holy Fair,
As forest fire
Leaps to the upper air,
Would we aspire.

Perish our leaf or bough
And ashes be,
If only here and now
We rise to Thee.

O Fairest, it were shame
Less to desire;
O turn us all to flame
Like forest fire.

Wg:

Thy Flames

Lord of bright ministers, burning and flaming,
Lord of the wind and the great wheeling star:
Speed us Thy servants who go forth proclaiming
Thee and Thy Christ to the peoples afar.

Angels and wind and star, pure and unfailing
In their obedience, fulfilling Thy word,
Shame us, confound us; but perfect, prevailing
Are the strong powers of Thy blood, O Lord.

Purge us and cleanse us, enfold us, inspire us;
We would be flames, O Lord, fervent and pure.
Jesus of Calvary, let Thy love fire us;
Give grace to suffer, give grace to endure.

Wg:

Dust and Flame

But I have seen a fiery flame
Take to his pure and burning heart
Mere dust of earth, to it impart
His virtue, till that dust became
Transparent loveliness of flame.

O Fire of God, Thou fervent Flame,
Thy dust of earth in Thee would fall,
And so be lost beyond recall—
Transformed by Thee, its very name
Forgotten in Thine own, O Flame.

TJ

Searcher of Spirits

Searcher of spirits,
    Try Thou my reins and heart;
Cleanse Thou my inward part—
    Turn, overturn and turn.
Wood, hay and stubble see
    Now spread out before Thee;
        Burn, burn.

Worker in gardens,
    Dig round my hidden root,
Let branch, leaf, bud and fruit
    Respond in quickened life.
Seek out the canker there—
    Cut out and do not spare
        Thy knife.

(Continued)

Savior of sinners,
Out of the depths I cry,
"Perfect me or I die—
Perfect me, patient One";
In Thy revealing light
I stand confessed—outright
Undone.

O to be holy!
Thou wilt not say me nay
Who movest me to pray:
"Enable to endure."
Spiritual cleansing Fire,
Fulfill my heart's desire:
Make pure.

MP, P

Make Pure

(Luke 3:17)

Lord, more and more
I pray: Whether by wind or fire,
Make pure my inmost heart's desire,
And purge the clinging chaff from off the floor.

I wish Thy way;
But when in me myself would rise
And long for something otherwise,
Then, Holy One, take sword and spear, and slay.

Oh, stay nearby,
Most patient Love, till, by Thy grace,
In this poor silver, Thy bright face
Shows forth in clearness and serenity.

What will it be
When, like the lily or the rose,
That in my flow'ry garden blows,
I shall be flawless, perfect, Lord, to Thee?

RFB

Cleansed

(Genesis 4:7; 2 Maccabees 14:36)

Sin crouched beside my door;
 It haunted all my room.
Polluted was the floor,
 The walls were hung with gloom—
When one of royal mien, before
Unknown to me, approached my door.
 Sin saw and fled away.
  "Come in, O Lord," I said;
 I knelt to Him to pray—
  But all the ground was red.
I knew Him then, the Crucified, and said:
"O holy Lord of all hallowing,
Keep undefiled forever
This house that hath been lately cleansed."

(Continued)

Dew lay upon His hair;
    Forspent was He, forlorn.
The face as flower fair
    A twisted thorn had torn—
And oh, the dewdrops in His hair!
It was the dew of blood lay there.
    But with my Kingly Guest
        Poured in a heavenly light,
    And all my room was dressed
        With Mary-lilies white
And passionflowers in bowls of chrysolite.
"O holy Lord of all hallowing,
Keep undefiled forever
This house that hath been lately cleansed."

MP

I See His Cross

(Philippians 3:8)

Christ my Master beckoneth,
    Christ my Lord, the Crucified;
He thus callèd reckoneth
    All the world as nought beside.
Show me not th' imagined loss—
    I see His Cross.

Nay, there is no loss to show;
    What is dust to pilèd gold?
Whom the Cross attracteth know
    Pleasure, sweetness, manifold;
Not the spirit of heaviness—
    Joy is their dress.

But if life of joy were bared,
  Stripped like to a leafless tree,
I, who know God hath prepared
  Treasures of eternity,
Could I for a moment's gain
  Turn from the pain?

Shame upon the coward thought!
  Shame upon the craven will!
Love of Loves, who for me fought
  Unto death on Calvary's hill,
Life's delight—I count it dross!
  I see Thy cross.

EHW, MP, P, Wg[1]

Let Me Not Shrink

O Prince of Glory, who dost bring
  Thy sons to glory through Thy Cross,
Let me not shrink from suffering,
  Reproach, or loss.

The dust of words would smother me;
  Be all to me anathema
That turns me from Gethsemane,
  And Golgotha.

If Thy dear Home be fuller, Lord,
  For that a little emptier
My house on earth, what rich reward
  That guerdon were.

(Continued)

And by the borders of my day
The river of Thy pleasure flows;
The flowers that blossom by the way,
Who loves Thee knows.

Wd

Where Thou Hast Trod

Lord Jesus, for me crucified,
Let not my footsteps from Thee slide,
For I would tread where Thou hast trod—
My spirit tender of the glory of God.

That glory which meant all to Thee,
Let it mean all, my Lord, to me;
So would I tread where Thou hast trod—
My spirit tender of the glory of God.

ACD, TG, Wg[1]

Why Hesitate?

March on in strength, my soul.
The sky is red;
I hear the drums' long roll,
I hear the tread
Of thousand tramping feet;
Say, must I still entreat?
Still do you hesitate?

(Continued)

The hour is late.
O stand not thus aloof,
Obey, obey.
Lest thou, a thing of ruth,
A castaway,
Grow deaf to trumpet note
That else had surely smote
Thy powers to vivid life,
And noble strife.

Away with coward fears.
Are battles won
Without shed blood or tears?
Have you begun
To count a pain too sore
Which Christ your Captain bore?
Would he choose ease who knows
What his Lord chose?

O stricken Savior Christ,
I yield, I yield—
With Thee I will keep tryst
On any field.
O Love that once I grieved,
O Love that has retrieved
All that there is of me,
I follow Thee.

MP, P

Following

I follow where Thou leadest; what are bruises?
There are cool leaves of healing on Thy tree;
Lead Thou me on. Thy heavenly wisdom chooses
In love for me.

Thy lover then, like happy homing swallow
That crosses hill and plain and lonely sea,
All unafraid, so I will fearless follow,
For love of Thee.

GBM, TJ

Our Undefeated Lord

O undefeated Lord,
Where Thou art, there are we;
Out on the battlefield
Our sword unsheathed would be.
We fall but to arise,
For Thou dost never fall—
And in Thy steadfast eyes
We read again our call.

We read it and rejoice;
Oh, perish every fear;
Thy pard'ning, heart'ning voice
Is sounding in our ear.
Thrice blessèd be Thy word
To us—to me—e'en me!
O undefeated Lord,
Lead on; we follow Thee.

Wg[2]

Make Me Thy Fuel

From prayer that asks that I may be
Sheltered from winds that beat on Thee,
From fearing when I should aspire,
From faltering when I should climb higher,
From silken self, O Captain, free
Thy soldier who would follow Thee.

From subtle love of softening things,
From easy choices, weakenings,
(Not thus are spirits fortified,
Not this way went the Crucified)
From all that dims Thy Calvary,
O Lamb of God, deliver me.

Give me the love that leads the way,
The faith that nothing can dismay,
The hope no disappointments tire,
The passion that will burn like fire;
Let me not sink to be a clod:
Make me Thy fuel, Flame of God.

ACD, GC, TJ, Wg[1]

Thou Dost Know the Way

My Father, to my heart I take
　　Thy simple word of truth today;
I shall not lose me in the brake,
　　For Thou dost know the way.

Before my face a mountain frowns,
　　Above me all the sky is grey;
The mist is lying on the downs;
　　But Thou dost know the way.

(Continued)

Around me various voices call,
But Thou wilt never let me stray;
For Thou, my Father, knowest all
The windings of the way.

Oh, music that the soft winds blow,
Sweet song of peace for troubled day—
I am contented *not* to know,
Since Thou dost know the way.

MP, P

I Would Climb

God of the heights, austere, inspiring,
Thy word hath come to me;
O let no selfish aims, conspiring,
Distract my soul from Thee.
Loosen me from Things of Time—
Strengthen me for steadfast climb.

The temporal would bind my spirit;
Father, be Thou my stay.
Show me what flesh cannot inherit,
Stored for another day.
Be transparent, Things of Time—
Looking through you, I would climb.

Now by Thy grace my spirit chooseth
Treasure that shall abide.
The great Unseen, I know, endureth;
My footsteps shall not slide.
Not for me the Things of Time—
God of mountains, I will climb.

ACD, TMS, Wg[1]

Make Me Thy Mountaineer

Make me Thy mountaineer;
I would not linger on the lower slope.
Fill me afresh with hope, O God of hope,
That undefeated I may climb the hill
As seeing Him who is invisible,

Whom having not seen I love.
O my Redeemer, when this little while
Lies far behind me, and the last defile
Is all alight, and in that light I see
My Savior and my Lord, what will it be?

GBM

Guided on the Heights

Make me to be Thy happy mountaineer,
O God most high;
My climbing soul would welcome the austere:
Lord, crucify
On rock or scree, ice-cliff or field of snow,
The softness that would sink to things below.

Thou art my Guide. Where Thy sure feet have trod
Shall mine be set—
Thy lightest word my law of life. O God,
Lest I forget,
And slip and fall, teach me to do Thy will—
Thy mountaineer upon Thy holy hill.

P, RFB

Heavenly Heights

Oh, there are heavenly heights to reach
In many a fearful place,
Where the poor timid child of God
Lies blindly on his face,
Lies languishing for light divine
Which he shall never see,
Till he goes forward at Thy sign
And trusts himself to Thee.

GC, RSP

Wilt Love Me? Trust Me? Praise Me?

O thou belovèd child of My desire,
Whether I lead thee through green valleys,
By still waters,
Or through fire,
Or lay thee down in silence under snow,
Through any weather, and whatever
Cloud may gather,
Wind may blow—
Wilt love Me? trust Me? praise Me?

No gallant bird, O dearest Lord, am I,
That anywhere, in any weather,
Rising singeth;
Low I lie.
And yet I cannot fear, for I shall soar;
Thy love shall wing me, blessèd Savior.
So I answer:
I adore;
I love Thee, trust Thee, praise Thee.

ACD, GBM, TJ

Like Homing Birds

Like the homing birds that fly
Through the untracked fields of sky
Till they find their place,
I would seek Thy face.

Like the homing birds whose flight
Dares the dark and cloudy night
Till they find their place,
I would seek Thy face—

Seek Thy face and find my rest,
Like the wild bird in her nest.
Where should my nest be,
Dear Lord, but in Thee?

P

No Wandering Bird Am I

Nearness to Thee, O God, is all my good;
No wand'ring bird am I in dark'ning wood.
In my tall Tree of Life my nest is set,
Sheltered by careful leaves from winds that fret.

No fowler climbs so high to fling his snare;
No prowling thing of night can breathe that air.
Under Thy covering wings Thy bird would dwell;
Safe nested in my Tree, all, all is well.

TMS

Strength of My Heart

Strength of my heart, I need not fail—
Not mine to fear but to obey;
With such a leader who could quail?
Thou art as Thou wert yesterday!
Strength of my heart, I rest in Thee;
Fulfill Thy purposes through me.

Hope of my heart, though suns burn low,
And fades the green from all the earth,
Thy quenchless hope would fervent glow,
From barren waste would spring to birth.
Hope of my heart, oh cause to be
Renewals of Thy hope in me!

Love of my heart, my streams run dry.
O Fountain of the heavenly hills,
Love, blessèd Love, to Thee I cry,
Flood all my secret hidden rills.
Waters of love, oh pour through me;
I must have love—I must have Thee!

Lord, give me love; then I have all,
For love casts out tormenting fear;
And love sounds forth a trumpet call
To valiant hope; and sweet and clear
The birds of joy sing in my tree,
Love of my heart, when I have Thee.

ACD, GC

Even as a Weaned Child
(Psalm 131:2)

And shall I pray Thee change Thy will, my Father,
Until it be according unto mine?
But no, Lord, no, that never shall be; rather,
I pray Thee, blend my human will with Thine.

I pray Thee, hush the hurrying, eager longing;
I pray Thee, soothe the pangs of keen desire;
See in my quiet places wishes thronging;
Forbid them, Lord; purge, though it be with fire.

And work in me to will and do Thy pleasure;
Let all within me, peaceful, reconciled,
Tarry, content my Well-belovèd's leisure—
At last, at last, even as a weaned child.

ACD, GC, TJ

Think Through Me

Think through me, Thoughts of God;
My Father, quiet me,
Till in Thy holy presence, hushed,
I think Thy thoughts with Thee.

Think through me, Thoughts of God,
That always, everywhere,
The stream that through my being flows
May homeward pass in prayer.

Think through me, Thoughts of God,
And let my own thoughts be
Lost like the sand-pools on the shore
Of the eternal sea.

GC, TJ, Wd, Wg[1]

Cause Me to Hear
(Song of Solomon 8:13)

O Thou that dwellest in the gardens,
As Thy companions hearken to Thy voice,
Love of my love,
May I not hear it there?
Cause me to hear it there.

Cause me to hear, for it is life to me;
I perish when I am away from Thee!
Love of my love,
Tell me, where walkest Thou?
I would be with Thee now.

Let me be Thy companion, even I,
For whom Thou once didst in a garden lie;
Love of my love,
Than all my dear, more dear,
Tell me, may I draw near?

I may, I may! Thou callest me to come.
O Dweller in the gardens, this is home!
Love of my love,
Dear Lord, what would I more
But listen, serve, adore?

GC, P

Lord God of Gardens

Lord God of gardens, Thou whose love disposes
 Sun, rain, wind violent,
So that our bushes flower to Thee in roses,
 We are content.

We do not ask to choose our garden's weather
 Too ignorant are we—
Only that we, Thy gardeners, together
 May pleasure Thee;

Only that till the time for gardening closes—
 Let skies be grey or blue—
Each dawn may find us bringing Thee fresh roses,
 Buds drenched with dew.

GBM, Wg[1]

Silent Desire

(Psalm 38:9)

As the misty bluebell wood,
 Very still and shadowy,
Does not seek, far less compel
Several word from several bell,
But lifts up her quiet blue—
 So all my desire is before Thee.

For the prayer of human hearts
 In the shadow of the Tree,
Various as the various flowers,
Blown by wind and wet by showers,
Rests at last in silent love—
 Lord, all my desire is before Thee.

RFB, TJ

Cross and Garden

As near Thy Cross a Garden lay,
So, as we follow in the way,
We find a garden. Pain and loss
Were not the last words of the Cross.

Beyond the sharpness and the strife,
The Easter lily reigns in life.
And singing birds are in the trees;
Were ever singing birds like these?

O Lord, the solemn mystery
Of Cross and Garden beckons me.
Thou who didst never turn Thee back,
Keep my feet steadfast in the track.

TMS

Waiting on Thee

O Lord beloved, my times are in Thy hand;
My very minutes wait on Thy command.
In this still room, O Blessèd Master, walk
And with my spirit talk.

GBM

The Prayer Cell

Lord of my life, I bless Thee for the cell
  Whereunto I resort so privily,
And on such quiet feet, that none can tell
  When I have slipped into that cell with Thee.
  That I, the least of all Thy company,
With Thee, my Lord, may dwell,
  Is wonder of all wonders unto me!

It passeth knowledge—like the fields of air,
  Kingdoms of light, the pathway of the sea,
And most of all—Thy love. I meet Thee there;
  Love's adoration do I offer Thee.
  Let the Much Incense of Thy merits be
The fragrance everywhere
  When Thou dost come and dost commune with me.

TMS

Shared Mystery

(John 11:4)

"Not unto death"—O Savior, who are we
  That Thou dost open mysteries to us,
As though we were Thy friends of Bethany,
  Martha and Mary or Thy Lazarus?

Blessèd be Love, that takes our creeping thought
  And gives it wings, and teaches it to soar
Until it touches fringe of what it sought,
  And learns to spell the words of heavenly lore . . .

And sees at last in fellowship of pain,
  In path that Lazarus through the valley trod,
Something that may be like the buried grain,
  Something that serves the glory of our God.

TMS

Thou Knowest and Carest

Savior who suffered, Thou dost know
The rankling thrust, the fiery dart,
How sharply little winds can blow
Upon the tired heart.

Thou knowest how the urgent call
Of love and life, so near, so far,
Can flash through window, pierce through wall,
Leap over bar.

Thou knowest and Thou carest too;
I lean like John upon Thy breast,
For there is nothing I can do
But lay me down and rest.

TMS

Thy John

As John upon his dear Lord's breast,
So would I lean, so would I rest;
As empty shell in depths of sea,
So would I sink, be filled with Thee.

As water lily in her pool
Through long, hot hours is still and cool,
A thought of peace, so I would be
Thy water-flower, Lord, close by Thee.

As singing bird in high, blue air,
So would I soar, and sing Thee there;
No rain nor stormy wind can be
When all the air is full of Thee.

And so though daily duties crowd,
And dust of earth be like a cloud,
Through noise of words, O Lord, my Rest,
Thy John would lean upon Thy breast.

RFB, TJ, Wg[1]

Peace and Gladness

Great peace and festal gladness
    And sweet tranquility—
These are the gifts Thou givest
    To him who lives in Thee.

Thine inner rooms are hallowed;
    No winds of time blow there,
But blessèd balm of quiet
    And joyance everywhere.

On him whom tempest buffets
    A sudden stillness falls,
And he is far from turmoil
    Within pavilion walls.

And heavenly places open;
    A heavenly feast is spread;
With oil of joy for mourning
    Dost Thou anoint his head.

There blame is all forgotten;
    There praise is all unheard;
He tastes the hidden sweetness
    Of far diviner word.

(Continued)

And cool, green leaves of healing
    Soothe every fretting sore;
He wonders at the trouble
    That stirred in him before.

The lot has fallen to him
    In fair and pleasant ground;
And multitudes of angels
    Encompass him around.

Then satisfied with favor
    His heart sings unto Thee
In whom is festal gladness
    And sweet tranquility.

MP, P

BREATHE, O BREATH

Breathe, breathe, O Breath,
And fill my sails
As I put out to sea;
Lord, I am Thine,
And Thou art mine;
I will go on with Thee.

Wg[2]

Content to Trust

(1 Corinthians 2:9)

Eye hath not seen, ear hath not heard,
Nor entered into heart of man,
The things that God delights to plan
For those who take Him at His word.

Now through a frosted pane we trace
The outline of His perfect will,
Content to trust His love until
We know and see Him face to face.

Wg[2]

Full Surrender

Father, who speakest to us by the way,
Now from a burning bush, now by a stream;
Father, whose loving kindness passeth dream,
Who makest music from the dust of spray;
Hidden my pool, where never man hath trod,
My pool where only reeds and marsh-flowers be.
O Beautiful, O Bountiful, my God,
Not one small reedful would I keep from Thee.

PVV

4 Poems of Ministry

Fire Words

"O God, my words are cold:
The frosted frond of fern or feathery palm
Wrought on the whitened pane—
They are as near to fire as these my words;
Oh, that they were as flames!"
Thus did I cry.

And thus God answered me:
"Thou shalt have words, but at this cost:
That thou must first be burnt—
Burnt by red embers from a secret fire,
Scorched by fierce heats and withering winds that sweep
Through all thy being, carrying thee afar
From old delights. Doth not the ardent fire
Consume the mountain's heart before the flow
Of fervent lava? Wouldst thou easefully,
As from cool, pleasant fountains, flow in fire?
Say, can thy heart endure, or can thy hands be strong
In the day that I shall deal with thee?

"For first the iron must enter thine own soul,
And wound and brand it, scarring awful lines
Indelibly upon it; and a hand
Resistless in a tender terribleness,
Must thoroughly purge it, fashioning its pain
To power that leaps in fire.
Not otherwise, and by no lighter touch,
Are fire-words wrought."

MP

Spirit, Work in Me

Spirit Divine, work in me holiness,
  Purity, pity for the world's distress.
But O let hope, Thy quenchless hope, prevail,
  Lest I should faint and fail.

Then as the incense from the golden bowl
  Rose up to Thee, so from my quiet soul
Let prayer arise—a little, quiet cloud—
  To Thee, my listening God.

Wg[1]

Hope Through Me

Hope through me, God of Hope,
  Or never can I know
Deep wells and living streams of hope,
  And pools of overflow.

Flood me with hope today
  For souls perverse, undone,
For sinful souls that turn away,
  Blind sunflowers, from their Sun.

O blessèd Hope of God,
  Flow through me patiently,
Until I hope for everyone
  As Thou hast hoped for me.

EHW

Our Unseen Guide

We know Thee with us, Thou who art
Our Lord, our unseen Guide.
O send us to the seeking heart,
The heart unsatisfied.

The sinful and the comfortless—
Great Healer, gather them
From out the careless crowd, to press
And touch Thy garment's hem.

K

That All Could See

Precious art Thou, Christ our Lord,
Light of light, Eternal Word;
O that all the world could see
What there is in Thee!

As the life in bud and leaf,
Wealth of blossom on the bough,
Gold of newly gathered sheaf—
So, my Lord, art Thou.

Glories of the earth and air,
Powers and splendor limitless—
All these forms and colors wear
Something of Thy dress.

But what words of man can show
That which happy lovers know?
O that all the world could see
What there is in Thee!

Wg[1]

Give Me Thy Thirst

No, not for you He thirsted as He died;
No, not for you my Lord was crucified:
Woods, streams and mountains, innocent are ye;
For you, no Bethlehem or Calvary.

Though dear as ye must be to Him, ye trees,
And running waters in your purity—
To heart that broke to save them, dearer these:
Sons of a poor, undone humanity.

O stainless things, I would not love you less;
How could I, you being what you are to me?
But I would love the unlovable—confess
Mankind as something more beloved than ye.

Give me Thy thirst; kindle, O Christ, Thy fire,
That passionate fire of love's sincerity.
My wild wind harp, take; make of it a lyre
Whose music shall win men to turn to thee.

DS, FF

Thirst-Quenching Streams

Lord, make of this our pleasant field
  A garden cool and shadowy,
A spring shut up, a fountain sealed
  For Thee, Lord Jesus, only Thee.

And fill it full of singing birds,
  On every bough of every tree,
And give the music and the words
  That will, Lord Jesus, pleasure Thee.

And as from far, untrodden snow
    Of Lebanon, the streams run free,
Dear Lord, command our streams to flow,
    That thirsty men may drink of Thee.

ACD, EHW, GC, MB

Christ's Fragrance

(2 Corinthians 2:15)

They say that once a piece of common clay
Such fragrance breathed as from a garden blows.
"My secret is but this," they heard it say,
"I have been near a rose."

And there are those who bear about with them
The power, with thoughts of Christ, men's hearts to stir;
For, having knelt to kiss His garment's hem,
Their garments smell of myrrh.

So grant, I pray Thee, Lord, that by Thy grace
The fragrance of Thy life may dwell in me,
That as I move about from place to place,
Men's thoughts may turn to Thee.

FTR

A Hint of Life?

We only see the scorching earth.
    Lord of the seed, we cry,
Our sowing seemeth little worth
    In ground so dry.

But if the eyes of angels see
    Some hint of tender green,
Anoint our eyes that they may be
    As angels', keen.

(Continued)

O mighty Quickener of the dead,
Dost Thou see life astir?
Dost Thou see harvest gold outspread,
As though it were?

Wg[1]

Sowing

Lord, we Thy sowers, at the set of sun
Come back to Thee to tell of sowing done;
And while the seed lies hidden in the ground,
O God of Hope, let hope in us abound.

Seed springeth up, we know not when nor how,
It is enough that Thou, O Lord, dost know.
To Thee the glory when it doth appear—
Blade, ear, and then the full corn in the ear.

Wg[1]

Love That Runs

(Luke 15:20)

A great way off, and lo, the Father saw him,
For keen the eyes that grief has washed with tears;
The son knew not that cords of love would draw him
From out the tangled snare of wasted years.

His Father ran: Love's feet were never holden;
The kiss, the robe, the ring, the shoes declare
Eternal love, and wandering son embolden
To seek his Father's heart and find it there.

My Father, very wonderful Thy loving—
The Father ran. Oh, give and give again
The love that runs, compassion ever moving
To welcome home the troubled sons of men.

Wg[1]

Make Me a True Lover

(Isaiah 42:3)

Mender of broken reeds,
O patient Lover,
'Tis love my brother needs;
Make me a lover.
That this poor reed may be
Mended and tuned for Thee,
O Lord, of even me
Make a true lover.

Kindler of smoking flax,
O fervent Lover,
Give what Thy servant lacks;
Make me a lover.
That this poor flax may be
Quickened, aflame for Thee,
O Lord, of even me
Make a true lover.

ACD

Love's Channel

"What wouldest thou that I should do for thee?"
My Lord, my Savior, pour Thy love through me.

As mountain river when its streams run dry,
So, but for Thee, Fountain of Love, am I.

If there be hindrance, sweep it all away;
O Love Eternal, pour through me, I pray.

EHW

Love Through Me

Love through me, Love of God;
Make me like Thy clear air
Through which, unhindered, colors pass
As though it were not there.

Powers of the love of God,
Depths of the heart Divine,
O Love that faileth not, break forth
And flood this world of Thine.

TJ

Through Me

Love through me, Love of God;
There is no love in me.
O Fire of love, light Thou the love
That burns perpetually.

Flow through me, Peace of God;
Calm River, flow until
No wind can blow, no current stir
A ripple of self-will.

Shine through me, Joy of God;
Make me like Thy clear air
That Thou dost pour Thy colors through,
As though it were not there.

O blessèd Love of God,
That all may taste and see
How good Thou art, once more I pray:
Love through me—even me.

EHW, Wg[1]

The Master's Way

Great Master, who didst always find
The way into the clouded mind,
O make me wise to find the way
To help the soul for whom I pray.

Give me the love that will not fail,
The hope that no rebuff can quail,
Thine insight—penetrating, clear—
Thy tender touch, direct, sincere.

O let me dwell so deep in Thee,
So close to Powers of Calvary,
That I shall never block the way
When streameth forth Thy healing Ray.

Wg[2]

Thy Love and Passion

(John 4:6)

Would anyone tell,
O wonderful Lover,
How precious to Thee
A single poor sinner?
Then let him behold
Wearied Love by a well—
Love urgent, intent,
One soul to recover.

(Continued)

Lord, what do we know
    Of love in this fashion?
Thy hunger and thirst,
    O give us, our Savior.
Though all hell oppose,
    Our fatigue lay us low,
O kindle in us
    Thy love and Thy passion.

Wg[1]

Bring Them Home

(1 Kings 19:10–12)

Oh, bring them home—what though their faint desire
Falter and fail before the piercing sword?
Yet in the wind, or earthquake, or in fire,
    Come to them, conquering Lord.

Or in the sound of gentle stillness, come,
Comforter, come. Let thought of us be far;
Not ours the light that leads them safely home,
    Not of us sun or star.

Dear Lord of Love, so boundless and so deep
That all Thy heart could yearn for us, accursed—
O Lord of Love, great Shepherd of the sheep,
    Give unto us Thy thirst!

GC, Wg[1]

A Passion for Souls

O for a passionate passion for souls!
  O for a pity that yearns!
O for the love that loves unto death!
  O for the fire that burns!
O for the pure prayer-power that prevails,
  That pours itself out for the lost;
Victorious prayer in the Conqueror's name,
  O for a Pentecost!

Infinite Savior, in mighty compassion,
  Take Thy poor child tonight;
That which she hath not in tenderness give her—
  Teach her to pray and fight.
Cost what it may of a self-crucifixion,
  So that Thy will be done;
Cost what it may of a loneliness after,
  So straying souls be won!

Jesus, my Savior, beyond telling rare
  The jewel I ask of Thee:
So much it meaneth, this talisman, Prayer—
  Wilt Thou not give it to me?
Intensely, intensely I long to know,
  Deep into this solemn thing:
Intensely, intensely I long to go
  All lengths with Thee, my King!

(Continued)

And now in the hush of this solemn hour,
    I would lie at Thy feet, O Christ,
While Thou, all majestic in love and power,
    Dost keep with Thy child a tryst.
Thyself unveiled, in Thy beauty fair,
    Would dazzle these earth-born eyes;
But oh, one day I shall see Thee there,
    In the glory of a surprise!

Speakest Thou now? Thou givest to me
    A choice, as in olden time?
Dear Lord, wilt Thou put the end of the rope
    That pulleth God's prayer-bell chime
In my little hand—enfolding it so
    That nothing may be of me.
When it soundeth above, our Father will know
    'Tis rung, O Belovèd, by Thee!

ACD, FSL, FTR, K

Give Thy Love to Me

Love that never faileth,
Love that all prevaileth—
Savior Christ, O hear me now
And give Thy love to me.

Round me souls are dying,
Deep in darkness lying;
Thou didst love them unto death;
O give Thy love to me.

Grant that I may reach them;
Grant that I may teach them,
Loving them as Thou dost love;
O give Thy love to me.

Love that ever burneth,
Love that ever yearneth—
Savior Christ, O hear me now
And give Thy love to me.

ACD, DS, K, Wg[1]

Cords of Love

O Belovèd of my soul,
 This do I desire:
Faith for the impossible,
 Love that will not tire.
Jesus, Savior, Lover, give me
Love for the unlovable,
 Love that will not tire.

O Belovèd of my soul,
 Yet again I come;
Give me cords of love to draw
 Many wanderers home.
Jesus, Savior, Lover, give me
Love that knows no strain nor flaw—
 Love to lead them home.

EHW

To Seek Thy Sheep

Good Shepherd, over whom no foe prevaileth,
    To whom the least of wandering lambs is known,
Grant us Thy love that wearieth not nor faileth;
    Grant us to seek Thy wayward sheep that roam
Far on the fell, until we find and fold them
    Safe in the love of Thee, their own true Home.

Wg[2]

The Shepherd's Heart

Thy Shepherd love impart,
    That never wearieth.
O give to me the Shepherd heart
    That loveth unto death.

Give me the love that led
    Unto Gethsemane.
That Thy dear sheep be shepherded,
    Lord, give that love to me.

Wg[1]

The Faithful Shepherd

As the faithful shepherd toileth,
    Through the briars, up the steep,
Lest some evil prowler spoileth
    His poor foolish wandering sheep,

So, great Shepherd, would we, caring
    For each several precious one,
Something of Thy travail sharing,
    Seek Thy sheep till set of sun.

Only twelve short hours—oh, never
Let the sense of urgency
Die in us, Good Shepherd, ever
Let us search the hills with Thee.

Wg[1]

Lead Onward

Step by step, Lord, lead us onward,
Walking barefoot with our guide—
Listening for Thy softest whisper,
Savior, for us crucified.

Lead us on, though flint and briar
Wound our feet at every stride,
Tireless, till we find the lost one,
Savior for him crucified.

Unp

Vigilance

Make me, my Lord, aware
Of peril in the air,
Or ever ravening wolf can leap
On the defenseless sheep.

Give me the eye that sees
When he is threatening these
Whom Thou hast trusted to my care.
Let me not fail them there.

Wg[1]

Seeking Thy Sheep

Sharp mountain briers intertwined
Have caught Thy willful, wandering sheep.
Long is the way, the rocks are steep—
"I seek," the Shepherd said, "until I find."

Good Shepherd, Thy poor sheep was blind
To all Thy love, to all Thy care;
Dews of the night are on Thy hair—
"I seek," the Shepherd said, "until I find."

O Shepherd, give to us Thy mind.
Thy hands and feet are tired and torn;
O let us share the toil, the thorn,
Seeking Thy sheep with Thee, until we find.

Wg[1]

Accountability

My God, who hast committed to my care
    Thy ransomed one,
Lest I be scattered, busy here and there,
    And he be gone,
Give me to hold me firmly to my trust.
Let all that would distract me be as dust.

"Thy life for his"—O solemn, urgent word.
    Lest I forget,
My sense of values waver or be blurred
    Or overset
By other things, take me and purge and bend
Each power and purpose to one single end.

Teach me to do the thing that pleaseth Thee,
O Lord, my God;
Give clearness, lest some byway tangle me.
Where Christ hath trod,
There would I tread, nor ever turn aside,
Lest he be missing for whom Christ hath died.
TMS

Resignation

There are some brave souls, and God knows them well,
Though magazines may not their praises swell,
Whose life breathes a fragrance, just felt, not seen,
Like the scent of the violet lost in green.
Trusted with pain in a shaded room,
Trusted with office, or shop, or loom,
Trusted with pen, or needle, or broom,
Such, day by day, toil, suffer and pray,
Contented to serve their God any way.

But some there are, superfinely molded,
Who sit with hands submissively folded;
Who vegetate rather than live, and suggest
Good cabbages—doing no harm at best.
Of the poor dark world's dark need they know;
They take a great interest in missions, and oh!
At times they are almost ready to go—
But then, by some flaw in their calculation,
They mistake laziness for resignation.

(Continued)

For they are so speedily persuaded
That all the reasons by which they are aided
    To gravitate back to the easy chair
    Are fully as solid as they are fair.
        They "can't be spared," they have surely heard,
        And they don't recollect the other absurd
        Little fact that, most certainly, never a word
    Would be raised did the question involve a *Ring*,
    For "Of course, that is quite a different thing."

They have "so few gifts," and they "cannot speak";
'Tis their "*cross* in life" to be timid and weak—
    Alas that we call by such sacred name
    Excuses, invented to save us from pain,
    Far, far removed from the Cross and shame!
        Perhaps the Society's door was locked
        When with somewhat uncertain knuckle they knocked,
    And everyone said, "Ah! now it is plain
    You cannot be meant to try again.
        How terrible should you the business shirk
        Of life's most serious fancy-work
        For our Father's business in temple's murk!"
    They sigh, and suppose so. The argumentation
    Transforms laziness into resignation.

If such a deluded one reads this rhyme
Oh, will not she waken while there is time?
    Don't think that "Sit still" must infallibly be
    A life-motto written expressly for thee.
        It may be the word is "Go forward"—if not,
        If before the Master you stand in your lot,
        He will flame your soul with a burning hot
    And passionate fire, and you shall know
    The joy of setting some other aglow.

And now, won't you face it, and have a cremation
Of the laziness which you called "resignation"?

FTR

Access

Lord God of all the great undone,
    They live by faith who with Thee dwell;
For Thou dost turn the flinty stone
    Into a springing well.

Lord God of doors we cannot pass,
    We go where Thou art leading on;
For Thou dost break the bars of brass
    And cut the bars of iron.

GC

Dust

God's walking the blue sky-roads today:
See, how lovely the dust of His feet.
"Clouds of dust," we say down here
As it whirls through our troubled atmosphere
And we walk in the thick of it; but up there,
"The clouds are the dust of His feet," they say.

Do the angels say, when they look at the crowd
And the crush on the roads of this dusty star,
As we toil along, nor strong, nor fleet,
And overwhelmed by the secular,
"How lovely the dust of their feet"?

GC

The Path of God

Across the will of nature
Leads on the path of God;
Not where the flesh delighteth
The feet of Jesus trod.

Oh, Jesus, Thy care is not to make
The desert a waste no more,
But to keep our feet, lest we miss the track
Where Thy feet went before.

CD, PU

Counting the Cost

Thou hast enough to pay thy fare?
Well be it so;
But thou shouldest know,
Does thy God send thee there—
Is that it all? To pay thy fare?
There's many a coin flung lightly down
Brings back a load of care.
It may cost what thou knowest not
To bring thee home from there.

GC

The Calm Community of the Criticized

If, though all unawares, and not of ill intent,
Thou steppest one inch outside the beaten track;
If thou in deed or word or preference
Depart from the accustomed, or ransack
The unexplored, bright treasure-mines of life,
And, drawing forth their jewels, make the House
Religious (as men call it) a glad place—

O then hide, hide thy face.
Or, quick make a pretense
Of suitable penitence;
For drum and fife
Are out against thee. Perish thy mad *nous*,
Or what it was that set thee grubbing where
A "decent" missionary never should be found.
They'll chase thee off the ground;
They'll harry thee,
Proclaim thee singular,
The while the truly sane and sober tar
Thy broken reputation for good sense.

At first, unconscious thou that things are thus—
Being innocent of all intentional wrong—
Thou wilt not know the fervent, general fuss
Pertains to thee at all. But gradually
It breaks on thee that various eyes are bent
Upon thy course, the lightness of thy gains
To scrutinize; and thou wilt see ere long
That certain hands hold firm a piece of chalk
To write thee up upon the wall. Advised
Be thou then, O my friend, in time;
Ponder the manner of thy careful walk;
See that thy very thoughts are close emmewed;
Tune all thy bells to play the usual chime—
Or brace thy spirit to be flayed alive
For its own good. The which, if thou survive,
Thou art labeled one of that community
Who loving much can suffer woefully,
And yet mix laughter with their foolish pains,
And go on unsubdued—
The Calm Community of the Criticized.

MP

Not Idle Ore

We are here to prove
To angels and to men:
That life is not as idle ore,
But iron dug from central gloom,
And heated hot with burning fears,
And dipped in baths of hissing tears,
And battered with the shocks of doom
To shape and use.

GC

By Thy Cross and Passion

O God of burning altar fire,
O God of love's consuming flame,
Make pure the flame of our desire
To win the lost to seek Thy name.

There is no coldness, Lord, in Thee;
O keep us kindled, lest we bring
To our dear Lord of Calvary
Dead ashes for our offering.

Dead ashes, husk of corn for wheat—
Lord of our Ordination vow,
We gather round Thy wounded feet,
We see the thorns about Thy brow.

Now by Thy Cross and Passion, Lord,
Grant us this plea, this sovereign plea:
Save us from choosing peace for sword,
And give us souls to give to Thee.

GBM

Faithful Warriors

Lord Jesus Christ, our Captain, we hail Thee Conqueror.
Ask what Thou wilt, we'll follow; we are Thy men of war.
We'll burn our boats behind us; we'll fling our ladders down;
No battle wound shall bind us, till Thou hast won Thy crown.
O Lord, our Leader, make us a faithful band
Till Hindustan from north to south is Thine, Lord—
Is Thine: Immanuel's land.

Wd

Over Foes Within

Make us valiant warriors, Jesus,
Over self and sin;
Lead us, lead us, on to triumph
Over foes within.
Lead us forth in any service
Thou, dear Lord, shalt choose;
Make us steadfast, make us faithful,
Meet for Thee to use.

BT

Gird Us Now
(2 Samuel 23:11–12)

"But he stood"—O let the words
Strengthen us in strong temptation.
Thou who art the God who girds
Soldier-souls for their vocation,
Gird us now that we may stand,
Strengthened by Thy mighty hand.

TG

The Call

Light of light, Light of light,
  Lover of children, hear.
Shine, shine through the night,
  Lighten the cloudy fear.
Little boats drifting over the bar,
Little lambs lost in fields afar,
Where is no moon nor star;
Call Thy little ones, call Thy little ones Home.

Far on fell, far on fell,
  Wander the lambs that stray.
Far, far from harbor bell
  Drift the small boats away.
Open to Thee are the paths of the sea;
All the world's corners are open to Thee.
Follow them where they be;
Call Thy little ones, call Thy little ones Home.

Deep to deep answereth now;
  Dimly I see a Cross—
Thirst, wounds, thorn-crowned brow,
  Stripping and utmost loss.
Over the bar the fret of the foam,
Rain on the fell where young lambs roam;
Lord, art Thou bidding me
Call Thy little ones, call Thy little ones Home?

ACD, BT

The Joy of Duty

For the quiet joy of duty.
Praise, praise I sing:
  For the commonplace and lowly,
  Set with pleasure high and holy,
  In each unromantic thing,
  Praise, praise to Thee, my King.

For the solemn joy of battle,
Praise, praise I sing:
  For the wounds and sore distresses,
  For the love that soothes and blesses,
  Strength in weakness perfecting,
  Praise, praise to Thee, my King.

For the splendid joy of triumph,
Praise, praise I sing:
  For the joy all joys excelling,
  Passing, passing human telling,
  Joy to see Thee conquering,
  Praise, praise to Thee, my King.

K, MP, P, WHP

In Any Office
(1 Chronicles 4:23)

My potter's busy wheel is where
I see a desk and office chair;
And well I know the Lord is there.

And all my work is for a King
Who gives His potter songs to sing,
Contented songs, through everything.

And nothing is too small to tell
To Him with whom His potters dwell,
My Counselor, Emmanuel.

Master, Thy choice is good for me;
It is a happy thing to be
Here in my office—here with Thee.

TJ

Love's Priority Over Music

Said one whose yoke
Was that of common folk:
Would that I were like Saint Cecilia,
And could invent some goodly instrument
Passing all yet contrived to worship Thee,
And send a love song singing over land and sea.

But when I seem
Almost to touch my dream,
I hear a call, persistent though so small,
The which if I ignore, clamors about my door
And bids me run to meet some human need.
Meanwhile, my dream drifts off like down of thistle seed.

A sound of gentle stillness stirred and said,
"My child, be comforted,
Dear is the offering of melody,
But dearer far—love's lowliest ministry."

TJ

The Humble Song of Deeds

Oh, that I were
As Saint Cecilia,
And could invent
Some goodly instrument
Passing all yet contrived, to worship Thee
In music great, celestial!
Or, if that cannot be,
Oh, would that I could break
With all conventions, and all trivial and low-roomed
Conceptions of Thee; being inwardly
Freed and informed by Thy pure Spirit, and consumed
By Fire of Love,
By Love majestical,
That I might sing that Love in words of glory
That should shake
The very firmament!

(Continued)

It may not be; for ever when I seem
Almost upon the border of my dream,
Cometh a call to some slight duty touching human needs,
Mixed in some small life-story.
And then, distinct above
The sound of music in me, it doth shout—
That call imperious—which, if at all
Ignored, is wont to make such deafening din
And clamor of displeasure, me within
And round about,
That all my shining thoughts affrighted fly
And scatter, as the wind-blown wingèd seeds
Of thistle weeds.
But, turning back from my poor strivings, I
Hear a low voice repeat
Over and over: "To thy Lord, most sweet
Of all sweet songs, the humble song of deeds."

MP

Mirth

(Ecclesiastes 2:2)

I said of Mirth: "What doeth it?"
Much every way;
For mirth is as the frolic of the spray
From the great ocean of eternal joy;
Or as the lovely, irresponsible play
Of sunlight upon water; or the coy
Touch of wind on leaves and meadow grass.
And all the common hours that else would pass
In dull procession, deaf and dumb and blind,
Sing with sweet Mirth a merry roundelay.

But whoso wooeth it
In devious ways may find—as did the king—
Of pleasant fruit only the rind.
For he, poor vexèd king, the peculiar treasure
Of foolish kings to amass,
Toiled knee-deep through a profitless morass,
Only to find Mirth fled,
Only to hear the knell
Of a far distant bell
Tolling his vain hope dead.
Therefore, in his displeasure,
"That which eludeth me,"
He said, "is vanity."

But Mirth is as a young, shy child
Who, caring not to be thus chased about,
Runneth away to hide, and maybe pout,
Embarrassed by her hunter's eagerness.
Let him forbear, and walk the common road,
Should'ring in patience his appointed load,
And he will catch a glimpse of a bright dress
Woven of sunbeams lighting a shadowy place;
Will presently feel a little, soft, warm hand
Slip into his; will look down, see a face
Lifted to meet his smile. The little maid
Will laugh with him until, as though he played
His boyhood's games, his very heart will laugh.

(Continued)

And he will understand
Why the king's epitaph
Is not believed by simple folk who say
They know the child, and call her Verity,
And love her well.
And he will join them, for sheer gaiety
Sing with her and the birds, and dwell
Under the happy blue of God's blue sky alway.

MP

In the Sickroom

Lord Jesus, Thou art here with me;
    I do not need to cry to Thee
To come with me, my loving Lord,
    For Thou art with me in the ward.

And though I may not see Thy face,
    Yet, as I go from place to place,
There is a hush upon my day
    That would not be, wert Thou away.

When in the still, white room I stand,
    Thy viewless hand will guide my hand.
Dear Lord, what joy, what peace to be
    About Thy healing work with Thee.

GC, Wd

A Nurse's Prayer

Let not routine make dull my quickened sense
Of Thee, Lord Jesus; give me reverence,
That in each wounded one I may see Thee,
My Lord, my Love, Savior of Calvary.

In dusty foot thorn-pierced, I would see Thine
Pierced by a nail for love of me and mine;
In each sore hand held out so piteously
I would see Thine, Redeemer, bruised for me.

For me be hallowed every common bed
Because Thou hadst not where to lay Thy head;
In common flesh, Lord Jesus, I would see
Thy sacred body laid upon the tree.

Should some I serve, unruly toss and fret,
And tire my patience, then, lest I forget
All that I owe to Thy long agony,
Show me once more, my Lord, Thy Calvary.

P

God's True Nurse

God's own true nurse is she who knows
"By constant watching, wise"
Just where the scalding current flows
That, hid from casual eyes,
Makes life an arid wilderness—
Then does the true nurse bless.

(Continued)

For she, without the noise of words,
Most lovingly will do,
Till, like the song of happy birds,
The joy of ease pours through
That which was arid wilderness—
So does the true nurse bless.

And when the spirit drifts afraid
To strange and unknown lands,
Then does the true nurse, undismayed
(Her dear love understands),
Follow and comfort and caress—
So does the true nurse bless.

O nurse, God-given, your ministry
Is something all divine;
With all you do, in all you be,
His love will intertwine
The gold threads of His gentleness—
So will His true nurse bless.

RFB

Sweetness Wherever
(Young Amy's Madonna Lily)

She grew, a plant of fair renown,
Where other lilies be.
They saw her white and golden crown,
And nevermore was she
Among the lilies of the wood;
For they that plucked her thought it good
That in another kind of room
That lily flower should bloom.

And to that room one day there came
A little wild-bird child,
But lately caught, and nowise tame,
And all unreconciled
To cages and to careful bars
That seemed to ban the very stars.
The lily looked at her and smiled,
As though herself a child.

And their eyes met; no word was said
That man could hear or say;
But thus the child was comforted.
And after, flown away
To far, far lands, rememb'ring this—
A comfort it were loss to miss—
Would even in this later hour
Sing joy to some dear flower.

O whosoe'er ye be, and where,
However straitly bound,
Your ministry is as the air
That sails the whole world round.
Do ye but fill your present room
With sweetness as of heavenly bloom,
Ye know not where it may be found:
Is Christ within you bound?

ACD, DS

Constant Victory

Before the winds that blow do cease,
   Teach me to dwell within Thy calm;
Before the pain has passed in peace,
   Give me, my God, to sing a psalm.
Let me not lose the chance to prove
The fullness of enabling love.
   O Love of God, do this for me:
   Maintain a constant victory.

Before I leave the desert land
   For meadows of immortal flowers,
Lead me where streams at Thy command
   Flow by the borders of the hours,
That when the thirsty come, I may
Show them the fountains in the way.
   O Love of God, do this for me:
   Maintain a constant victory.

EHW, RFB

Medals and Titles?

(A religious paper lately complained that "Christian workers" as such were neglected in the distribution of honors.)

Medals and lighted titles? Who but is ashamed
That such, for such as we, should ever be claimed
As our just due? Perish the paltry plea,
The sordid thought. Oh little, little have we
Done for our kind; that little, how faultily.
And yet what joy to do it! Has the day
When "The Offscouring of All Things" could be
An apostle's title wholly passed away?

Ah, but if one among us covets famed
Great Orders—recognitions—let him lay
Close to his heart two ancient words, and say
Them over and over till he be
Somewhat attuned to them: Gethsemane
The first; the second, Calvary.

MP

5 Poems of Wartime

This Great Obedience

(Lieut. Chorlton Nosworthy, reported "Missing" in May 1915.

Till August 1916 nothing further was known of him; but in that month his soldier servant, a prisoner of war, was traced to Oldenburg, and through him the first news of their only son reached his parents. He was wounded near Ypres on the morning of May 8, and was left by his own desire to meet his death alone. "He told us," writes the soldier simply, "to go on with our duty.")

Oh, triumph of the Spiritual! Struck down quick
On the rough edge of battle; boy in years
But man in fixed resolve; his disciplined powers
Firm, undiminished in him; and his life
Pulling at him with eager holding hands.
Thus suddenly he entered his great hour,
How great none but hath entered it may know
Or can conceive.

(Continued)

Oh, triumph then,
If in the tremendous hour, when desperate pain
Tramples the body down and weakening flesh
Aches for the touch of flesh, the Spiritual
Proves conqueror; and Duty's quiet voice,
Being recognized through the confused turmoil
By ear that death is deafening, is obeyed.

O English nurseries that trained such sons—
O schools and playing fields that sent them forth—
Where is your like? Decadent have we grown?
Steeped in the spirit of the earth, consumed
By lesser fires than the pure altar fire
Of love of duty? Well we know our sins;
But if we are wholly degenerate
Whence came this great obedience? Will such fruit
Spring from a tree-stump rotting at the root?
Form on the instant, ripen in a day?
Never: but its stern nurturing has been
Through valorous centuries of sun and rain
And beating wind that dealt with vital force,
The sap of life.

Now may the Lord our God
Grant to our Empire this one golden boon:
That the pure light—
The light that streams from the black fields of war—
Being the chiefest glory of the War,
May light our very cradles; that our race
May will to keep its high tradition whole,
Contemn the sensual, crown the Spiritual.

MP

Battle Burial

Where is his grave? Only the angels know,
    Who companied about him to the end.
What was his winding sheet? Ah, very low
    All heaven did stoop, and of its glory lend
A robe of light. Was ever funeral
Like battle burial, sweet, mystical?

But oh, to know how the last hour went by,
    The thoughts he thought, the words he would have said
Had any listened! Wist thou not that nigh
    To him was One who loved him? Comforted,
He communed with his Father; roar of gun
Was hushed that God might listen to His son.

Did he regret the vanishing life that beat,
    Hurrying within him, fierce with mortal pain?
Nay, never, never! Doth the corn of wheat
    Mourn that it fall into the ground in vain?
Oh, that thou couldst have seen his steadfast eyes
Lighted and filled with joy of sacrifice!

How did he die? Somewhere a bugle blew,
    And he was gone; I know not any more.
Only I was aware, as he passed through
    The quiet borderland of air, a door
Opened in Paradise. And musical
Sweet welcome led him in to festival.

MP

Missing

The telegram said "Missing" and she said,
"Would God that he were dead,
For this is worse." And for a terrible hour
The enemy had power.

And he painted grievous wounds,
Tortures unsuccoured,
Insults dastardly,
A lingering piteous death,
Or misery of crowded hospital
Or hateful prison.
All sights, all sounds, sharp-edged imaginings
That cut into the soul, had power with her,
Until she turned from all, and moaned, "My God!"

And God said to an angel, "Go to her,"
(He named the house and room),
"Show her the things that be."
The angel flew.
And shortly after she was made aware
Of movement all about her; and her gloom
Rolled up like fog at dawn; a glorious air,
As from far mountains blown,
Like wine revived her spirit. She could see
On to blue distances—eternity
Opened its spaces; and she tasted powers
Of the world to come, and knew
As she was known;
Knew herself not forsaken.
Then as she waited, a great brooding calm
Filled all her being; and as dew
Rises in stillness from a field of flowers,

So from her heart, quieted now as any summer field,
Soft thoughts rose gently, soothing as a psalm
Familiar, cadenced; and she looked and saw
Deep into mysteries; but by the law
(Which rules the place to which she had been taken)
Directed, she was careful not to say
What she had seen; except, being free to tell
The comfortable word that healed
Her sorest hurt, she chose
This as the sweetest: that before they
Wrote her belovèd "Missing," One
Well-skilled in finding lost things said to those
Who stood about Him, "Lo, another son
Has need of Me," and went . . .
But where,
He did not tell;
Only she knew He found him. "It is well,"
She said aloud, being unaware
That she was home, till fearful, violent
As waters that have sudden broken bound,
Strong doubts turmoiled her. "Drown,"
They cried, "Yes, drown,
Poor foolish hope! Who heeds thee?" and they tossed
Its folly aside,
And shouted, whispered, cried
About her hope, "Drowned! Drowned!
The vision is vain
For he is lost!"
But she again
Affirmed her faith, and on the telegram crossed
The "Missing" out, and wrote instead, "Nay, Found."

MP

Spray

(An allegory)

An upland valley, a bright mountain stream:
By either bank, calm flow of water, taking
Its usual course; but in the center where
Rocks bar the way,
A silver disarray—
All in impetuous vehemence forsaking
The gentler curves, and leaping towards the race
In straight simplicity,
A light upon its face.

For now the sun fills every several globe
Of that fine, hurrying spray, as if he, knowing
Its purpose and being tenderly aware
How brief its day,
Made beautiful its stay;
Made still more beautiful its going.
The drops spring in their myriads; see them shine
Each individually,
As touched by the Divine.

A moment's flash, a fall, a vanishing;
And marvelous veils, woven by their great lover
Of rainbow thread on gossamer mist, are flung
Across the abyss. My soul, be not thou rude;
Respect the river's reticence;
Refuse to intrude;
Quiet thyself, for thou art now among
Wonders and mysteries; be hushed and feel
If texture of the curtains can discover
Such glories, what the glories they conceal.

Yet may we not without discourtesy
Pursue those shining drops in happy dreaming,
See them refresh the forest tree, the fern,
The plain that gasps in heat, city and village—
Relieving toiling man's suspense,
Blessing his tillage,
Themselves a benediction till they turn
The last bright curve; then out into the sea
That lies like a long, luminous ribbon gleaming
Upon the far horizon's boundary?

O Parent-springs in lonely watershed,
The sky smiles down on you. The glad winds' voices
Talking to one another, say, "These gave
(Not lent in loan,
For hardly could their own
Return to them): oh, choice of all great choices."
Thus the glad winds, who with the angels saw
The deed from their high places:
"So to obey Love's law!"

They did not disappoint you, Parent-springs—
Those plunging drops that from your fountains parted.
Yours was the impulse that constrained to brave
Self-heedless deed;
Your sons but lived their creed.
And when you meet them, and the joy departed
Returns tenfold, will you not recognize
Them by their sunlit faces,
And their rejoicing eyes? . . .

MP

Is There No Balm in Gilead?

("So many of the uncomforted are turning to spiritualism"—from a letter written in the winter of 1916. Here, a despairing mother broods over the loss of her soldier son, and messengers from Above and Beneath vie for her attention.)

As on calm, sunlit days
By tropic shore,
We see, through fathoms of liquid fields of green,
Faint glimmerings that wander hither and thither,
And shuffling shapes that thread the roots of rocks;
So in our aerial greys
And blues, the mystery
Of that which is about us we
At times explore—
Catch glimpses of the radiances that, whither
We go, attend us. And a worse than kraken's dread
(Though maybe faintlier seen) comes,
Haunting our human ways.

• • • • •

She sat "alone" beside the fire,
Her boy's last letters in her lap;
And all in her was one desire—
To pierce the mist, to leap the gap.
And as she sat, the clear fire-light
Showed a tall angel on her right;
And on her left the flicker fell
On a dim shape I saw not well.

That mother in her secret pain
Upon a rack whole nights had lain,
While he who did the pulleys ply
Kept muttering "Why?" and ever "Why,
Why all this woe?" The question stole
The seeds of peace from her sad soul.

Now he of the dim shape
Drew nearer, urged escape
From bars of the material,
Painted mirage, and called it spiritual;
Wearied her with the same insistent "Why?"
Suggested, "Why not there
The answer?"—till her being lay bare
To subtle influences drawing otherwhere;
Whispered, "A touch, a push, and you may enter in,
The veils being spun so thin."

The angel meanwhile waited, shone
Upon her, though she saw him not;
For what she wistful gazed upon
Dazzled her vision: she forgot
The true in the illusion. He
Touched her tired eyes, that she might see
Another, far more glorious, Whom
She, seeing, recognized. The room
Lightened! I saw the dark shape pass—
As a breath breathed upon a glass.

The Lord said little: "What I do
Thou knowest not now." "Ah true, ah true!"
Her heart moaned back. "But thou shalt know
Hereafter." Then she looked and, lo,
The world had rounded to a hill
Awful with crosses. There all ill
Met, mingled, boiled up; and a cry
On a black wind went flying by:

"*Why? Why? O Why?*"
And none did make reply,
Or none she heard. Her own distress
Paled before this; became as nothingness.
Why? Why? O Calvary,
Was this thine agony, too? Gethsemane,
Didst know it, too? Yea, verily, verily.

(Continued)

From winepress of the wrath of God,
In garments stained by wine's red stain,
On wounded feet He came, unshod
To walk her rough path with her. Pain
Lost power to torture her; a new
Comfort consoled her. And the blue
Forget-me-nots began to blow
Along the road she had to go.

Today, upon the clan
We call mankind
Falls such a woe, that hadst Thou passionless
Spent easy days, O Christ, known only joy's dear kiss,
Walked on safe, sandled feet
In meadowlands—Ah, who that ever ran
Naked across the plain,
Scourged by the vehement, bitter rain
And fearful wind,
But turning to Thee desperate, would miss
Something in Thee, yea vital things?
Tears were Thy Meat,
A spear stab, Thy caress,
Thou suffering Son of Man.

MP

The Medical Way

(Having recently reenlisted, the army doctor went out at night to the trenches at the front, to attend the wounded. He was found with surgical dressings in his hand, shot through the head.)

In England

A brave young mother and her little ones—
Babes born and nurtured in the air austere
That blows upon the land
Where Sacrifice and Duty glorious reign
Eternal king and queen,
Inviolate, sincere;
Look and rejoice, ye angels.

In France

A doctor seeking other mothers' sons—
Their desperate need being call. Hushed be the dear
Home voices, because the Hand
Pierced once for him has beckoned. What is pain,
Of what account things seen,
That they should hinder here?
Look and rejoice, ye angels.

• • • • •

Forward he presses through the dangerous field,
He whom we met clad in such simple guise
That hardly had we known
Him hero. But the usual medical way
Is noble, though not esteemed
A thing for praise—or ignorant surprise.
Rejoice, rejoice, ye angels.

They found him in the morning. He who healed
So many hurts now very quiet lies,
No skill to heal his own
Being granted to him. Ah, but he would say
It was the death he dreamed—
The joyfulest road unto his Paradise.
Rejoice, rejoice, ye angels.

MP

To Agatha and Evelyn

Children of sacrifice, to Him who reigns
Sitting above the waterfloods, all pains
Apportioning—and joys and blessèd gains—
I, loving you, commit you.

Dear little nestlings, born while war's wild wind
Swept round your nest, will you not surely find
Your Father very pitiful and kind?
Yea, verily, you will.

Will He not comfort you when comfortless?
Will He not shelter you when shelterless?
Being a Father to you—fatherless—
Yea, verily, He will.

O children, in a night of weeping born,
Live to be comforters, to pluck the thorn
From wounded hearts—till comes the joyous morn—
As, verily, it will.

MP

6 Poems of Encouragement

In Acceptance Lieth Peace

He said, "I will forget the dying faces;
The empty places—
They shall be filled again.
O voices moaning deep within me, cease."
But vain the word; vain, vain:
Not in forgetting lieth peace.

He said, "I will crowd action upon action;
The strife of faction
Shall stir me and sustain.
O tears that drown the fire of manhood, cease."
But vain the word; vain, vain:
Not in endeavor lieth peace.

He said, "I will withdraw me and be quiet;
Why meddle in life's riot?
Shut be my door to pain.
Desire, thou dost befool me; thou shalt cease."
But vain the word; vain, vain:
Not in aloofness lieth peace.

He said, "I will submit; I am defeated.
God hath depleted
My life of its rich gain.
O futile murmurings, why will ye not cease?"
But vain the word; vain, vain:
Not in submission lieth peace.

He said, "I will accept the breaking sorrow
Which God tomorrow
Will to His son explain."
Then did the turmoil deep within him cease.
Not vain the word, not vain;
For in acceptance lieth peace.

ACD, GC, MP, TJ

Rose from Brier

Thou hast not *that*, My child, but thou hast *Me*;
And am not I alone enough for thee?
I know it all, know how thy heart was set
Upon this joy which is not given yet.

And well I know how through the wistful days
Thou walkest all the dear familiar ways
As unregarded as a breath of air;
But there in love and longing, always there.

I know it all; but from thy brier shall blow
A rose for others. If it were not so
I would have told thee. Come, then, say to Me:
My Lord, my Love, I am content with Thee.

RFB

Like Rain and Snow

Returneth the rain, returneth the snow?
Their secret ministry, who may know?
For never all they do is seen
Although the world is dressed in green
Because of the rain, because of the snow.

So vanisheth sound of preaching away;
Like rain and snow, it maketh no stay,
But it shall do as He shall please,
That souls of men may dwell at ease
When sorrow and sighing shall flee away.

Wg[2]

The Promised Harvest

(Psalm 126:5–6)

We will not fear; we will believe to see.
O Lord our God, our eyes are unto Thee.
Thy promise is our stronghold; not in vain
The sower soweth Thine eternal grain.

And Thou hast said that he shall doubtless come
And with rejoicing bring the harvest home.
Of what account are tears and toil and heat,
If we may garner golden sheaves of wheat?

Wg[1]

Not in Vain

(Habakkuk 3:17–18)

Not in vain, the tedious toil
On an unresponsive soil,
Travail, tears in secret shed
Over hopes that lay as dead.
All in vain, thy faint heart cries.
Not in vain, thy Lord replies:
Nothing is too good to be;
Then believe, believe to see.

Did thy labor turn to dust?
Suff'ring—did it eat like rust
Till the blade that once was keen
As a blunted tool is seen?
Dust and rust thy life's reward?
Slay the thought; believe thy Lord!
When thy soul is in distress,
Think upon His faithfulness.

(Continued)

Though there be not fig nor vine,
In thy stall there be no kine,
Flock be cut off from the fold,
Not a single lamb be told,
And thy olive berry fall
Yielding no sweet oil at all,
Pulse-seed wither in the pod—
Still do thou rejoice in God.

But consider, was it vain
All the travail on the plain?
For the bud is on the bough;
It is green where thou didst plow.
Listen, tramp of little feet,
Call of little lambs that bleat;
Hearken to it. *Verily,*
Nothing is too good to be.

MP, P, TJ

God's Asphodels

Once, heaven's door being opened, I looked in,
Saw all good men's good purposes alive,
Flowering like glorious flowers in the sun:

The thing conceived to better their own kind—
Which the wise world, desiring not, being blind,
Had carefully killed by calumny;
The young, glad hope that hardly had begun
To walk when it—being pierced by some sharp javelin,
Or strangled by a small, invisible thread—
Drooped its bright head
And seemed to perish.

What they did contrive
With pains but could not effect, I saw, and knew
God hath not given the spirit of fear that quells
All noble risings of the soul to do
Difficult, right things—immortality
Being in men's honest strivings.

Not as weeds
  Are such things regarded on the heavenly meads:
    The angels call them all God's asphodels.

MP

Calvary's Elucidation

Yet listen now,
Oh, listen with the wondering olive trees,
And the white moon that looked between the leaves,
And gentle earth that shuddered as she felt
Great drops of blood. All torturing questions cease
In him who girds his soul to listen there.
There, only there, can we take heart to hope
For all lost lambs—aye, even for ravening wolves.
Oh, there are things done in the world today
Would root up faith, but for Gethsemane.

For Calvary interprets human life:
  No path of pain but there we meet our Lord;
    And all the strain, the terror and the strife
      Die down like waves before His peaceful word.
And nowhere but beside the awful Cross,
  And where the olives grow along the hill,
    Can we accept the unexplained, the loss,
      The crushing agony, and hold us still.
And nowhere is that clearer vision given
  Which pierces a bewildering providence,
    And opens windows upon highest heaven,
      But where we see Suffering Omnipotence.

PVV, RFB

The End

Will not the End explain
The crossed endeavor, earnest purpose foiled,
The strange bewilderment of good work spoiled,
The clinging weariness, the inward strain;
Will not the End explain?

Meanwhile He comforteth
Them that are losing patience; 'tis His way.
But none can write the words they hear Him say,
For men to read; only they know He saith
Kind words, and comforteth.

Not that He doth explain
The mystery that baffleth; but a sense
Husheth the quiet heart, that far, far hence
Lieth a field set thick with golden grain,
Wetted in seedling days by many a rain;
The End—it will explain.

ACD, GC, MP, TJ

Comforted

(Matthew 14:24–27)

A great wind blowing, raging sea,
And rowers toiling wearily,
Far from the land where they would be.

And then One coming, drawing nigh;
They care not now for starless sky.
The Light of Life says, "It is I."

They care not now for toil of oar,
For lo, the ship is at the shore,
And their Belovèd they adore.

Lord of the Lake of Galilee,
Who long ago walked on the sea,
My heart is comforted in Thee.

GBM, TJ

The Age-Long Minute

Thou art the Lord who slept upon the pillow;
Thou art the Lord who soothed the furious sea;
What matter beating wind and tossing billow
If only we are in the boat with Thee?

Hold us in quiet through the age-long minute
While Thou art silent, and the wind is shrill.
Can the boat sink while Thou, dear Lord, art in it?
Can the heart faint that waiteth on Thy will?

EHW, GC, TJ, TMS

Reassurance

Lord, is all well? Oh, tell me; is all well?
No voice of man can reassure the soul
When over it the waves and billows roll;
His words are like the tinkling of a bell.
Do *Thou* speak. Is all well?

Across the turmoil of the wind and sea,
But as it seemed from somewhere near to me,
A voice I know: "Child, look at Calvary;
By the merits of My *Blood, all is well.*"

Whence came the voice? Lo, He is in the boat;
Lord, wert Thou resting in Thy love when I,
Faithless and fearful, broke into that cry?
O Lord, forgive; a shell would keep afloat
Didst Thou make it Thy boat.

(Continued)

And now I hear Thy mighty "Peace, be still";
  And wind and wave are calm, their fury, froth.
  Could wind or wave cause Thee to break Thy troth?
They are but servants to Thy sovereign will;
    Within me, all is still.

Oh, was there ever light on land or sea,
  Or ever sweetness of the morning air,
  Or ever clear blue gladness anywhere
Like this that flows from Love on Calvary—
    From Him who stilled the sea?

Father and Son and Spirit be adored;
Father, who gave to death our blessèd Lord;
Spirit, who speaks through the Eternal Word,
By the merits of the Blood, all is well.

P, RFB

Tides of Healing

Blown by wind and wet with spray,
  Buffeted by many a blow,
Master, whom our times obey,
  Never one Thou didst not know—
Lash of bitter, biting rain,
  Toil beneath the heavy load,
Baffling weakness, crippling pain,
  Heat of sun, and dust of road.

It is true; but happier times
  Thou hast tasted, Thou dost give.
Then the man who stumbled, climbs,
  Hears the mighty "Look and live,"
Looks upon the generous sea,
  Tides of healing through him pour.
As of old in Galilee,
  Thou dost meet us on the shore.

P

The Sun Will Come Back

The world is black;
The eastern sky's grey rack
Lies like a waste of sullen sea,
Void of all hope of joy to be.
O Sun, come back;
Come back.

Of voices none
(Save alone only one)
Answers the low wind's faltering lute,
For all earth's singing things are mute.
Come back, O Sun,
O Sun.

No faintest spark
Strikes from the east; but hark,
Like some small, cheery, woodland elf,
A stream is singing to itself
All in the dark,
The dark.

For, oh, not dumb,
As he that would succumb
To wistful doubt, the running stream
Makes a sweet music of its theme:
The Sun will come,
Will come.

My Lord, I see
What Thou wouldst have me be;
Through darkened hours, before the Sun
Comes back again, O let me run,
Singing to Thee,
To Thee.

MP

Clearing and Cover

Mountains swallowed up in darkness,
Say, are you lost?
See, the mist is torn asunder
By great winds crossed.
See, through ragged rifts appearing,
Forms familiar, quick uprearing
Crag and peak, triumphant clearing
Clouds, tempest-tossed.

Forest shivering in your rain cloak,
Are your birds drowned?
See the sudden burst of sunshine—
Hark, the glad sound;
All the wood with bird calls ringing,
Not a little bird but's flinging
Thought of rain afar and singing—
All joyful, found.

Then, my heart, be strong, be joyful;
Let be what be.
Mist and rain are not appointed
Perpetually.
He who built the mountains, cover
Found for wild bird; He thy Lover—
He it is, and not another—
Plans life for thee.

DS

The Mist Will Pass

Where are ye, O ye mountains? Not a peak
Has looked on me throughout this heavy day.
Where is your purple? I see nought but grey;
The place you once made glad is cold and bleak.

See, wind and sun perform their ministry.
Watch the tossed mist shape silver frames of cloud,
Until the crags, like friendly faces, crowd
To look through clear, large windowpanes at Thee.

Where are ye, O ye little birds that made
The forest sing before the rain began?
How gay ye were. How pitiless to ban
Your simple pleasure. Have you flown, afraid?

The sun streams out and shines through wetted leaves,
And strikes the fern like golden rain aslant.
Hark to the birds; the wood is jubilant,
As if the world held nowhere one that grieves.

Then, O my heart, be comforted; be strong.
The mist will pass; the mountains will remain;
The sun will shine; the birds will sing again.
In mist, in rain, look up and sing thy song.

MP, P

Grasses in Storm

Brown mountain grasses, fiercely tempest-tossed,
What do you say to me?

The great wind shaketh us
But never breaketh us,
Beateth and bendeth,
Flingeth low and raiseth;
And the sharp rain
In gusty spurt
Smiteth us sore, and lendeth
Sting to the wind, and dazeth
Us for a little hour.
But never a feathery flower
On our spiked head is ever so lightly hurt,
Nor awn nor glume nor green-veined palea lost.
All weathers feed our grain:
Say, canst thou read our allegory?

MP

Life From Fire

O fire-swept mountain slope,
I never saw thee so:
Thy grass is green as youngest hope,
Thy woods aglow.

Ruby and blood-red sard,
Art thou all precious stone,
Budding in jewels, jewel-starred
With flowers fresh blown?

Never this carnival
Of color to desire
But for that fierce, effectual,
Swift flame of fire.

O Fire and Heat whose breath
Scorches the shrinking soul,
Blind, blind I stood and saw as death
Life's aureole.

As death, I saw, being blind;
But now, come Fire or Frost,
In your great mystic touch I find
Life I thought lost.

DS

Fire and Dews

Velvety darkness of a tropic night
Shot through with venomous darts of red.
Sinister, fleet,
A mile-long fiery snake
Curves up the mountain, coils about his brow.
What panic there, what flight
On frightened wings and eager, furry feet
Before the hiss of the fire-serpent! Wake,
Awake, good forester!

But long ago he woke;
Above the crackle of the flames his shout
Clamored, and woke the coolies. And they fight
The fire with counterfire, as if to scorch
That glitt'ring skin; and vehemently they clout
The orange serpent on his evil head.

Alas for massacre
Of woodland beauty! See the poor, charred cone
Black on the morning blue. For not
A green thing lives from saddle to summit now.
But like a torch,
Half burnt, blown out, and left to smoke,
The mountain stands alone. . . .

(Continued)

Hot months have crawled past since that furious fray.
This year the sky has carelessly forgot
To send her rains. The mountains wear a cloak
Of faded stuff they do not care to own;
From its drab folds the little birds have flown. . . .

A misty, gusty day;
A knife-edged ridge
Between two mighty cloud-scapes, like a bridge
Flung across time; emerging from the mist
As the wind blows it back, a shining green,
Green summit, like an emerald set in snow—
To which the forester, pointing, "See that head?
A forest fire there some six months ago
Gave us a hard night's work; licked the top clean
As my bare fist."
"New grass then? with no rain?" "Where fires pass,"
The forester said,
"The dews of the night make grass."

MP

Listening

I sat in a greenwood.
  A foaming torrent drummed,
"The Lord is great!" "And He is good,"
  A tiny insect hummed.

A wild bird sang, "And kind,
  Oh, we have found Him so."
And then a soft and pleasant wind
  Sang, "Kind," as he did blow.

The young leaves whispered, "Yes."
  The mosses by the mere
Murmured, "We love His gentleness."
  A fern said, "He is dear."

A little flower looked up,
  A smilet on her face;
Sweet food lay in her open cup.
  A butterfly said grace.

• • • • •

The good sun clouded o'er—
  Birds, butterflies withdrew;
The wind shook leaves down on the floor;
  The sky hid all her blue.

Mist lay upon the hill;
  Sharp rain the river smote;
But on its glancing surface still
  I saw bright bubbles float.

They caught the fading light
  That was so fain to go;
The waterway was as the white
  Of moonbeams upon snow.

And as they shone and broke
  In simple gaiety,
I was aware of One who spoke
  By bubbles unto me.

MP, P

Words of Light

Fear thou not the cloudy evening.
  By dim waters fireflies glisten;
'Mid the dark leaves of the tree
  Starry hosts are moving; listen,
Listen, for they speak to thee:
  "My Lord will take care of me."

(Continued)

Fear thou not the moonless darkness.
    Moonless nights discover fireflies,
Star-seeds of eternity,
    Luminous when common day dies.
Words of light are sown for thee:
    "My Lord will take care of me."

PU

Fern and Waterfall

O fern behind the avalanche of foam,
Why hast thou chosen so disturbed a home?
Great voices thunder, waters fret thy ledge;
Thy tender lace has patterned all its edge.

The waters boil, and vehemently hurl
Defiance at thee; thy young fronds uncurl
Each in his order, and thy gentleness
Seems the more lovely, set in such great stress.

Then, then is wrought the wonder that restrains
And turns the threatened loss to joyful gains:
The furious menace as light mist of spray
Breathes blessings on thee as it floats away.

O Lord my God, do not great waters flow
Above, about me, where Thou bidst me grow?
And dost Thou say, "Come, child of Mine, and learn
Again and yet again from this My fern"?

Yea, it is true, Thy world's a picture-book,
Mountain and forest, falls and fern-dressed nook:
The waters flow, O God, at Thy command,
I hide me in the hollow of Thy hand.

MP, P

Heart's-Ease

Oh, there was never a blossom
 That bloomed so blithe as she,
On the bitter land, by the salt-wet sand,
 On the margin of the sea.
Where never a flower but the gorse can blow,
And the dry sea-pink that the mermen sow,
 There grows she.

Oh, there was never a blossom
 That bloomed so brave as she,
On the narrow ledge of the mountain's edge
 Where the wild fowl hardly be.
And over her head the Four Seasons go
With a rush of wings when the Storm Kings blow—
 There grows she.

Oh, there was never a blossom
 That bloomed content as she,
In the heart that burned, and loved and learned
 Of the Man of Galilee.
And plant her high, or plant her low,
In a bed of fire, or a field of snow,
 There grows she.

PVV, TJ

Bud of Joy

Come, bud of joy, the driving rain
 That all thy young, green leaves doth wet
Is but a minister of gain
 To that which in thy heart is set.
Come forth, my bud; awake and see
How good thy Gardener is to thee.

(Continued)

And pass, my bud, to perfect flower,
    Dread not the blast of bitter wind;
Thy Maker doth command its power;
    It knoweth not to be unkind.
Haste thee, my flower; unfold and see
How good thy Gardener is to thee.

O fruit that cometh after rain,
    O fruit that ripeneth in the sun,
Now praised be God that not in vain
    For Thee the changeful seasons run.
O fruit of mine, make all men see
How good thy Gardener is to thee.

Great Gardener, whose grey rain beat,
    And sudden blasts of grievous wind,
Whose sun devoured me with his heat,
    I know Thee wise, I know Thee kind.
Let all who look be caused to see
How good my Gardener is to me.

And when the sap in me doth fail
    And natural vigor of my youth,
Then may Thy life in me prevail,
    That I may still show forth in truth
By flower and fruit on this my tree,
How good my Gardener is to me.

MP, P, TJ

Irresistible Power

Glory to Thee, O God of mighty forces;
Glory to Thee for mystic voices' thunder;
Glory to Thee for these Thy watercourses—
Whispers of wonder.

How calm thy flow, thou stream of golden glances
Frail water-plumes, why fret ye at his flowing?
Will thine array of frothy spears and lances
Bar his great going?

It may not be. Oh, see the white mist creeping;
The hurrying wheels of cloud-land—hear them, hear them!
The rains, the falls—Oh, tumult of their leaping—
Vain ripples, fear them!

O splendors, powers, deep in the silence hidden—
Today these bars; tomorrow and thereafter
Triumph of flood and glorious, unforbidden,
Snow-foam of laughter.

DS

A Cry for Rain

O poor, dry earth,
Where is thine ancient glorious mirth?
I listen; everywhere
Thou art one cry for rain;
Thy heart being vexed in thee, thou dost complain.
Are the heavens brass unto thy prayer?

The heavens are brass?
Whence then this splendid mountain grass?
What secret fountains fed
The scattered, hidden roots
That they should put forth such bright shoots
From that which had appeared as dead?

Akin am I
To thee, O Earth: my wells run dry;
And in me everywhere
Is one long cry for rain.
My heart is vexed in me, and I complain.
Are the heavens brass unto my prayer?

(Continued)

Thus, I in haste:
Oh, dull and slow of heart to waste
My Secret Waters! Lest
It should be even so,
God took me out to where His grasses grow
And bade me turn again unto my rest.

DS

Withered Lawn

(John 4:14)

"'Shall never thirst'—My God, what does it mean?
My wells of joy are dried up, and the dawn
Of this strange day discovers all my lawn,
That yesterday lay green,
A stretch of withered grass; and the white may
That bordered it is gone. My desolate day
Lengthens to weeks; will the long weeks be years?
Henceforth must only tears
Suffice me? 'Never thirst'! Are the words mockery,
Framed to ensnare?
Nay, God be true though my own heart be liar!
When was He ever a wilderness to me?
As waters that fail?
Thou pricking, stinging brier,
False stabbing thought—go trail
Thy venomous thorns elsewhere!
O God, my Father, help me."

Thus he spoke—
The man whose heart God broke,
But broke in pitifulness. Though by a stroke
He took the dear desire of his eyes,
It was but to surprise
Him with greater Love. For far more full
Of incommunicable delights,

The fountain on the heights,
Than wayside pool,
However sweet with fringing flower and fern;
And those who learn
The secret path that to the fountain goes,
Whence comfort flows,
Would tread it ever. But just then, of this
Only the border of the coming bliss
Was shown to him—as in the desolate dawn
Father and son
In a new union, one,
Walked hand in hand across the withered lawn.

MP

Rise and Fly

House of the greenwood,
Patterned the carpet
Thy weaver weaves;
Grey are thy walls,
Fitly carved thy staircase,
Purple thine eaves;
High is thy house roof,
Fashioned for beauty,
Very far spread;
Mighty thy lamps
And thy candles forever
Bright overhead.

Various thy music:
Over thy harpstrings
Great fingers sweep;
Light lilt of lullaby
Floats where the wind rocks
Treetops to sleep;
Hark to the lovable

(Continued)

White waters singing
Carols and glees;
Hark to the bird whistle,
Whispers of grasses,
Hum of the bees.

House of the greenwood,
Cleansing and healing
Thine influence;
Pure are thine airs,
Every room in thee holy
With Innocence.
And all throughout thee
Thy manifold voices
Speak the word plain:
"Grovel not, rise ye;
Be bird-like, be dove-like;
Rise, fly again.
Down among pots
Though ye lay, yet aspire ye.
Was it not told,
God has prepared for you
Wings as of silver,
Feathers of gold?"

MP, P

The Cool, Green Mere

I see a little cool, green mere
  Like to a ruffled looking-glass;
Where lovely green lights interfere
  Each with the other, and then pass
In rippled patterns to the grey
  Of rocks that bar their further way.

I hear a mingled music now:
  A streamlet that has much to tell,
And two sweet birds that on a bough
  Nearby love one another well.
And like a flake of summer sky,
  A pale blue butterfly floats by.

A sudden sun-flash, and below,
  Upon a rock of amber brown,
Bright golden sparkles come and go,
  As if in their dim water-town,
Set on that lighted pedestal,
  The water things held carnival.

• • • • •

The mountain wind blows in my face;
  I see the water, smell the rain;
Yet I am here in mine own place
  With duties thronging me again—
But the more welcome, the more dear,
  Because of you, my cool, green mere.

MP, P, TJ

Winter

When my leaves fall, wilt Thou encompass them?
  The gold of autumn flown, the bare branch brown,
The brittle twig and stem,
  The tired leaves dropping down—
Wilt Thou encompass that which men call dead?
  I see the rain, the coldly smoth'ring snow;
My leaves, dispirited,
  Lie very low.

(Continued)

So the heart questioneth, white winter near;
  Till, jocund as the glorious voice of spring,
Cometh His "Do not fear,
  But sing; rejoice and sing,
For sheltered by the coverlet of snow
  Are secrets of delight, and there shall be
Uprising that shall show
  All that through winter I prepared for thee."

RFB, TJ

Fear Not—Sing!

Have I a fear that Thou dost know?
Fear of weakness, fear of failing
(Though Thy power is all-prevailing)
Or a haunting fear of bringing
Care to others?

"Share it not with a weakling;
Whisper it to thy saddle-bow,
And ride forth singing."*

Many fears can murmur low:
Fears of ills the future holdeth
(Though, indeed, Thy grace upholdeth)
Dulling fear and fear sharp stinging,
Fear that tortures.

"Share it not with a weakling;
Whisper it to thy saddle-bow,
And ride forth singing."

*King Alfred the Great

EHW

FRET NOT THYSELF

Far in the future
Lieth a fear,
Like a long, low mist of grey,
Gathering to fall in dreary rain;
Thus doth thy heart within thee complain.
And even now thou art afraid, for round thy dwelling
The flying winds are ever telling
Of the fear that lieth grey
Like a gloom of brooding mist upon the way.

But the Lord is always kind;
Be not blind, be not blind
To the shining of His face,
To the comforts of His grace.
Hath He ever failed thee yet?
Never, never. Wherefore fret?
O fret not thyself, nor let
Thy heart be troubled,
Neither let it be afraid.

Near, by thy footfall,
Springeth a joy,
Like a new-blown little flower
Growing for thee, to make thee glad.
Let thy countenance be no more sad,
But wake the voice of joy and health within thy dwelling,
And let thy tongue be ever telling,
Not of fear that lieth grey,
But of little laughing flowers beside the way.

For the Lord is always kind,
Be not blind, be not blind
To the shining of His face,
To the comforts of His grace.

(Continued)

He hath never failed thee yet.
Never will His love forget.
O fret not thyself, nor let
Thy heart be troubled,
Neither let it be afraid.

K, MP, P, TJ

God's Thread

"An ill dread is hanging over me,
Slung on a single strand of cobweb thread.
I do not know how I can live today
The usual life of common duties, turn
A calm front to the day's perplexities,
A smile upon its small, persistent cares—
While inwardly a raging fear devours
Courage in mouthfuls; and my chariot wheels
Drag heavily; and gladness flies from me,
Leaving me standing shivering on the edge
Of unknown desolation; and all things
Look dark to me. O God, Thou knowest my fear;
Go Thou not far from me lest trouble be near."

"An ill thou dreadest hanging over thee,
Slung on a single silken strand of cobweb thread—
Think: Is it cobweb thread? No spider of chance
Spun that fine-twined thread from out herself
In blind obedience to some unknown law.
But I, thy God, thy Father, spun that thread
Whose very substance is My eternal will,
My eternal Love. And in My hand I hold
The further end and guard its whole long length
From human intermeddling. I may use
Some visible hand to operate and loose
The seeming ill; but I alone am He
With whom thou hast to do. And I, thy God,

The Father of Lights in whom no variableness
Nor shadow cast by turning ever was,
Am with thee, to be light to all thy days,
Even to the end. Therefore, thou wilt be strong
And more than conqueror; for I am here:
I go not from My own when trouble is near."

MP

A Quiet Mind

What room is there for troubled fear?
I know my Lord, and He is near;
And He will light my candle, so
That I may see the way to go.
O Love, O Light, I sing to Thee,
And in my heart make melody.

There need be no bewilderment
To one who goes where he is sent;
The trackless plain by night and day
Is set with signs lest he should stray.
O Love, O Light, I sing to Thee,
And in my heart make melody.

My path may cross a waste of sea,
But that need never frighten me;
Or rivers full to very brim,
But they are open ways to Him.
O Love, O Light, I sing to Thee,
And in my heart make melody.

My path may lead through woods at night,
Where neither moon nor any light
Of guiding star or beacon shines;
He will not let me miss my signs.
O Love, O Light, I sing to Thee,
And in my heart make melody.

(Continued)

Lord, grant to me a quiet mind,
That trusting Thee—for Thou art kind—
I may go on without a fear,
For Thou, my Lord, art always near.
O Love, O Light, I sing to Thee,
And in my heart make melody.

MP, P, TJ

THE CLOUD

I thought the way upon the mountainside
Would lead to certain clearness; but my Guide,
Whose thought was otherwise,
Led to a cloud which blotted out the skies.

I feared to enter into that great cloud,
And fearing, cried aloud,
"O patient Guide, I fear;
Be not far from me now, with trouble near."

"Let not thy heart be troubled. Could I cease
To care for thee?
Can vapors cancel peace, My gift of peace?
O rest in Me.
I wait to meet thee in that cloudy place,
And in that cloud thou shalt behold My face."

FTR

THINK IT NOT STRANGE

Think it not strange, if he who steadfast leaveth
All that he loveth for the love of Me
Be as the prey of him who rendeth, reaveth,
Breaketh and bruiseth, woundeth sore and grieveth,
And carefully a spray of sharp thorn weaveth
To crown the man who chooseth Calvary.

Count it all joy, the blaming and the scorning,
  Ye who confess love's pure, transcendent power;
Stay not for speech, heed not the wise world's warning;
  Thine is an incommunicable dower.
What will it be when sudden, in the morning,
  From brown thorn buddeth purple Passion flower?

TJ

Thou Canst Not Fear Now

My soul, thou hast trodden down strength,
And fearest thou now?
The noise of the whips and the rattle
Of wheels in the hurry to battle,
The thunder of Captains, the shouting,
Bewilderment, weariness, flouting—
Are these new things to thee?
The Lord thy God is a Man of War;
Verily thou hast followed afar
If thy garments have never been rolled in blood
In the place swept through by the red, red flood,
Where battles be.

My soul, art thou dreaming?
Thou hast felt the keen edge of the sword,
The thrust of the spear;
Thou hast fallen and risen,
Hast fainted, revivèd, and striven,
Forgetting to fear.
Thou hast trodden down strength in the battles of old,
And fearest thou now?

(Continued)

My soul, thou hast proved thy God,
And fearest thou now?
Behold Him, thy Light and thy Cover,
Thy Champion, Companion, Lover,
Thy Stay when the foeman oppresses,
Thy Song 'mid a thousand distresses.
Is this all new to thee?
The Lord thy God—hath He stood aloof?
(Verily thou hast put Him to proof)
Hast thou ever, resisting alone unto blood,
Betrayed, overwhelmed by the red, red flood,
Sunk shamefully?

My soul, learn to triumph;
Thou hast felt the keen edge of the sword,
The thrust of the spear;
Thou hast fallen and risen,
Hast fainted, revivèd and striven,
Forgetting to fear.
Thou hast trodden down strength in the battles of old;
Thou canst not fear now.

MP, TJ

Death Is Conquered

Death hath no more dominion over Him.
O Prince of Life, when all our stars burn dim,
And hope is like a slowly with'ring flower,
Command this truth to shine upon that hour.

Close round us throng vast armies of the night;
Closer art Thou, O radiant Lord of Light.
Precious the gains won on the shameful Tree:
Death hath no more dominion over Thee.

Therefore, to Thee be glory, glory given;
Glory to Thee, Lord Christ of Highest Heaven;
Glory to Thee, Thou royal conqueror;
Glory to Thee, O Lord, forevermore.

TMS

Be Triumphant

(Luke 10:19; Jeremiah 46:17)

Be triumphant, be triumphant;
  Stake thine all upon thy Lord.
Stake thine all upon His Word;
  It is shield for thee and sword.

For the Lord thy God hath giv'n thee
  Power over all the power
Of the enemy, His foeman—
  Claim thy heritage of power.

Be triumphant, be triumphant;
  Let the spiritual watchers see
That thy God doth strengthen thee,
  That in Him is victory.

For Pharaoh, king of Egypt,
  Saith the Lord, is but a noise;
He hath passed the time appointed;
  He is nought, is but a noise.

RFB, Wg[1]

The Lord's Army

On earth, confusion, land by land;
And heart by heart is riven.
But, as of old, unshaken stand
The battlements of heaven.

On wings of wind, from all their coasts,
Angelic armies speed;
The Lamb of God, the Lord of Hosts,
That shining band doth lead.

O cause our stumbling prayer to soar;
Let joy be our array;
For art not Thou whom we adore
Already on Thy way?

TMS

The Impossible

For all that seems impossible,
For all things hard,
I thank Thee who art my exceeding Joy
And great Reward.

For what I have not strength to do,
Where I must fail,
All glory to the Victor in the fight,
Who will prevail.

Unp

My Quietness

O Thou who art my quietness, my deep repose,
My rest from strife of tongues, my holy hill,
Fair is Thy pavilion, where I hold me still.

Back let them fall from me, my clamorous foes,
Confusions multiplied;
From crowding things of sense I flee
And in Thee hide.
Until this tyranny be overpast,
Thy hand will hold me fast.

What though the tumult of the storm increase,
Grant to Thy servant strength, O Lord,
And bless with peace.

MP, P, RFB, TJ

How Can We Fear?

How can we fear?
  For love delighteth ever
To meet our need—
  And great it is indeed.
For we go forth
  To meet a foe who never
Before mere man doth cower.
  But God, our Tower,
Is our defense; He is our Power.

Our fingers He
  Doth teach the art of fighting;
His bugle call
  Hath summoned soldiers all
To rise and go,
  In faith and love uniting.
This war is His affair;
  Unseen as air,
Upon the field, He will be there.

ACD, EHW

God's Laugh

(Psalm 2:4–6)

Thou art here—Emmanuel;
Therefore shall the evil fall.
Rage the powers of death and hell?
Laugh the hosts satanical?
But the Lord shall laugh at them;
Short their day and fleeting fast.
And the Child of Bethlehem
Shall be King at last, at last.

Wg[2]

Close Up the Ranks

Let us close up the ranks;
The tireless enemy would fain break through.
Cause us to stand our ground; this one thing do.
Thou hast enrolled us, armed us for the fight;
From our weakness to Thy valor, look we, Lord of Might.

Let us close up the ranks.
Long is the line and very few are we,
But One is with us whom we cannot see;
Lo, Thou art with us always. Blessed Lord,
Thou hast said it; we believe Thee; changeless is Thy word.

Let us close up the ranks.
There is an end appointed soon or late;
Back shall the foe be turnèd at the gate.
The Risen Christ shall death and hell confound.
Christ enabling, Christ inspiring, we shall stand our ground.

Wg[2]

The Enemy Retreat

Refuge from storm, a Shadow from the heat
  Of glowing sand;
Fierce though their blast, the Terrible Ones retreat
  At Thy command.
We hear them rage, like wind against a wall;
At Thy "Be still," we see them sink and fall.

K

Our Strong Captain

(1 Kings 20:27)

Like two little flocks of kids,
We are scattered on the hill;
Of what avail our puny might?
Of what avail our skill?

But with us is the Lord of Hosts;
He is the Lamb that was slain;
What matter though the Syrians fill
The valley and the plain!

Unp

Undefeated Captain

Christ Jesus, Unseen Leader,
  Thy sword is in Thy hand;
As Captain of the hosts of God,
  Thou takest Thy command.
No ambush can surprise Thee;
  We hear the trumpets blow
Or ever wall has fallen
  Of mighty Jericho.

(Continued)

We hear and we will follow,
And compass round about,
Until the seven great trumpets sound
And Thou dost bid us shout.
As seeing the invisible,
We follow, for we know,
O undefeated Captain,
We'll hear the trumpets blow.

Wg[2]

Beatitude

(Romans 8:28)

The foe meant thine ill,
The Father, thy blessing;
Always 'tis so.
O heart, be thou still,
However distressing
Sharp winds that blow.

The Seen and the Unseen,
The stars in their courses,
All own His sway;
His powers intervene,
His heavenly forces
Compass our day.

If truly all things
Are working together
Only for good,
The trusting heart sings,
Whatever the weather.
Beatitude.

FTR

A Burdened Awakening

My thoughts had said:
Lord, I am weary of the way;
I am afraid to face another day—
Frustrated, limited,
Guarded, confined wherever I would go
By close-set "cannots," that like hedges grow
About me now. And then our dear Lord said,
"I am about thy bed."

TMS

Grey Evening Sky

(Ephesians 5:19)

Thy day is almost done;
How few the victories won;
How slow thy crawl, thou who didst hope to fly!
Thou who has often told
Of shining, heavenly gold,
How grey thine evening sky!
Why art thou thus, merely a cumberer?
Was ever broken vessel emptier?

Be still, mine enemy;
I hear another word:
"Make melody
With music of the heart
Unto thy Lord."

FTR

I Will Refresh You
(Matthew 11:28)

Heart that is weary because of the way,
Facing the wind and the sting of the spray,
Come unto Me, and I will refresh you.

Heart that has tasted of travail and toil,
Burdened for souls whom the foe would despoil,
Come unto Me, and I will refresh you.

Heart that is frozen—a handful of snow,
Heart that is faded—a sky without glow,
Come unto Me, and I will refresh you.

Heart that is weary, O come unto Me.
Fear not, whatever the trouble may be;
Come unto Me, and I will refresh you.

K

Nearness

Thou hast renewed us in Thy love today,
And countless are the touches that declare
Thy hand upon our way;
    Thou hearest prayer.

How often Thou hast drawn us close to Thee,
And spoken to our tired but listening ear;
And though we could not see,
    We knew Thee near.

So near that "near" is but a phantom word
For that which is indeed our heart's delight,
Thy blessed presence, Lord,
    By day and night.

Wg[1]

Too Great for Thee
(1 Kings 19:5–8)

An angel touched me, and he said to me,
"The journey, pilgrim, is too great for thee;
But rise and eat and drink;
Thy food is here,
Thy Bread of Life,
Thy cruse of Water clear,
Drawn from the brook that doth as yesterday
Flow by the way.

"And thou shalt go in strength of that pure food
Made thine by virtue of the sacred Rood,
Unto the Mount of God
Where thy Lord's face
Shall shine on thee,
On thee in thy low place,
Down at His feet who was thy Strength and Stay
Through all the way."

O Cake of Bread, baken on coals of fire—
Sharp fires of pain;
O Water turned to Wine—
The word is true; this food is daily mine.
Then never, never can the journey be
Too great for me.

RFB, TJ

We Shall Know

He will renew us in His love always.
Ours is a weary, clogging flesh,
But we shall know
Patience of comfort, peace and fortitude,
Shall drink where fresh waters flow,
Taste angels' food;
For, loving, Thou dost love until the end.

O great and dear Redeemer, we have proved
What Love Divine can spend
On its beloved.

RFB

Sweetened Waters

(Exodus 15:23–25; John 14:1)

O Marah pool, set in the desert sands,
How can we drink; how can we drink of thee?
But Moses cried, and he was shown a tree.
Did ever heart in vain Thy grace entreat?
Touch of the tree made bitter waters sweet.

So, blessèd Lord, in all our Marah days,
Show us the Tree; one thought of Calvary's Cross
Makes bitter sweet, discovers gain in loss.
"Let not your heart be troubled," Thou didst say
Long, long ago. It is Thy word today.

EHW

Provision
(Psalm 78:19)

Can God spread a table
In the wilderness?
Is our Father able?
Praise Him, *Yes!*

Glory, Alleluia,
Gratefully we sing
To our Unseen Leader,
Lord and King.

For His word is stable,
He who yesterday
Spread a bounteous table,
Does today.

BT, NS

Confirm Thy Word
(Psalm 119:49)

Confirm, O Lord, that word of Thine,
That heavenly word of certainty;
Thou gavest it; I made it mine,
Believed to see.

And yet I see not; he for whom
That good word came, in Thy great love,
Is wandering still, and there is room
For fear to move.

O God of Hope, what though afar
From all desire that wanderer seems—
Thy promise fails not; never are
Thy comforts dreams.

TG

A Lost Care

(What the ticking of the clock said)

Commit your care; commit your care
For I am here, and I am there.
Commit, commit, and do not fear
For they are dear and you are dear.

Where is your care? Where is your care?
You cannot find it anywhere;
You cannot find it anywhere.
I heard your prayer; I heard your prayer.

EHW

Leave It to Me

Leave it to Me, child; leave it to Me.
Dearer thy garden to Me than to thee.
Lift up thy heart, child; lift up thine eyes;
Nought can defeat Me, nought can surprise.

Leave it to Me, child, leave it to Me;
Trust in the Wall of Fire. Look up and see
Stars in their courses shine through the night;
Both are alike to Me—darkness and light.

Leave it to Me, child, leave it to Me.
Let slip the burden too heavy for thee;
That which I will, My Hand shall perform—
Fair are the lilies that weather the storm.

ACD, WHP

HARVEST

O God, wert Thou plowing
    Thy profitless earth
With the brave plow of love
And the sharp plow of pain?
    But hark to the mirth
Of wheat field in harvest!
    Dear Plower, well worth
That plowing, this yellow-gold grain.

PU, PVV

DISAPPOINTED?

Art thou disappointed? Come to Me;
I will never be a grief to thee.

Hurt by hand thou trusted? Come to Me;
Leaves of healing I will lay on thee.

Art thou broken? Come, My child, to Me;
I, thy Comforter, will comfort thee.

Even friends can sometimes changeful be;
I will always be the same to thee.

K

Joy Comes, Singing
(Psalm 30:5)

Lord, I would take Thy comfortings
With both hands gratefully,
And grief's dark overshadowings,
As lightly as may be—
For they belong to evenings;
Joy comes with day to me,
Comes running with the day to me.

Although my wayside inn at night
May harbor grief as guest,
With dawn he swiftly takes his flight—
And like a bird to nest,
Dear joy comes singing with delight,
As she comes home to rest;
Dear joy comes singing home to rest.

TG

Joy in the Morning

As surely as the shadows of night
Give way to the splendor of morning,
So, sorrow may lodge for a night,
But joy shall come in the morning.

O Giver of songs in the night,
O Lord of the stars of the morning,
We praise Thee, for Thou art our Light,
And Thy kindness is new every morning.

Unp

I Promise Thee

I promise thee
That I, to whom the pillars of the earth belong,
Will bear thee up and keep thy spirit strong.

I promise thee
That none shall add a furlong to the mile
That thou must walk through this long, little while.

I promise thee:
Thy private shadow shall not shadow ever
The path of thy belovèd fellow lover.

I promise thee
That though it tarry, yet the day will come
When I shall call thee Home.

TMS

Jesus Walks With Thee

(John 21:18; Luke 24:15)

Are these the days when thou dost gird thyself
And walkest where thou wouldest—battle days,
Crowded and burdened and yet lit with praise,
Days of adventure; eager, glorious choice
Folded in every hour? Rejoice, rejoice,
O happy warrior, if so it be,
For surely thou shalt see
Jesus Himself draw near and walk with thee.

Or doth another gird thee, carry thee
Whither thou wouldest not; and doth a cord
Bind hand and foot and flying thought and word?
An enemy hath done it; even so,
(Though why that power was his thou dost not know)
O happy captive, fettered and yet free,
Believe, believe to see
Jesus Himself draw near and walk with thee.

(Continued)

So either way is blessèd; either way
Leadeth unto the Land of Heart's Desire;
Thy great Companion's love can never tire;
He is thy Confidence, He is thy Song;
Let not thy heart be troubled, but be strong,
    O happy soul, to whom is given to see
    On all the roads that be,
Jesus Himself draw near and walk with thee.

RFB, TJ

A Presence in Prison

(Matthew 25:36)

"I was in prison."
O Breath of heavenly air
Blown by the winds of heaven,
Let come what may,
Our hearts will not despair.
Thou wilt not stay away
From any prison
When friend of Thine is there.

"I was in prison."
So art Thou with them there.
The door that opened to them, unaware
Of Thy great Presence, opened unto Thee,
Whom no man can gainsay.
The warders never knew,
Nor had they eyes to see,
Whose feet passed through
The door that day.

FTR

THE SHEPHERD'S FLUTE

Once, being of a flute in need,
  The Heavenly Shepherd sought
Until He found a bruisèd reed;
  It was as if He thought
It precious; for aloud said He,
  "This broken reed will do for me."
It heard the kind word wonderingly,
  Being a thing of naught.

And then that Lover of sweet sound,
  No single note to lose,
Himself repaired the reed He found,
  Well skilled such things to use.
This done, a happy melody
  He whistled through it; "Now," said He,
"This flute of mine shall stay by me."
  Thus He His flute did choose.

He said, "I play My country airs
  The which do some displease;
But others, listening, find their cares
  To pass and sweet heartease
Begin to blossom; and," said He
  Unto His flute, "Thou, dear, with Me,
Wilt, making gentle minstrelsy,
  Be comforter to these."

"Be comforter!" O bruisèd reed,
  Dost seem a thing apart
From usual life of flowery mead?
  What if, by His great art,
Perceiving what thou know'st not, He
  Saith even now, "Yea, thou shalt be,
O broken reed, a flute for Me"?
  O broken life, take heart!

MP, RFB

The Embrace of Peace

The rocks of pain stand up and shout,
  "No peace, no peace for thee!"
O rocks, what can you do to flout
  The flowing of the sea?
The great sea waves flow over you,
  And peace embraceth me.

TMS

Unfathomable Comfort
(Revelation 2:9–10)

"I know": The words contain
Unfathomable comfort for our pain.
How they can hold such depths I do not know—
I only know that it is so.

"Fear not": The words have power
To give the thing they name; for in an hour
Of utter weariness, the soul, aware of One beside her bed,
Is comforted.

O Lord most dear,
I thank Thee, and I worship—
Thou art here.

ACD

Light in the Cell
(Acts 12:7)

"And a light shined in the cell,"
And there was not any wall,
And there was no dark at all,
Only Thou, Immanuel.

Light of Love shined in the cell,
Turned to gold the iron bars,
Opened windows to the stars;
Peace stood there as sentinel.

Dearest Lord, how can it be
That Thou art so kind to me?
Love is shining in my cell,
Jesus, my Immanuel.

ACD, GC, RFB, TJ

God's Caress

What is this hush, that like a heavenly air
  Of clearest blue
Enfoldeth me, a Presence everywhere—
  Or like the dew
White on the grass, cooleth, refresheth me
Until the dawn is all alight with Thee?

"Child, it is I; for I, thy Lord, am here—
  Beneath, above,
Around, within thee, nearer far than near—
  An air of Love,
A dew of peace to cool thy weariness.
Child, it is I. This hush is My caress."

TMS

Lest We Forget

Home of our hearts, lest we forget
  What our redemption meant to Thee,
Let our most reverent thought be set
  Upon Thy Calvary.

We, when we suffer, turn and toss
  And seek for ease, and seek again;
But Thou upon Thy bitter cross
  Wast firmly fixed in pain.

And in our night star-clusters shine;
  Flowers comfort us, and joy of song.
No star, no flower, no song was Thine,
  But darkness three hours long.

We, in our lesser mystery
  Of lingering ill and wingèd death,
Would fain see clear; but could we see,
  What need would be for faith?

O Lord beloved, Thy Calvary
  Stills all our questions. Come, oh come,
Where children wandering wearily
  Have not yet found their home.

EHW, GC, P, RFB, TJ

Life's Autumn

Great Giver of my lovely green in Spring,
A dancing, singing green upon my tree,
My green has passed; I have no song to sing;
What will my Autumn be?

Must it be, though alive, as all but dead,
A heavy-footed and a silent thing?
Effectless, sapless, tedious, limited,
A withered vanishing?

• • • • •

Thus I; but He to me: "Have I not shown
In Autumn woodland and on mountain fell
The splendor of My purpose for Mine own?
Fear not, for all is well.

"And thou shalt see, My child, what I will do,
For as thy lingering Autumn days unfold,
The lovely, singing green of hitherto
Will come to thee in gold."

TJ

Growing Old

What is it to grow old?
To trudge across a plain with stunted palm trees set
And flattened, bent acacia; overhead
Blazes a sky, like to the plain, all bare,
No sudden lights and shadows, one hot glare
Of day that long since shed
Her morning mysteries and would fain forget,
Except to regret,
The passing of her glories manifold?

(Continued)

What is it to grow old?
To climb a hill by shadowy forest path;
To hear the sound of murmuring waters call
To one another, waterfall
Shout in great voice of triumph. Each new turn
Of winding track high up the mountain pass
Opens on widening view, discovers fern
Unknown before, or slope of cool green grass—
Windswept, and jeweled with flowers, an aftermath
From recent rains,
An angel's garden. These, our precious gains,
Are ours to share; for never lonesomely
We climb, being well refreshed by dear companionship.
And if a younger climber slip
Behind a little, fearing the prophesied
Drear waste in front, how good to call quick back,
"Nay, I have tried
And proved the fallacy
Of that delusion. Come, let us explore
To the far reaches of this mountain track.
Come, let us prove the word—that never less, but more,
Joy's blessèd light will shine for thee,
For me."

But of the end? Who knows?
No one is sent to tell of it, God being aware
That it exceeds our power to imagine, were we told.
Only we know: towards evening, all the gold
That the sky treasures pours into the air,
Brightening the last, short mile
As we in single file
Toil, maybe a little tired—till suddenly
Years fall from us; we feel their weight no more.
Pains fall from us; the sorrow that we wore
Like to the very vest of life, that ever next

Unto our hearts we wore—the heart that vexed
Itself in vain so often—all is gone!
To reconcile
All variance within us, music flows
About, around us, as we, clothed upon
By youth of immortality, go on,
By strong new energies thrilled,
By limitless enthusiasms filled,
All we thought past returns—
Feel it rush through thee,
This quickening bliss, by thousand signs foretold,
This quickening joy that burns
Like to a lamp new lit,
A star new set aflame, is it—
This, what God meant should be
When men say "growing old";
Still more, when they have said
Of thee or me,
"He's dead."

MP

No Strength to Pray

(Psalm 141:2)

When vision fadeth, and the sense of things,
  And powers dissolve like colors in the air;
And no more can I bring Thee offerings
  Nor any ordered prayer . . .

Then, like a wind blowing from Paradise,
  Falleth a healing word upon my ear:
"Let the lifting up of my hands be as the evening sacrifice";
  The Lord doth hear.

EHW, TJ, TMS

It Will Be Clear

Thy touch hath still its ancient power,
  Thy loving touch that healeth all;
And yet we wait from hour to hour,
  Nor see Thee come by evenfall.

We bow before Thy Calvary;
  The twilit hour shall find us dumb,
And unoffended, Lord, in Thee:
  It will be clear when Thou dost come.

RFB

In Sleep

He gives to His beloved in sleep,
For when the spirit drifts from fields of time
And wanders free in worlds remote, sublime,
  It meets Him there—
  The only Alone Fair.
  But were it bidden to tell
  The heavenly words that fell,
Dropping like sunlit rain through quiet air,
It could not, though it heard them everywhere.

Were some small fish, in rock-pool close confined,
Swept in the backwash of a wave of sea,
Could it describe that blue immensity?
  Could the caged bird,
  Whose happy ear had heard
  The lark sing in high heaven,
  And had escaped, be bidden
To bind that rapture fast in earthly words?
Not so is bound the song of singing birds.

Nor can I tell what He gave me in sleep.
The mind, still conscious of the body's stress,
Hindered awhile—and in a wilderness
  I walked alone,
  Till One a long time known
  Drew near. "Lord, may I come?
  For I would fain go Home."
"Not yet, My child"—then waves on waves of blue,
Like the blue sea, or air that light pours through.

This is not much to bring of that land's gold.
But one word lingers of the shining dream:
"Be comforted, all ye who by a stream
  Watch wistfully,
  Lest your belovèd be
  Swept to some shore unknown,
  All desolate, alone;
It is not so; but now, as heretofore,
The Risen Christ is standing on the shore."

RFB, TJ

Homecall

Out of the heat and out of the rain,
Never to know either sin or pain,
Never to fall and never to fear—
Could we wish better for one so dear?

What has he seen and what has he heard,
He who has flown away like a bird?
Eye has not seen, nor dream can show
All he has seen, all he may know,

For the pure powers of Calvary
Bathe little souls in innocency.
Tender, tender Thy love words be:
"Dear little child, come home to Me."

PU, TJ

Angelic Transport

(Luke 16:22)

"Carried by angels"—it is all we know
Of how they go;
We heard it long ago.
It is enough; they are not lonely there,
Lost nestlings blown about in fields of air.
The angels carry them; the way, they know.
Our kind Lord told us so.

K, TJ

River Comfort

As Time counts time, two years ago
One with whose life my life did flow
Hastened her Homeward to the Sea
That changes all things. Can it be
That she is still herself to me?

Am I myself to thee, my brother,
Or am I changed into another?

Stream, as two years ago thou art;
I look into thy very heart:
Thy colors are as they have been—
Amber and beryl and tourmaline.

Yet neither rocks nor pebbles show
Just as they did two years ago.

But I was never reckoned blind;
Where the green bank is undermined
I see, as oft with joy I saw,
Thy yellow lights like sunlit straw.

And yet the bank we used to know
Slipped down the fall six months ago.

Small flowers and grass and ferny moss
Grow round thine islet; thou dost toss
Bright showers upon it in thy play—
It was thine old, familiar way.

Yet there are differences; that isle
Is slowly changing all the while.

My stream, I know thee; changeling thou?
As thou wert then, so thou art now.
I know thy voice: it is thine own;
I know thine every bubble blown;
Thou dost but mock. Assure me now
That thou art thou, and very thou.

Yes, I am I, the very I
Whom thou by love didst certify.
And yet, indeed, the word is true
That all within me is made new.
And shall it not be even so
With her with whom thy life did flow,
But parted from, two years ago?

TJ

Ours Forever

All that was ever ours is ours forever:
Glory of greenwood and the shining river,
Joy of companionship of kindred mind;
All, all is ours. It is not left behind
Among the withered things that must decay;
It is stored up for us, somewhere, and for another day.

K, TMS

To My Friends

What are ye, O my friends?
As charm of light on leaves
And grass and fields of wheat
And fresh-plowed earth and rain-washed mountain slopes—
So are ye, O my friends.
As trees that face all weathers; flowers that meet
Me, new every morning; comforting moss
That to the bare rock cleaves
Only the closer for its poverty;
As waterfalls that toss
Perpetual joys to me,
Perpetual hopes;
Or as the pool below the waterfall
Whose clearness is as your dear loyalty—
All this, and far, far more are ye
Whom I may call
My friends.

MP

Patmos

Lying asleep on a wine-dark sea, a lonely isle—
Shadowy shore where a captive stood, but mile on mile,
Rippling away in a radiant sheen to sky afar,
Like a ribbon of silver, a road leading on to a silver star.

Glisten of delicate, tumbled shell the wavelet kissed,
Glitter and jangle of steel that locked wrist to wrist—
Ah, but forgotten chain and scourge and burning scar
For the joy that was singing and calling to him from the silver star.

Then, on the silver-white road, he walked to Otherwhere;
Pain was not; death was not, nor defeat nor despair.
Things that were seen appeared no more as things that are
But the foam of the surf by the fair, shining road to the silver star.

King of stars, whom a star foretold long ago,
Hail we the sign of the star that lies bright and low,
Low on the land and low on the sea, for oh, not far
Is the dawn that follows on golden feet—the silver star.

P

Wind

A wind blows through the book*
Right healthily,
Scant in its sympathy
With groveling things of earth,
Barren of worth,
And scant in courtesy
Toward mean suspicions, peevish moodiness
Of mind or manners. All such pettiness—
A huddle of loose straw—it sweeps away,
Whistling as if in play,
Yet serious,
Discoursing thus,
In words untrimmed and only vigorous:
"Gird up thy loins.
Come, climb the heights with me.
The mountains, the great mountains beckon thee;
Here, here,
The air is clear;
The lowland glooms lie far beneath thy feet;
The flowers are sweet
In upland places;
Bright new faces
Are here to greet thee;
Bracing influences await thee;
And to fête thee,
Hosts of angels
With whom thou may'st company.
But how clothed upon? Oh, white—

(Continued)

* *Charles Kingsley's Life*

White as light—
Are the garments that they wear
Who are there
On the mountain top. Refuse
Then for dress
Fleshliness.
Choose, O choose
As he would
Who, though still a mortal, stood
Fronting immortality."
Thus the great wind, becoming vocal, spoke;
And none the silence broke;
Only the sound of gentle stillness made reply
Till the blue sky
Persuasively
Sang soft in color-music: "Soul forgiven,
Be not tired out by loving; this is Heaven."

MP

Let Us Go Hence

The world is bright:
A room set all alight,
As if the House-Lord did employ
All that He had to give us joy.
The world is bright.

And life is good;
Who doubteth never stood
A happy lover in the room
Glowing with flowers of love abloom.
Yea, life is good.

Though it be true
Who loveth suffereth too,
Do not love's unimagined gains
Far more than balance all life's pains?
They do! They do!

Let us go hence;
Dost apprehend a sense
Of something moving thee away,
Something that stirreth thee to say,
"Let us go hence"?

Not here thy rest;
Thou art a passing guest.
But if life's lower rooms appear
So dear to thee, how much more dear
Thine own true rest.

MP, P, TJ

Look Toward the Light

(Night reflections in a pool)

Mountains, dreaming in the quiet of the young moon's light,
Forests, all at heart a-glimmer, and ye falls, snow white;
        And thou, pool, so palely gleaming
        Like a pearl set in the greenwood,
Of what think ye through the silence of the night?

Hark, a whisper, and a calling: "Child of man, come to me."
'Tis our moonlit pool that calleth; well content are we—
        Drop within her, feel her open
        To embrace us; pass from moonshine
To the deeps within her, know how dark they be.

Yea, how dark; but pressing upward, open new-washen eyes,
Meet the welcome of the moonbeams from the far, far skies—
        Meet it in the lightening water,
        Hint of radiance swift becoming
Myriad dance of silver sparkle as we rise.

(Continued)

O ye mountains, forests, waters, have I read you right?
Doth your young moon sing her story through the dark of night?
"Not toward darkness are our faces—
Towards the light creation moveth.
Lift your heads up; lift your hearts up to the light!"

DS

Discouraged?

But when from mountain top,
My Lord, I look with Thee,
My cares and burdens drop
Like pebbles in the sea.
The air is clear;
I fear no fear;
In this far view,
All things are new.

EHW

Arise, My Soul

Wood violets lent their blue;
The plain, like sea at rest,
Lay calm, composed, as slowly grew
A glory manifest—
Of water, earth or air,
Of gold or precious gem?
Who gazed could only think of fair,
Far New Jerusalem.

O thought in me, take wings,
And further, further fly;
Hath entered heart of man the things
That wait beyond the sky?
O Light that shall prevail,
O Powers that yet shall be!
Arise, my soul; cast loose, set sail:
Before thee lies the sea.

DS, TJ

The Moon Rainbow

It was a chilly night
    At the end of a showery day,
And the air was full of a silver light
    And rain like the dust of spray.

And softly the woodland folk
    Moved here and there; and, dumb,
The night-bird flew; and suddenly broke
    Through the silence, a voice calling, "Come."

And we stood in the dim moonshine
    And saw a wonder grow
Like a moonflower's delicate, curving line,
    A floating phantom bow.

The glimmering colors hung
    Over mountain, forest and stream.
Was ever a radiance so lightly flung
    In a faint and vanishing dream?

What lay beyond? We shall know
    When the King of Eternity,
Whose fingers fashioned the moon rainbow,
    Calls, "Children, come and see."

P

Perspective

Down on the plains they gazed upon a rainbow
Laid on the blue of the familiar hills,
Faintly discerned, but they knew it enfolded
Forest and fell, sweet nooks by ferny rills.

We on the mountains at the same bright moment—
Distance behind, like some forgotten fence—
Traced one by one each dear, familiar feature,
Known in a new and joyous immanence:

Saw the fall flash, entangled in the colors;
Saw the trees bathe in waves of colored air;
Saw the grey crags, astonished, jewel swiftly;
Climbed with the grass from painted stair to stair.

Will it be so where that fair Other Rainbow
Springs from the sapphire? And to those who stand,
Life's fences passed, does all feel dear, familiar—
Only seen nearer in the Fatherland?

DS

Safely to the Fatherland

(Deuteronomy 33:27)

"The eternal God is thy refuge sure;
Underneath are the everlasting arms";
And the word is true: He will keep secure
His beloved, from the enemy's alarms.

How blessed are those who this song do know;
They shall walk in the light of the Lord.
And from strength to strength they shall onward go;
And His triumph shall be their great reward.

Oh, what will it be when at His command
The trumpets of welcome sound,
And all at home in our Fatherland,
We see our Redeemer crowned.

Wg[2]

Swords Drawn

For us, swords drawn, up to the gates of heaven.
Oh, may no coward spirit seek to leaven
The warrior code, the calling that is ours;
Forbid that we should sheathe our swords in flowers.

Swords drawn,
Swords drawn,
Up to the gates of heaven—
For us
Swords drawn,
Up to the gates of heaven.

Captain belovèd, battle wounds were Thine;
Let me not wonder, if some hurt be mine.
Rather, O Lord, let my deep wonder be
That I may share a battle wound with Thee.

Oh, golden joy that Thou, Lord, givest them
Who follow Thee to far Jerusalem.
Oh, joy immortal, when the trumpets sound,
And all the world is hushed to see Thee crowned!

GC, RFB, P

Welcome, Coming King

Wars and battles, shocks and heartbreaks,
Weariness and hidden scars;
But a vision of the triumph,
Glorious glimpses of the stars.
  Wounded, let us rise and sing
  Welcome to our Coming King.

Sunrise, sunset, fling their carpet,
Gold and orange, grey and rose,
Welcoming His royal footsteps—
Every heart that loves Him glows.
  Joyful, let us rise and sing
  Welcome to our Coming King.

GC

His Footfall

Do we not hear Thy footfall, O Belovèd,
  Among the stars on many a moonless night?
Do we not catch the whisper of Thy coming
  On winds of dawn, and often in the light
Of noontide and of sunset almost see Thee—
  Look up through shining air
And long to see Thee, O Belovèd, long to see Thee,
  And wonder that Thou art not standing there?

And we shall hear Thy footfall, O Belovèd.
  And starry ways will open, and the night
Will call her candles from their distant stations;
  And winds will sing Thee; noon, and mingled light
Of rose-red evening thrill with lovely welcome.
  And we, caught up in air,
Shall see Thee, O Belovèd; we shall see Thee—
  In hush of adoration see Thee there.

GC, RFB, TJ

Song of Faith

O little bird that sings
Long before the glad day springs,
What radiant victory
You show to me.

You sing of conquering faith,
And of life subduing death,
And of joy before the light
Has vanquished night.

God of the sweet bird-song,
Let us all be borne along
By this triumphant mirth
That's not of earth.

Foreseeing dawn, would we
Now exult melodiously,
And sing before the light
Has vanquished night.

RFB

How Long?

O Star, whose sweet, untroubled song
  Floats tranquil down the moonlit blue,
Do you not see the ages' wrong?
  Nor hear the cry, "How long, how long,
    Till all things be made new?"

The wounded silence aches with prayer;
  Do broken prayers not rise so high?
A sound of tears disturbs the air;
  Does it not beat upon you there?
    Nor pain of human cry?

• • • • •

(Continued)

Lo, Dawn has lit his beacon fire;
The Conqueror rides in His car;
He comes, He comes; yea nigher, nigher,
The nation's hope, the world's desire,
The bright and morning Star.

GC, PVV, TJ

Easter Day

Lord Christ of Easter Day, Christ the victorious,
On this most radiant of all radiant days
Thee do we worship, Redeemer, all-glorious,
Offer Thee hearts' adoration and praise.

Sealed was the stone, and the rock did enfold Him,
There in the silence of moonlight and stars,
Till the hour struck; then the tomb could not hold Him:
Snapped like a straw, death's omnipotent bars.

Evil may triumph today, but tomorrow
Seeth the end of satanical strife.
Fear not and falter not; sin, pain and sorrow
Fall when He cometh, the Christ, Prince of Life.

Sound the word over the land and the waters;
Let it sound over the air once again:
Christ hath arisen! His sons and His daughters,
Lift up your heads, for He cometh to reign!

EHW

The End of India

We have come to the end of India
Where the rocks run into the sea,
The wonderful, blue-green, boundless sea,
That moves and murmurs constantly
About the rocks at the end of the land
That is greater than we can understand,
And dark with a terrible mystery—
The mystery of iniquity.

For at the end of India
A temple stands on a rock,
As if to block
The way of the God of the sea
From entering in at His gate;
But He is patient to wait
Till the towering temple wall
Shall shiver and totter and fall
With a plunge into the sea—
And the land shall be cleansed from iniquity.

So, at the end of India
Where the rocks run into the sea,
The wonderful, blue-green, boundless sea,
Mystery touches mystery;
And every thud of the waves on the shore
As they break in might,
And leap in white
Of majestic, prevailing purity,
Is a solemn stroke on Eternity's drum,
Saying, "Lo, I come;
In the roll of the book it is written of me."

MP

The River That Makes Glad

There is a river—dost thou know it, friend?
A river full of water, bordered by great trees
That hold the breeze
Entangled in their branches; dim
Small grottos plumed with fern adorn its ways;
Through drowsy days,
The fishes swim
In circles in the pool below the waterfall,
Where furtive creatures crawl
Each on his separate little business bent.
And all delightsomeness
Is there to bless
The lover of my river. For him, Solitude
Waits with her benedictions. Good
Is she to him who trusts her. Wild flowers bloom
At her command for him; their delicate bells
Ring merrily to pleasure him; she tells
Her grass and mosses to be ministers
To his contentment; and house-room,
In her economy, she finds for all things innocent.
For her low voice it is which says, "Uncurl,
Shy thoughts, with the young fern fronds." To the merle
She says, "Sing sweet, dear bird; a tired man is here."
And to the flickering butterflies, "Come near."
Melodious pauses
Deep in the heart of silence—these are hers.
And it is she who causes
All sinless things to look at him and smile
And speak soft words of cheer,
Till they beguile
His soul to rest.

Then, lovingly, lest
Aught should be lacking to him, the kind stream

Conspiring with her, calls to him to dream
Great dreams, fair dreams, dreams that shall flower and fruit,
Having their root
Set deep in quietness. And clear,
My river sings to him in her mysterious language, eases
His knotted burden-cords, appeases
Intrusive things, persuading them away.

The dust of day
Washes clean off him; she purges his dim eyes,
Braces his sinews, strenuously denies,
He being a man, his right
To miss life's gladness; says to him, "Perceive
The spiritual in the visible and receive
Refreshment manifold!"

She touches him, and, behold,
In him arise
Jubilant fountains of a new delight;
And waxing strong,
Being comforted,
And wonderfully fed
With food convenient for him, he decries
Untrodden paths that beckon him; along
The watercourses lets his spirit travel;
In brimming brinks
Of carvèd basins, stoops and drinks
And bathes, a man renewed. And the bright play
Of sunbeams on the brown and amber gravel
Is as the light that fills him, till the boy
Buried in him—made bold
By the excess of joy—
Awakes, upsprings,
Laughs, mixes with the life of things
About him—while upon
Him waits God's gracious peace. Gone, gone

(Continued)

The usual sense of cankering, cumbering care.
Gone where?
Who knows?
He only knows it gone.

MP

The River's Word

River, river, interpret thy sound;
Open its word to me.
Charms of all ages in thee meet;
Joys of all joyance wait to greet
My spirit that moveth forth to thee.
Thy beauty is magic; and yet I found
Or felt something beyond it when my ear
Fancied it pierced through the sweetness, heard
A secret Word;
But now I fear
I shall never attain to the song in whole.
Jubilant soul
Of the running river, be kind, expound
This, thy great Word, to me.

"Thou art of time, ephemeral fool;
How canst thou fathom me?
Chant of the ages is my song.
Thou who by nature dost belong
To trivial things of today, to thee
Pertain but the passing seasons, the rule
Of the futile gnat. Wouldst thou penetrate
Through to my heart? Hast thou inferred
My secret Word?
What if too late
In creation's scheme thou'st appeared, to win
So far within
Mystic harmonies? Thus do I school
Those who would question me."

River, river, it cannot be thou;
Never was scorn in thee!

"Hushed be thy heart, for even now
I open my Word to thee:

"Before I was, thou wast: the eternal Mind
Framed thee eternal. Time can never bind
Thee to today; for thee is life's tomorrow.
For that the seasons borrow
All lovely colors, all enduring joy—
For that employ
All processes to make eternal Spring.
And I, rejoicing, sing
As one aware, informed
By that which is to be;
And it is thus my song,
And I am beautiful to thee.
I sing to thee . . .

"Of the time when the marred shall be mended,
And the bitter wrong be ended,
And the pain be comprehended
In a peace that endeth not;
And no blot
Stain life's landscape; and to sever
Hearts united, knife shall never
Be upraised;
And the good alone be praised;
And the praised unconscious be
Of his crown. I sing to thee . . .

"Of the love that shall know no depletion;
Of the joy that shall know all completion;
Of the gracious power that—mating
Will to force and dedicating

(Continued)

Every energy to use,
Every use to perfect scope—
Shall clasp hands with glad-eyed hope
And be satisfied. Then loose
From thy shoulders faithless weakness
As a castoff garment; nought
Being too good to be.
O thought,
Wingèd thought, fly higher, higher,
For thou canst not fly too high—
Nay, nor high enough. O fly
Out of time's detaining fingers
Into thine eternity!

"Mortal who hast listened to me,
Thou'rt immortal; thou belongest
Wholly unto that good day
That my music celebrateth,
For the which creation waiteth.
Wild confusion of my steeps,
Rippling shallows, silent deeps,
Strange aloofness of my lone,
Shadowy pools where bubbles blown
By the quiet things below
Come and go;
All gentle glancing
Golden lights low in me lying,
Silver lights on me replying
Unto my gay colors' dancing;
All my illusive beauty; sense
Of triumphant joy in me,
And transparent innocence—
All I am now singeth *to thee*,
Singeth *through* thee,
The one Word that thou hast heard—
That great Word, that deep, wide Word:
Eternity, Eternity."

MP

So He Bringeth Them to Their Desired Haven

Soft thunder of great waves and splash of spray
And little, sparkling laugh of breaking bubbles,
And then a gradual glory swept the sea
And thrilled the air (the outgoings of the day
Rejoicing thus). While moving as aware
Of measured music beating time for him,
The sun descended, touched the waiting sea,
And with majestic movement—and yet swift—
Sank till the utmost rim of ocean drowned
His last, thin line of light.
A pause, and then
A luminous loveliness, as if all precious things—
All crystals, jewels, creatures iridescent—
Lent of their spirit to the atmosphere.
All colors mingled, and all glories met
In that bright moment. And the track of sun,
Himself departed but still looking back,
Lay red-gold on a waste of violet.

Then, while the hush of golden afterglow
Held us in silence, a small fishing boat
Sailed on the darkening sea that pressed upon
The lighted path, until she entered it.
And now no more could we perceive her form
Or dull brown sails distinguish, but she seemed
An amethyst that hung in amethyst air,
A pearl that floated on a sea of pearl
Mingled with fire. And all the colors bent
To welcome and embrace her as she passed
Within their radiant kingdom.
Then my soul
Sprang forth to meet Him who is ever wont
To speak in parables. For often I,
Smitten by fear, despondent, dare not think

How it may fare at the far end with me
Who am the least of all my good Lord's ships,
Not worthy to be reckoned in His fleet.
For see, my hull is battered, my sails torn,
Not one fair space of deck is found in me—
Oh, not in me is any single good!

Yea, but that fishing boat, that three-logged boat,
Was not in itself worthy, but rough hewn,
Like other Indian boats, and nowise meet
To take a place in any battle line,
Or sail in a regatta of swift yachts,
Or even carry costly merchandise;
Not of itself, its glory.
O most good,
Most reassuring thought. Go on, pursue
Thy healing ministry, for shall it not
Be even thus, my Lord, with this, Thy ship?
Once, all but wrecked, it drifted;
Rocks roared to devour it,
Sending fierce outriders bidden to seize it;
Winds howled about it;
Whirlpools sucked beneath it;
And neither sun nor stars in many days appeared.

Then, at what time the wild storm fell upon me,
I called, and on the instant, Thou didst draw me
Out of those many waters. Thy right arm
Doth still sustain me, and I cannot fear
Abandonment; O Lord, I will not fear
Ill (Thou granting succor) for my last voyage.
No shock of tempest, no supreme eclipse,
No inward deviation of my helm,
Will Thy long provèd love permit to end
What that same love began. Thy word is pledged

To perfect that which doth concern the least
Of Thy small fishing boats.
I shall not slip
Out of Thy love and find myself forlorn,
Lost in the dark upon an unknown shore;
But drawn by invisible currents, I shall move
Upon the golden pathway of the sea
At sunset, with my old, torn sails full set
To catch the colors, till (for sweet,
Sweet is Thy mercy to Thy wind-worn ships)
I shall be changed and fashioned otherwise.

And I who long time bore in heaviness
The image of the earthly then shall bear
The image of the heavenly; and this flesh
Being no more, my base corruptible
Shall put on incorruption. Mortal, I
Shall put on immortality, and pass
Out of the temporal into the eternal—
Out of night into the welcoming light
Of the pure shining of Thy countenance.

MP

Illumination

(Ecclesiasticus 25:11)

The Sky

In me is light:
Consider well my sun, his rise, his setting;
My glory of noon.
Let there be no forgetting
My sparkling dust of stars; my exceeding bright
And quiet moon;
My swift, forked lightnings. Where, if not in me,
Is there illumination? Filled am I
With light that passeth all things.
Thus, the sky.

(Continued)

The Sea

In me is light:
Most wondrous is the glory of my gleaming;
My waterways,
With delicate sunbeams dreaming
In intricate, netted dances do unite.
My very haze
Is luminous; and my night is lit with lamps
Mysteriously moving. Yea, in me
Is all illumination.
Thus, the sea.

The Earth

In me is light:
My flowers are dressed in garments light-enwoven;
My creatures reign
Royal in colors. Cloven
By fire or frost, my substance, depth or height,
Discovers vein
On vein of lustrous metals, jewel beds,
Hidden illumination. All the mirth
Of lightsome things possess I.
Thus, the earth.

• • • • •

I listen to the voices of the sky;
I listen to the voices of the sea;
The earth, with all her various loveliness, sings
Sweet songs to me.
But something in me wanders wistful still,
Unsatisfied;
Beyond the light of earth and sea and sky
Is there no light beside?
I stand outside life's shining palace halls,
Disconsolate;
Will no one come, interpret mysteries,
Unlock the gate?

• • • • •

After this I looked, and behold,
A door was opened in heaven.
And by desire made bold,
Forward I ran, and saw the Colors Seven,
Entangled as a rainbow caught in spray,
Over-arch the way;
Whence issued pure, foam-white,
From fountain springs of light,
The exhaustless love of the Lord.
(O rich reward
For poverty of yearning!)
Glowing, burning,
I had felt the heats of the world's brilliance pass;
As withered grass
They left me, scorched by the very glow.

Now penetrating
Through the last layers of the dusty clod
I call my soul, the love of God,
Lover of lovers, came
Keen as a flame,
Illuminating
By that strange, spiritual brightness, my waste lands.
And lo,
The whole wide world did to my Lover sing
In colors; even the desert sands
Were quickened and were green, recovering
All in a moment, verdure. And a rain
Mixed with the light, swept by and cleansed the air.

Oh, it was beautiful,
Beyond the reach
Of mind to think it, heart to adore it—
Beautiful.
All previous lights paled utterly before it.
I stood upon the beach
Of infinite joys and gazed

(Continued)

And gazed again,
All humbled and amazed
By the tumultuous rush of mine own happiness,
And only knew to bless
The Giver and confess
Myself content to be forever there.

Till a familiar voice came unto me and said:
"Although life shed
Her visible glories, still do thou believe.
Doubt not what thou hast seen; rather, retrieve
Thine own—for no deceptive dream,
To fade or fail,
That vision beautiful.
But thou must learn to prevail
By force of faith. Be humble, dutiful,
Sincere, without offence,
And quick to penitence;
And put far from thee vanity and lies,
Thy stedfast eyes
Set on the invisible. And know
Assuredly: above, below,
Behind the changes of thy changeful heart,
Behind the fluctuations of thy will,
Uninfluenced by the influences of time,
The love of the Lord, once thine,
Continues with thee. Part
In no wise from this assurance; let it fill
Thy being with its gladness. In thy God
Learn thou to hold thee still.

"Then, in those desperate moments when there slips
Sense of possession from thee,
And fear strips
Feeling from off thee,

And thou standest alone—
Then, then, oh be it known
Through to the core of thee, that Love remains!
For no bewildering pains
Of life or death can wrest her from thee,
No, nor even stains
Or shadows of thy sin dim her illumination;
Her tranquility
Shaming thy restlessness,
Her light, like to a pearl most precious."

Fell quietness then, and hushed me. All creation
Lay back from me, as owning
Itself surpassed. And as a homing,
Tired bird returns into her nest,
My soul returned unto her rest.

MP

Even There

"Thou hast fared far, my friend, and sounded depths.
Hast thou touched bottom?"

"Once I reached the place
Where all illusions die, and platitudes
Shrivel and shrink, ashamed. Some time I was
Detained in that drear land where all the guests
Are held in thrall; struck dumb by strong distress,
They neither strive nor cry; there the tears
Do not flow easily but sting and scald.
And hearts are broken very silently."

"Deeper than this, far deeper lie the depths,
The deepest depths."

"Deeper I went: I walked
For many days of years with one beloved

(Continued)

Across a scorching country, till I came
To a wild valley called the Shadow of Death,
Where dreadful power is given unto pain
To rack the limbs and fill the eyes with fear
(Dear eyes that beamed with love-light) and to wring
Low, broken moans that strike against the air
Of that hot region (voice that once caressed
By lightest intonation)—until I,
Forgetting all desires save only one,
Called upon Death, kind Death, to set her free.

"But, even as I prayed, the tide of life
Came creeping, bounding through the reluctant veins;
And sense, asleep awhile, awoke and felt
The sharpness of the flints strewn on the way
Prepared for naked feet. And then I, pitifully
Counting the possible miles of jagged flints,
Sickened at heart, and suffered many things
From scorpion thoughts that from black darkness crawled
And set upon me, and from thoughts like whips
That lashed me, and from thoughts like claws
That tore me. For my near, familiar woe
Into the mass of the great, sad world's woe
Passed undistinguished, fearfully darkening
The black confusion."

"*Nay, not even thus*
We sound the deepest depths."

"I know it well
For once a scale was given to me by which
All anguish may be measured. On that day
I stood fast bound, whilst hurrying down the road
Fled a young life, and after it in haste
The shape men call Pollution. And I saw
It gaining ground upon the hunted thing,

The little, innocent, cherished, hunted thing
That ran with all its impotent strength. I strained
Hard at the cords that bound me, till they cut
Into my flesh. And then a great wind blew,
And the dust blinded me, and the great wind
Swept them away, hunter and hunted.

"Then one insidious—Despair his name—
His nature venomous, of torturers chief,
Approached me, and with ancient, subtle darts
Assailed me inwardly: 'Dost still believe,
Still tarry, O deluded, the Lord's leisure?
Perished thy hope, for were the angels given
A charge concerning her, the innocent one?
Thou sinkest in deep mire; there is no standing;
Over thy head the sullen floods are flowing;
Thou art cut off—thy hope clean gone forever.
For God—He hath forgotten to be gracious;
In anger He hath shut His tender mercies.
God—doth He reign? How canst thou know He reigneth?
Is the world God's or Devil's?'"

"Thou hast touched
The deep place, than which deeper there is not;
Thou hast touched bottom. Oh, in such an hour
Of sudden fallings off of trusted things,
Of gloom of moonless night appalling thee,
And winds tempestuous, tell me if thou didst then
Perceive a light, a glorious certainty?
Feel under thee the Rock of ages, know
It stood unshakable? Discover God,
The living God?"

"Yea, verily, the rock
Was underfoot, and overhead, a light!"

(Continued)

"Then joy! Rejoice, again I say, Rejoice!
And offer in His temple an oblation.
An oblation of great gladness. For be sure
And sing for sureness, thou, thus having stood
Even there, and proved Him true and very God—
His beacon unextinguished and Himself
Thy stony rock, thy castle, thy deliverer—
Wilt never, happen what may to thee, arrive
At any place forsaken. Even there,
In unimagined utmost of distress,
His hand shall lead thee; His right hand shall hold thee
Until the path, compassed so far by Him
Whom thy soul loveth, turn, and lead thee straight
Home to the Land Celestial where, unveiled,
He welcometh His travelers, healing them,
By that sweet welcome, of all weariness.
Then He who aforetime met thee, nourished thee
In barren, blistering wastes and desolate depths,
Will lead thee unto fountains of cool waters
Flowing about the roots of fair, green trees
And by the river of God that maketh glad
The city of God.

"Therefore, I say, Rejoice,
Again, and yet again, I say Rejoice,
Such joy being set before thee. Even now
Lift up thine head above thine enemies;
Yea, lift it up, and learn to wear thy pain
As night doth wear her diadem of stars."

MP

Dost Thou Care?

A sea that fell along an alien shore;
Grey evening, and a man with a heart all gloomed
By thoughts that seemed part of the sullen roar
And crash of waves along that iron coast;
And, singing to herself and gathering shells,
A young, untroubled child. "Are we all doomed
To perish?" the man cried. "The heavenly host
That tarries round Thine own—where is it? Hell's
Let loose, and he that loosed it stands
With dripping hands,
And kinship claims with Thee, the Holy One!
God, smite him on the cheekbone! Let us have done
With his iniquity. But dost Thou care?
Or has our age's sin
Caused Thee to hide Thy face from us? Has the din
Of our mad clamor quenched Thy Spirit?" And his mood—
Embittered by the exceeding bitter food
That nourished it—no comfort anywhere
Could find, but bled
In words: "The shambles cry to Thee; the ground is red;
The very air is red, and dost Thou care?"

Across the darkening sea, a ship toiled slow.
  He watched her, thinking, "She has far to go;
    Will wind and tide be friend to her or foe?
And will she ever reach the port where she would be?
  O God! O Christ, great Ruler of the Sea,
    We toil at rowing, going heavily.
For it is night with us; oh, for the dawn of day!
  The wind is contrary; the blinding spray
    Is breaking on the boat—and Thou away.
Calm Watcher on the hill, to whom, if not to Thee
  Can we appeal to save us from the sea?
    Walk on the water! Come to us, to me!"

(Continued)

Hark to the waves that roll and swell and comb;
Hark to the hiss of the indifferent foam—
Is there no other answer? As the wild
Sea voices moaned about him and beguiled
Him further into sadness, the young child
Beside him still was crooning her soft song,
A nursery song of simple things. And he,
All quick and raw and rasped with sense of wrong,
Unwittingly
Listened to this, her song:

God made the shore,
  Rocks and sand and sea,
Little lovely shells;
  He made me.

God feeds the fish
  Swimming in the sea,
Feeds them every day;
  He feeds me.

God rules the tides
  Of the mighty sea;
God will never fail;
  He guides me.

God's behind the storm
  Lashing up the sea;
God's within the calm;
  He loves me.

Though I may forget,
  He loves faithfully:
Always God goes on
  Loving me.

And the song dropped into the heart of the man,
And he suddenly knew
That the God who was loving the child
Loved the universe too;
It was love's fiery law he saw working,
And not love's decrease.
And he blessed the young child and her God—
And had peace.

MP

Lift Up Thy Heart

The child lay dying, and I looked and saw
Through the open nursery window, pale blue hills
In quiet folds beyond the garden wall.
And as I looked, I thought: If I could see
God's angels standing on those blue hillsides,
With faces turned in welcome towards the child,
And hands outstretched to take her, would I toil
So hard to keep her from them? Would I not
Loose her and let her go? And then this song awoke:

"If we could see all the surrounding spaces,
    Blue hills or gardens, or the common street,
Bright with the heavenly people's welcoming faces.
        Say, would we still entreat
        In desperate prayer
For sojourn in the broken house of clay?
    Oh, could we hear the music in the air,
        Would we then toil or pray
        For long imprisonment?

"If we could see the quickened powers awaken,
    Each from its sheath, like buds newborn on earth,
And the free spirit, wind-swept, overtaken
        By racing waves of mirth,
        Jubilant spray,

(Continued)

Breast the great breakers of its happiness,
Would we not rise up then and quietly say,
'My God, I acquiesce;
Yea, I am well content.'"

• • • • •

O thou bereavèd and not comforted,
Lift up thy heart, lift up thine eyes, and look
And see the things that are.
A singing land
Lies there above the clouds and the grey rain:
Sighing and tears have never found the way
That leads from earth to it—nor pain, nor sin;
Baffled, they fall back on the troubled world
And walk about down here. Dost thou love rivers?
A river flows through all that goodly land.
Dost love the sunshine and the shade of trees?
There is no night there; but lest any heat
Should hurt, the light comes filtered through the leaves
Of the immortal Tree. The flowers there,
Colored with happiness, forget to fade;
Each fern uncurls in individual joy;
The very mosses and the lichens paint
The rocks with conscious pleasure; and the birds—
Oh, they are eagerer than even ours
To pour live joy into the air, an air
That seems alive, instinct with joy of life.
And the earth underfoot laughs softly, buds;
And the dear, shy buds smile.
The children, see,
Gayer at games they are than even here,
Keener at work; for, look, the Wonder Schools
Open their secrets to them, secrets shut
Fast from us mortals. And the men and maids
Do nobler deeds than ever they had dared
To dream in limited days; for never bar

Is set to high endeavor; but to think—
So pure their thoughts—is gloriously to do,
And with swift ease. For the city is not paved
With wasted powers; no lost or futile loves
Lie like fair fallen petals on the walks
Of its great gardens; else the word that calls
Him blessèd whom God, choosing out, receives
And satisfies with the pleasure of His house,
Were dust and ashes. And it never was God's way
To feed the soul He made on vanity.

Therefore, I take it to be verity
That these things are, yea, tenfold better things,
And that our own enjoy them, they being still
Our own, not stranger folk of alien mind,
Removed, aloof. The love we knew is there,
The cheerfulness, the courage, faithfulness
To duty, and forgetfulness of self—
But perfected in holiness. And they,
Living their stainless lives in joyousness,
Are still themselves, and wait to hear thy step
(Their hearts will know it, though a thousand thronged
Together at the door); yet they, having seen
The end of the Lord, are well content to wait.

• • • • •

My soul, wait thou as they. Though silence holds
The space between us, 'tis but for today.
Tomorrow's near; wait thy tomorrow, my soul.

MP

7 Youthful Thoughts

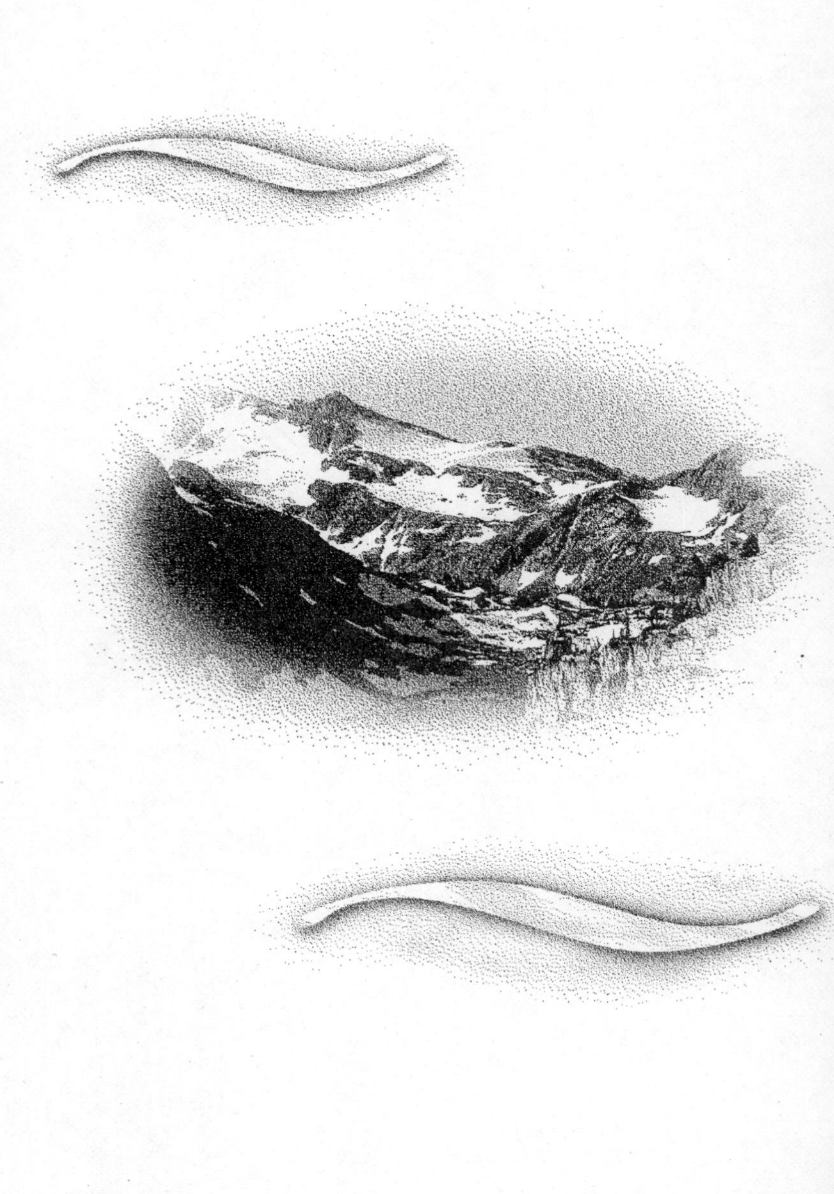

The Angels' Song

The Lord of Love, on a certain night
  Said, "Lo, the world's lamp grows dim."
And He made a Song, and filled it with light;
  And He called His angels to Him,
And He said in His kindness, "My poor people lie
All in the dark; take this new Song and fly
Down to them; sing it to them, or they die."

In each angel's heart, like a little bright sun,
  Was the beautiful Song—and new.
And they wanted to sing it to everyone
  As the Lord had told them to do.
"For," said the angels, the one to the other,
"Whoso that sings it will know his great Lover—
See in the light of it each man a brother."

So they flew past many a burning star
  That sails in the outermost deep;
And they passed the white moon, and they traveled far
  Till they came to a field of sheep.
And the men that tended them woke as the light
Of the wonderful Song broke forth in might;
And the world has been lighter since that night.

DS

God's Nursery

There was snow on the hearts of the children of men;
  There was cold like the cold of snow,
When the Child came down to Bethlehem's town
  And asked for a place to go.
And they said, "Nay we
    Have no nursery."
      And He made Him a place where the oxen be—
For they said they had no other nursery.

(Continued)

But the dear, good beasts—they were glad and proud,
And did their Creator know;
And they wondered then at the ways of men,
That they should treat Him so.
And they said, "Ah, we
Have a poor nursery,
But, oh, He is welcome as welcome can be."
And they gave Him their straw for His nursery.

But afterwards some of the children of men
Were sorry when they did know
How sore was their sin when they went to the inn
And left Him with nowhere to go.
And they said, "Will He
Make a nursery
Here in our hearts, for sorry we be?"
And so He came home to His own nursery.

DS

The King in a Manger

When the morning stars sang together, and all
The sons of God shouted for joy,
He was there—who was laid in a manger made
For the little calves of the stall:
The King, the King of Eternity,
Laid His glory by for thee and for me.

Who hung the round world upon nothing—He lay
A babe on His mother's lap.
Who made of the clouds swaddling bands for the sea,
Her gentle hands did Him wrap:
The King, the King of Eternity,
Laid His glory by for thee and for me.

Oh, well may we love our kingly Lord,
Oh, well may we love our King
Who for love of us all became weak and small
As any baby thing.
The King, the King of Eternity,
Laid His glory by for thee and for me.

DS

The Wise Men

Once a star rose in the sky,
Silver star of mystery,
But the wise men, pondering, knew
What it said that they must do.

So, in that first Christmastide,
On their camels they did ride—
Rode to far Jerusalem,
Rode to farther Bethlehem;

Found the little, precious child,
On the ground before Him piled
Gold and frankincense and myrrh;
Hailed Him Royal Conqueror.

Once again, led by a Star,
Do we come from near and far,
Drawn by Love's belovèd cords,
Hail our Savior, Lord of lords.

And as holy seraphim
Veil their faces, worship Him,
Pray we now this Christmas grace—
Reverence as we seek His Face.

EHW

Christmas Gifts

Did Mary say to Joseph tenderly,
"Such little hands, such little feet! They be
Like little shells we've found beside the sea,
The Sea of Galilee"?

And did wise Joseph answer, "For love's sake
Our love shall shelter Him, enclose, and hold,
As the low hills about that silver lake
Shelter it, fold on fold"?

Across the stable, like a wind—a breath—
"The wicked have enclosed Me," it saith.
"Thou hast brought Me into the dust of death."
Into the dust of death.

And then did Joseph's father-like surprise,
As round his finger little fingers curled,
Call smiles and tears to Mary's mother-eyes?
He clings who'll save the world.

And as the Child in His soft manger lay,
Did gentle oxen in their language say,
"A mangerful of our sweet-smelling hay—
Our gift this Christmas Day"?

Again that breath—An unregarded tree
Is growing somewhere, making wood to be
One awful day, the Cross of Calvary—
The Cross of Calvary.

O Lord, we adore Thee!
The wicked did enclose Thee;
Pierced were Thy hands and feet for us—for me—
 O Child of Bethlehem.

Christ our dear Redeemer,
We come and we adore Thee,
We come and we adore Thee,
We come and we adore Thee,
 Christ our Lord.

WHP

For You and Me

Silver moon, did you see
 Kneeling in Gethsemane,
One who made you and me—
 Praying under an olive tree?

Golden sun, did you see,
 On the hill called Calvary,
One alone on a tree,
 Dying just for love of me?

And did you veil your face?
 Darkness, did you fill the place
When, alone on a tree,
 Love gave up His life for me?

Silver moon, you saw more,
 Saw the opening of a door.
Little birds, did you sing
 In the moonlight to your King?

BT, P

THE PASSIONFLOWER

Dear flower, you tell a story
  Of suffering and glory.
I softly, softly sing to you,
  O purple passionflower!

A little child am I;
  I often wonder why
Your story is so sorrowful,
  O purple passionflower.

Three nails, five wounds you show;
  And I can never know
The pain you try to tell me of,
  O purple passionflower.

A crown of thorns you show,
  And I can never know
The pain you try to tell me of,
  O purple passionflower.

And yet beyond the sadness
  There is mysterious gladness;
And reverently I sing to you,
  O purple passionflower.

For now the Crown of Glory
  Encircles all your story.
With solemn joy I sing to you,
  O purple passionflower.

DS

Ants: A Child's Question

Each has its little life to live;
Each has its death to die.
But each is such a minute speck of life
That though we may fervently try,
We cannot concern ourselves very much
Whether it live or die.

Are we as minute to the angels who look
Down from their place in the sky?
Do the great people there
Very greatly care
Whether we laugh or cry?
To them are we mere little atoms of life
That are born, grow old, and die?

No, no,
It is not so;
For One who is higher than they
Took flesh of our flesh and stooped to die
In pitiful, human way.

And ever since that wonderful day
When the Highest lifted us high,
To the angels we are not common clay,
Not morsels and motes to come and to go,
But beings belovèd, in whom they know
Is the mystic seed of eternity;
They see in us that which yet shall be.

MP

A Little Bird-Song

Once I heard
A little bird
Singing very clearly;
And the bird
That I heard
Sang: "God loves me dearly."

Please stay now
And tell me how,
Little bird, you know it.
"Every day,
Come what may,
Many kind things show it.

"Sun and rain,
Ripening grain,
Food and water given,
Leafy trees—
All one sees
Under the blue heaven."

Then the bird
That I heard
Sang it very clearly:
"God loves you"
(Off it flew)
"Loves you very dearly."

BT, P

God Cares For Me

God made the shore,
Rocks and sand and sea,
Little, lovely shells.
He made me.

God feeds the fish
Swimming in the sea,
Feeds them every day.
He feeds me.

God rules the tides
Of the mighty sea;
God will never fail.
He guides me.

God's behind the storm
Lashing up the sea;
God's within the calm.
He loves me.

Though I may forget,
He loves faithfully,
Always God goes on
Loving me.

BT, P

Commelina

(A little blue grass-flower)

O wonderful and dear,
My Lord, my God; and art Thou here?
Could any mere imagining
Make me so glad that I must sing?
'Tis true as this blue flower is blue:
My Lord is here.

(Continued)

The sun is in the sky;
The sky is vast and very high,
But the blue flower beside me drinks
Her little fill of sunshine, thinks
Not one so near as her dear sun,
    Though he be high.

And now and every hour.
As if there were no other flower
In all the world for Thee to tend,
Thou dost stay by me, love me, spend
On me all I can use of Thee,
    I being Thy flower.

DS

Bladderwort

Brave blue bladderwort!
Down the water dashes
In a swift, tumultuous leap,
Over you he flashes—
  With a mighty, mighty roar
  On the black rock flashes.

Brave blue bladderwort!
Well you know your river;
Could a thousand thousand falls
Make your blue bells quiver?
  You are not a coward flower,
  So, why should you quiver?

King of water-floods,
Maker of the wild flowers,
Raging forces own Thee Lord;
Thine are all the world powers.
  What can hurt what Thou dost guard:
  Little child or wild flower?

DS

The Angels and the Tiger

I think the careful angels walk
    Where little children be.
One night a tiger came to stalk
    His game quite near our nursery.

On our verandah, as we slept
    In the warm, open air,
We dreamed good dreams; they kindly kept
    Their watch around us everywhere.

And in the morning, when we saw
    And counted eagerly
The marks made by each great big paw
    A stone's throw from our nursery,

We wondered what the angels said
    To make him go away.
Perhaps they patted his soft head
    And whispered, "Tiger, you're astray.

"See, we will show you by our light
    The way that you should go,"
And gently led him through the night—
    I wonder, was it really so?

BT, DS

God's Messages

Little flower,
New this hour,
What do you say to me?
 "God came near,
 So I'm here;
 Think of Him reverently."

Dear wild bird
That I heard,
What do you say to me?
 "God is good,
 Gives us food;
 Think of Him gratefully."

Blue, blue sky,
Very high,
What do you say to me?
 "God is true,
 God loves you;
 Think of Him lovingly."

Evening star,
Shining far,
What do you say to me?
 "Go to sleep,
 God will keep;
 Think of Him peacefully."

BT, P

It's True

O dear Lord Jesus
Thou lovest me.
I do not know at all
How that can be.

But, dear Lord Jesus,
I know it's true,
True as that grass is green
And skies are blue.

So, dear Lord Jesus,
Help me to be
Thy loving little child,
Pleasing to Thee.

BT, P

Loranthus

(A parasitical plant)

As this green thing that I see,
Drinking sap from his tall tree,
Climbing fearless, I would be.

Thou, my Tree of Life, art tall;
Though my roots be weak and small,
If I cling, I shall not fall.

If I drink, I shall not die,
Nor in longest drought be dry;
In my Tree is my supply.

Thou who didst in olden time
Use low things to teach sublime,
Teach me, by this, how to climb.

DS

LORD JESUS, LIVE WITH ME

Dear Lord Jesus, will You come
Into such a little home?
    It is poor, and it is bare;
    Dear Lord, You'll find nothing there.
        It is very dusty, too—
        Oh, it isn't fit for You.

Not a flower has bloomed for me;
There's no fruit upon my tree.
    And, Lord Jesus, have You heard?
    I have not one singing bird.
        Dearest Lord, how can You come
        Into such a dismal home?

"But, My child, I want to come,
Want to make your house My home.
    If I come, it shall be fair,
    In and out and everywhere.
        I will clear the dust away,
        Make it clean and make it gay.

"All its flowers will bloom for Me;
Fruit will ripen on your tree;
    In your garden will be heard
    Many a merry, singing bird.
        Dearest child, I want to come.
        May I make your house My home?"

O my Savior, Lord and King,
Come, I give You everything.
With my whole heart I say, Come—
Come and make my house Your home.

PU

Angels Near Us

(Gideon—Judges 6:20–24)

Once a man stood near a stone,
Thought that he was all alone,
Spoke a little, frightened word;
        But an angel heard,

Heard and answered him and said
Kindly words, and comforted,
For the man was not alone
        By the altar stone.

Nor are we alone today
When we work or when we play;
Angel people—they are here
        And they hold us dear.

When we're good, then they are glad;
When we're naughty, they are sad;
Could we see our angels' eyes,
        Would we see surprise?

Would we see them in their place
Where they see the Father's face,
Shamed and grieved to have to tell
        How we children fell?

Lord of angels, make us good;
Help us do the things we should;
Keep us so that we may be
        Pleasing unto Thee.

BT, P

Daydreaming

Hurry scurry, worry flurry,
Such a fuss and such a hurry.
Down I slid by a private stair
To a room in a forest of maidenhair.

The glistening walls were of mother of pearl;
The roof was a moonstone; the delicate twirl
Of a kind of coiled ladder sprang up from the floor
Of loveliest opal. The low, swinging door
Had a way of opening silently
To people like you and me.

In the room was a sea pool made
In a hollow and carven slab of jade.
And coral polyps and corallines spread
Their pink and purple; and sea things fed
Each in his fashion. The room, like a shell,
Curved softly and smoothly; for a lamp, there fell
A great white Indian star from the sky.
And into that room slipped I.

Hurry scurry, worry flurry,
"Where's the child? Catch her. Hurry!
Absent-minded again!" My ear
Thought it heard, but it did not hear
Really and properly, you know,
For I was slipping and sliding so
That I couldn't listen. At last I curled,
Safe in my dear little inside world,
In the cool, green forest of maidenhair fern,
As they clawed the outside of me and said,
"Come, learn your Tamil grammar, and do your sums."

But I was away where nobody comes
But foolish people like you and me
Who are far, far, far from what they should be.

GC

FINDING JOY
(Ecclesiasticus 7:15)

Hate not laborious work;
Joy, joy is in it.
Do not thy duty shirk;
Joy, joy is in it.
Welcome the daily round,
On, and be faithful found,
On, and thou shalt be crowned;
Joy, joy is in it.

Scorn not monotony;
Joy, joy is in it.
Blessèd be drudgery;
Joy, joy is in it.
Welcome the daily round,
On, and be faithful found,
On, and thou shalt be crowned;
Joy, joy is in it.

Toil unto weariness;
Joy, joy is in it.
Live but to help and bless;
Joy, joy is in it.
Welcome the daily round,
On, and be faithful found,
On, and thou shalt be crowned;
Joy, joy is in it.

Come then—if cold or heat;
Joy, joy is in it.
Be thou God's corn of wheat;
Joy, joy is in it.
Welcome the barren ground;
Hereafter will be found
Fruit to abide, abound;
Joy, joy is in it.

MP, P

Do Your Best

Donkey's bray
    Seems to say,
        "Oh, to sing a song!
But though I
    Really try,
        Somehow the tune goes wrong.

"*Ai-yai-yo!*
    Well I know
        I can only bray."
Do your best,
    Leave the rest;
        That's a good donkey's way.

"In the Ark,
    In the dark,
        All the poor things wept.
'Twas my time
    And my chime
        Up to the high roof swept.

"They looked 'round
    At the sound—
        Shouted, 'Hip Hooray!'
Rubbed their ears,
    Wiped their tears,
        All on a wisp of hay.

"So, you see,
    If like me
        You are only you,
Do your best,
    Leave the rest;
        That's what you'd better do."

FTR

Scrub and Sing

I scrub my pots, I scrub my pans;
I scrub my brasses and my cans;
I sweep and scrub each red floor tile
Till I can see it smile.

And as I scrub, I feel so gay
It might be my own Coming-day;
For work is such a jolly thing
It makes one want to sing.

K

For Jesus

Jesus, Savior, dost Thou see
When I'm doing things for Thee?
Common things, not great and grand:
Carrying stones, and earth and sand?

"I did common work, you know,
Many, many years ago;
And I don't forget. I see
Everything you do for Me."

K

Jesus' Ways

If Jesus built a ship,
    She would travel trim;
If Jesus roofed a barn,
    No leaks would be left by Him;
If Jesus planted a garden,
    He would make it like Paradise;
If Jesus did my day's work,
    It would delight His Father's eyes.

GC

What Is Discipline?

When I refuse the easy thing for love of my dear Lord,
And when I choose the harder thing for love of my dear Lord,
And do not make a fuss or speak a single grumbling word;
That is discipline.

When everything seems going wrong and yet I will not grouse,
When it is hot, and I am tired, and yet I will not grouse,
But sing a song and do my work in school and in the house;
That is discipline.

When Satan whispers, "Scamp your work"—to say to him, "I won't,"
When Satan whispers, "Slack a bit"—to say to him, "I won't,"
To rule myself and not to wait for others' "Do" and "Don't";
That is discipline.

When I look up and triumph over every sinful thing,
The things that no one knows about—the cowardly, selfish thing—
And when with heart and will I live to please my glorious King;
That is discipline.

To trample on that curious thing inside me that says "I,"
To think of others always—never, never of that "I,"
To learn to live according to my Savior's word, "Deny";
That is discipline.

K

Square Prayers

Oh, I wonder how my prayer
Finds its way up through the air
To God's palace in the sky,
Very far and very high.

Once I threw a little stone
Far, far up; it was alone
And it couldn't find the way.
Is it like that when I pray?

Down my stone fell on the ground,
Though it was quite small and round.
Prayers, you know, are long or square;
How do they get through the air?

I was thinking this when, deep
In my heart—I was asleep—
I heard someone saying, "No,
Prayers have never far to go.

"And they never are alone
Like your little, lonely stone."
And I saw a shining spread
All about me on the bed.

And I knew it was moonlight
All about me in the night;
But the moon was in the sky,
Very far and very high.

Then, although it was the moon
Shone about me, it was noon,
And the garden flowers were bright
In the happy, golden light.

(Continued)

"Open, rose buds, in the sun,"
Said the rose trees one by one;
But the sun was in the sky,
Very far and very high.

Then deep, deep inside of me
Said a voice, "God's nearer thee
Than the sunshine to the flower
In the sunny noontide hour,

"Nearer to thee in thy place
Than the moonlight on thy face;
Never far to go has prayer
To the One who's everywhere."

BT, DS

Jesus Always Answers

(An incident of Amy's childhood)

Just a tiny little child
Three years old,
And a mother with a heart
All of gold.
Often did that mother say,
"Jesus hears us when we pray,
For He's never far away;
And He always answers."

Now, that tiny little child
Had brown eyes,
And she wanted blue instead
Like blue skies.
For her mother's eyes were blue
Like forget-me-nots. She knew
All her mother said was true.
Jesus always answered.

So she prayed for two blue eyes,
Said "Good night,"
Went to sleep in deep content
And delight.
Woke up early, climbed a chair
By a mirror. Where, oh where
Could the blue eyes be? Not there!
Jesus hadn't answered.

Hadn't answered her at all!
Never more
Could she pray—her eyes were brown
As before.
Did a little soft wind blow?
Came a whisper soft and low,
"Jesus answered. He said, 'No';
Isn't '*No*' an answer?"

ACD, BT, P

Thoughts in Childhood

Behind me, yellow gorse and grey-green grass,
Before me, the great moving, sounding sea;
The sky is growing golden. People pass
And shout and laugh; and on the clean white sand
I lie and wonder things. . . . And quietly
New thoughts come; but I cannot understand
What they are saying, for I cannot touch
Even their edges; like the little boats
Out on the sea, each little boat-thought floats
Quite out of reach of me as I lie here
Until the colors come and talk to me,
As they so often do; for they are dear
And faithful friends to me, and very much
I love their talk. . . . And from the far skyline
My thoughts come dancing toward me: "Oh, this time
They will come near," I think; but no, away
They slip again, as they did yesterday.

MP

My Questions

My mind has five large windows looking out,
And in the roof a skylight; and the wind
Blows through it always for, of course, my mind
Will never shut its windows or its door.
And lying on the floor
Are many things I want to know about.

And morning, noon, and evening, and at night
(If it is moonlit, and the world is clear)
As I look out, I find new questions here;
They walk in without knocking at my door
And lie down on my floor
And whisper softly to me through the night.

I let them lie—my questions—and I wait
And hope one day someone will answer me;
And in the evening, when the moon is late,
And only star-shine falls upon my floor,
I, sitting, at my door,
Do wonder when that friend will come to me.

P

I Wonder

Dim, green forest
Of a thousand secrets,
When you were planted
Did the angels sing?
Many things I wonder;
Are they all your secrets?
Won't you ever tell me anything?

Great white waterfall
Breaking through the forest,
Where do you come from?
Where do you go?
Had you a beginning?
Will you spout forever?
Forever and forever will you flow?

Great black, glistening wall
Veiled in shining glory,
Piled among the waters,
Rock upon rock;
Oh, to have stood and seen
Hands at work upon you,
Shivering you and shattering shock on shock.

Deep, dark, silent pool,
Hollowed at the fall's foot,
What do you think of
All the long day?
Do you hear the thunder
Of tremendous waters?
Do you hear the laughter of the spray?

ACD, FF, P

God's Secrets

I push a little way
  Behind the thing I see,
And something seems to say,
  "Hush"—very quietly.
That is God's private secret; He
Has not told it to me.

Why is this rose leaf green?
  Between transparent walls
Inside it, I have seen,
  Afloat, small clear green balls;
But how they come and how they go—
Does anybody know?

Why is this rose bud pink?
  All colors live in light;
And the rose bud, I think,
  Chose pink, and she's quite right,
For it is beautiful; but oh,
How does she make it show?

And so it is indeed
  With everything I see.
The smallest little seed
  Is Wonderland to me,
Full of God's secrets. When will He
Explain them all to me?

DS

Wonderland

Lord, Thy little children stand
At the opening of the day
Bordering on Wonderland.

Very near to us it lies,
Gathers round us as we play,
Waiting for our seeing eyes.

Wonderland is everywhere;
Can we go where it is not?
When we go, we find Thee there.

And Thou art so very kind;
Thou hast never once forgot
To put things for us to find.

Oh, a thousand voices call,
"Come and find what has been hidden;
All the world's a Wonder-ball."

Father, may we take Thy hand?
We will do as we are bidden.
Come with us to Wonderland.

DS

The Butterfly

Our mother was a butterfly;
We are her little eggs;
Inside us caterpillars lie,
Young things with many legs.

I am a little caterpillar,
So very soft and fat;
I'll change into a chrysalis;
What do you think of that?

I am a little chrysalis,
And very still I lie,
For folded up inside of me
Is a little butterfly.

I am the little butterfly;
I want to fly about;
I am so tired of being here—
Oh, now I'm out! I'm out!

O kind wind, come and fan my wings;
O sunshine, make them dry;
O flower, I come to you! Away,
Away, away I fly.

ACD

The Lizard

The lizard runs along the ground,
And then runs up a tree;
He turns his funny little head,
And then he looks at me.
He wiggle-waggles up and down,
And then he looks at me.

K

Bear Talk

Said a baby bear
To his mother:
"Which paw shall I move,
This or t'other?
Right or left, or all
Four together?"

So he stood in doubt
Asking whether
Front or back should go—
This or t'other.

"Do not talk. Just walk,"
Growled his mother.

K

Elephant Tracks

The elephant comes with a tramp, tramp, tramp;
The elephant comes with a stamp, stamp, stamp;
Through forest and over marshy ground,
His great big flat feet pound and pound
With a rumpety-dumpety-crumpety sound.

See, here's a tangle of maidenhair,
Among the pandanus spikes down there;
And right through the very middle of it,
He's trampled exactly as he saw fit.
With his blundery-wondery-dundery wit.

A fool, do you think? No, he's no fool:
Look at the track; it leads to a pool,
And on and on to a shady place,
Where he can fan his beautiful face
With a jingelly-tumbelly-scrumbelly grace.

ACD

Looking Through the Microscope

I looked, and saw through the transparent depths
Of a thin film of water many things
Too wonderful to tell in any words
That I can find. And yet I want to try;
For as I try, I see the things again.
And you must see them too.
                                        I saw a bell
Like lily of the valley, but alive
With fringing petals that whirled round like wheels,
One fringe after the other, and in time,
As if to water music. And I saw
Small, spinning specks sucked down into the bell
That suddenly dived—curling its slènder stem
Quick to a spiral—which uncurled again,
Flinging its bell afar.
                                And then I saw,
Or thought I saw, a carvèd, crystal vase
With two fringed heads that, like the lily's, whirled.
And once again I saw the spinning specks
And sudden vanishings. And then the vase,
Like Alice when she ate the magic cake,
Lengthened amazingly and stooping, strode
Across the small, smooth floor of its round pool,
Walking on two transparent, pointed toes—
A vase alive! And sometimes it would draw
Its wheels into itself; sometimes its toes.
I wondered as I looked.
                                    And then, surprise
Of all surprises! A great trumpet swung
From off a glistening leaf. It was snow-white;
And now it swayed and swept from side to side;
And now it stood in quietness, except
That without pause its delicate fringes moved,
Sweeping the waters till its whole length curved
In a long, lovely outline—and then passed,
Even as I looked, into an oval pearl
And floated out of sight.

MP

Nature's Joy

Low laugh of water and sparkle of spray—
Father, how lovely Thy river, how gay,
Or in the light,
  Or in the night,
Rippling in laughter and silver array.

Chirp of the nestling and flutter of wings—
Father, how peaceful Thy feathery things,
Waiting up there,
  High in the air,
Waiting content for what mother bird brings.

Flame of the forest, bright blossom afire—
Father, how radiant Thy flower of desire,
From the bare bough,
  Springing forth now,
Singing in color, "Look higher, look higher."

P

Everywhere

Have you found Him, little bird,
All He said that He would be?
Have you found Him in the air,
On the land, on the sea—
Have you found Him there?

Everywhere, everywhere,
Everywhere His winds do blow;
Everywhere His waters flow;
I have found Him there.

Wd

Nature's Praise

O rippling water,
Clear, rippling water,
  I can understand your language:
  Praise the Lord.

O hills and mountains,
Upland and lowland . . .

O trees and blossoms,
Ferns and all grasses . . .

O joy of bird songs,
Pure joy of bird songs . . .

O woodland creatures,
Furry, wild creatures . . .

O golden sunshine,
Sunrise and sunset . . .

C rain and rainbow,
Moonlight and starlight . . .

And we together
Through all life's weather,
  Join and sing your mighty language:
  Praise the Lord.

P

Sunbeams and Moonbeams

I've seen the sunbeams play
Through the long, golden day
On mountain pool,
All colorful;
I've seen their dance so gay.
Have you,
    Have you
Been there when sunbeams play?

I've seen the moonbeams dance
With softest radiance
On wind-swept mere
And river clear.
Have you, by any chance,
Been there,
    Been there
When silver moonbeams dance?

I've seen the tangled maze
Of rippled waterways
On some grey stone—
And all alone,
Enchanted, stood to gaze.
Have you,
    Have you
Seen that bright, darting maze?

Shadow and sunlight play
On many a merry day:
Like brother, he,
Like sister, she—
He serious, and she gay.
Have you,
    Have you
Delighted in their play?

BT, P

Fairy Rainbows

Have you seen my fairy rainbows
    Flashing in the air?
Coming, going, coming, going,
    Coming, going—where?

They are not like other rainbows
    Painted in the sky,
That come slowly, and as slowly
    Fade away and die.

For they dart and dance and sparkle
    In the dust of spray
Where the children of the water
    And the sunbeams play.

O my little fairy rainbows
    Flashing in the air:
Tell me, tell me where you go to
    When you are not there.

P

THE DREAM POOL

Deep down under the water
Wonderful things are done;
Deep down under the water,
Far from the eye of sun,
Down, down, where the water-weed waves
Small green flags over small lost graves;
Down, down, where the rotifer whirls
Little twin wheels, and the lily curls
Her living stem, and a thousand things
Happen forever . . . and no bell rings
But the silent bells of the water school
Where the babies play—O Pool, my Pool,
I am coming to you when the moon is bright;
I am coming to you tonight.

I am coming to you tonight, my Pool,
When the moon and the stars come out;
And the big people say, "O sleepy head,
It is time you were fast asleep in bed."
But they never know
Where I always go
When the lamp is turned down very low;
For neither of us tells
In the least little tiny whisper about
The Real Things that we know
In the land of the waterbells—
O Pool, where I'll be tonight.

There all my dreams come true;
None are too strange to be.
And things I long to know
Are shown to me.
And I lie low among
The water-green grass,
And watch the friendly folk
That shyly pass
On noiseless little feet
And noiseless spin
Such dresses for themselves
As never in
The grown-up people's world
Were ever seen:
That flash now ruby-red,
Now emerald green,
And sometimes amethyst
And violet,
With sparkling dust
Of diamond, set
In patterns; and like pearls
Some are, and crystals, too,
That catch the light and show
A sapphire blue.
And joyful, lovely things
Are everywhere.
O Wonderland, tonight
I shall be there.

(Continued)

Sky, sky, where are your colors
When all the air is grey?
Flowers, flowers, where are your colors
When they have faded away?
Down, down where the water things swim,
In the place the earth-world fancies dim,
Down, down, in that radiant land
Where the floor is sprinkled with sparkling sand,
And the flowers are alive and build fairy towers,
And jewel grottos and garden bowers;
And wonderful changes mix and flow
In circles forever—there they go,
Your poor, tired colors. I know, I know,
For I have been there. When they feel the cool,
Soft wash of the water in my Pool,
They are comforted, and they drop down deep,
Through its coolness, as I do when I'm "asleep."
And they find it a pleasant place to be;
And we all are happy, they and we
Who belong to the Pool. O Pool, my Pool,
When the moon is full
And the path through the wood is all alight,
I am coming to you; I am coming to you;
I am coming to you tonight.

MP, PVV

Bubbles

What are bubbles made of? Tell me:
Diamond flashes?
Film of pearls?
See, the smooth green water curls
Round the shoulder
Of a boulder;
Something shatters,
Something scatters,
Dances on the polished floor;
More and more
Come and go;
Underflow
Of swift water hurries past;
Bubbles frolic on it, last
Just a moment; others run
In their myriads, and are spun
Down the shining, sunlit river,
On and on, and on forever.

MP, PVV

The Call of the Waterfall

I sat beside the waterfall
A little while yesterday,
And I think I heard the words of its call
To the waters far away.

For, behind, in the watershed
They loitered most lazily;
But the waterfall—it laughed as it sped
On, on to the deep blue sea.

And it splashed on its crystal floor,
And its call was glad and clear:
"Come on! Come on! 'Tis better on before;
For the way is wider here."

(Continued)

"Beckon, spray!" was its quick command.
I saw little spray people spring,
And each one waved with a little white hand;
I could see them beckoning.

"Come on! 'Tis better on before,"
Was the word perpetually,
"For our riverbed widens more and more,
And leads to the deep blue sea."

DS

The Lovely, Glad Seashore

I sing the gaiety
Of the lovely, glad seashore,
Where the young ripples play
And the white dancing spray
Laughs back to the wild waves' roar.

You may watch the blue sea melt
Like a dream in the blue, blue air.
You may hear it, too,
Sing in words of blue;
And the song is a kind of prayer.

You may hear bubbles laugh on the beach,
As the wave runs down the sand;
You may lean low and listen
To the wet seaweed glisten
Just for joy that it doesn't grow on land.

And the endless surprise of the pools
With their silver glimmerings—
Can you bend very low
And not hear and know
The laughter of jubilant things?

Oh, the lovely, the wonderful shore
Is a place of gaiety;
    And the longer I stay
    Where the sea things play,
The dearer it is to me.

P

Observe the Rocks

My stately friends, the rocks,
    Whom to know indeed is good,
Have a gracious fashion of their own—
    For every lovely mood
Of earth and air finds answer where
They lift their hoary heads on high,
Or on their mother's green lap lie.

Be it sunrise, rose-red they—
    Their jeweled thoughts aglow;
See them meet the happy blue with blue;
    See them white as driven snow
When deep in the heart of the moonlit part
Of the woods, where the leaves grow thin,
The moon's round face looks in.

And hidden away in them
    What precious things there be:
All the colors that we dream are there,
    Though few the eyes that see.
And who can tell, for they keep it well,
Their sparkling secret, through and through?
I cannot, nor, I think, can you.

P

Earth's Carpet

Said the Father of us all:
"Some of these I love are tall—
They can almost fly with wings;
They can see My highest things;
  Some are very small."

Then unto His world He said:
"Let thy floor be carpeted
By what pleases children's eyes;
Let them have some good surprise
  Everywhere they tread."

And the earth at once began
To make pretty things that ran
Up and down and everywhere—
Flew low in the children's air.
  Count them if you can.

And the greenwood—when she shed
Her tired leaves, painted them red,
Orange, too, and golden brown;
So the children looking down
  Never thought them dead.

And the garden painted, too,
Every color that she knew,
Every color you can think—
Yellow, purple, violet, pink,
  And, of course, dear blue.

And the rocks and stones took grey
And soft greenish paint; and they
Strewed themselves about the floor.
And the sea shells asked for more
  Colors, and were gay.

So, just as the Lord God said,
All the world was carpeted.
And though it's so long ago,
Everything is new, you know,
  Everywhere we tread.

BT, DS

A Garden Gay

A garden gay is my garden dear,
In it the trees grow tall;
My shining flowers are seen
The little leaves between—
The joyfulest things of all.

When the glad sun calleth, "Here I am,"
Looking the green leaves through;
Then over tree trunks brown,
Joy danceth up and down;
My heart, it danceth, too.

The good rain causeth in all my buds
A stir, a laugh, a voice;
Then doth each little spray
Swing merrily and say,
"Rejoice, rejoice, rejoice."

(Continued)

On moonlit nights many angels come,
Stepping most delicately.
Then is my garden dressed
In colors full of rest,
The loveliest that there be.

A garden gay is my garden dear,
Of gentle joys the prime,
Where often He doth talk,
Whose wont it is to walk
In gardens at evening time.

MP, P

Lovely Lily

Oh, lovely lily,
Growing in our garden,
    Who made a dress so fair
    For you to wear?
    Who made you straight and tall
    To give pleasure to us all?
Oh, lovely lily,
Who did it all?

Oh, little children
Playing in our garden,
    God made this dress so fair
    For us to wear.
    God made us straight and tall
    To give pleasure to you all.
Oh, little children,
God did it all.

LB

Yellow Flowers

Up in Heaven, the golden street
    Trodden by so many feet
Must get dusty; without doubt,
    Tidy angels sweep it out.

Dust of gold then falls and falls
    Past the shining, jewel walls,
Through the quiet dark blue air—
    Making stars come here and there.

And the moon—who cannot sleep
    And whose thoughts are very deep—
Says, "My flowers are silver; go,
    They have need of you below."

So dust falls into our world,
    And the little flower bud curled
In her pale green envelope
    Wakes, a golden flower of hope.

And more wake, and more and more,
    Till the world's big, grassy floor
Laughs with flowers of hope, and all
    The round world's a flowery ball.

"Flowers of hope": because they say
    Softly, gladly, all the day,
"Only dust of glory we;
    What then must the glory be?"

DS

Friends Angelical

Far beyond the shifting screen
Made of things that can be seen,
Are our friends angelical
Of the Land Celestial.

Thence they come to tend the flowers
That we thought were only ours.
What their toils, we may not know,
As they come and as they go.

Only this we know: they see,
As we cannot, what shall be;
Watch the hidden buds unfold,
Dream of color, heart of gold.

Therefore, look behind the screen;
Trust the powers of the Unseen.
Neither vague nor mystical
Are our friends angelical.

TJ

Blue Morning-glories

Quiet voices calling,
  Calling through the air;
Gentle sunbeams falling,
  Falling everywhere;
And the blue flowers open
  Each her lovely bell,
Knowing by some secret token
  All is well.

And within the blue shrine
  Is a tiny light,
Faint and far like moonshine,
  Pure and clear and white;
Blue flower, will you open
  This to me? The bell
Answers, "Can you show the token?
  Is all well?"

P

I Want To Climb

I want to climb the air;
I want to find the stair,
But I cannot find it anywhere.

I know quite well there are
Great things up there—far, far;
I should like to stand upon a star.

But though I cannot go
So far away, quite low
Many little, lovely, dear things grow.

K

Oleander

We grow beside the shining sea
  Set round with hills in Galilee.
We often saw our Lord, and knew
  He saw us—and He loved us, too.

For He loved all the little flowers
  That smiled at Him through sunny hours;
And when the sky was dark and grey,
  Still smiled and did not go away.

We tried to make the world more sweet
  For Him who walked with holy feet
Along its way—and by its sea
  Set round with hills in Galilee.

DS

Songs For Jesus

No music set in golden bars
  Floats down from heaven to me,
Nor silver words shine forth like stars
  To make great songs for Thee.

But long ago, when Thou wert here,
  Field flowers grew round Thy feet,
Just little things—but they were dear,
  And to Thy love, how sweet.

And so, Lord Jesus, may I bring
  My small field flowers to Thee?
And wilt Thou listen when I sing
  Because Thou lovest me?

P

Sing the King of Heaven

O ye mountains, valleys,
  Waters, forest ways,
Sing the Child of Bethlehem,
Kingly Child of Bethlehem,
The Lord Christ, Ancient of Days.

O all ye green things
  Brought forth by the sun,
Sing the King of Heaven,
The Holy One.
O Creation, praise Him!

O ye little children,
  Pause you in your plays;
Sing the Child of Bethlehem,
Kingly Child of Bethlehem,
The Lord Christ, Ancient of Days.

O all ye peoples,
  But for Him undone,
Sing the King of Heaven,
The Holy One.
O Creation, praise Him!

DS

Together

No purer joy can be
Than to be one in Thee;
Bound by one golden cord
Of love to our dear Lord.
Together, together, together,
Made one in Thee,
All one in Thee,
Come, let us flow together.

Come, let us flow together
    To the goodness of the Lord,
        Together, together, together,
            Alleluia.

Than song of sweet, wild bird,
Deep in the greenwood heard,
More sweet the melody
Of such a unity.
All singing, all singing, all singing,
Made one in Thee,
All one in Thee.
Come, let us flow, all singing.

Come, let us flow together
    To the goodness of the Lord,
        Together, together, together,
            Alleluia.

GC

Singing Music

Why do we love singing music?
Don't you know?
'Tis the sweetness of a heavenly
Overflow.

In that singing land, they often
Let it go,
Whispering softly, "Be their comfort
Down below."

To the music of the wild wind
Tall trees grow;
To the music of the wild bird
Flower buds blow.

To the music of the waters
As they flow,
God made mountain land and forest
Long ago.

Listen, listen, overhear it
And you'll know
Joy of sunrise, peace of quiet
Sunset glow.

P

Flowers and Ferns

Flowers and ferns and trees and skies,
Singing birds and butterflies—
    These praise the Lord;
    Allelulia, Amen.

Silver stars and silver moon,
Sunrise, sunset, sunny noon—
    These praise the Lord;
    Alleluia, Amen.

Let us all with one accord
Sing and magnify the Lord;
    O Praise the Lord;
    Alleluia, Amen.

P.

Humbly We Worship

Blessèd and holy,
Blessèd and holy,
Blessèd and holy, O Lord, art Thou.
Humbly we worship,
Humbly we worship,
Blessèd and holy, O Lord, art Thou.

Good and forgiving,
Good and forgiving,
Good and forgiving, O Lord, art Thou.
Humbly we worship,
Humbly we worship,
Good and forgiving, O Lord, art Thou.

Gracious and loving,
Gracious and loving,
Gracious and loving, O Lord, art Thou.
Humbly we worship,
Humbly we worship,
Gracious and loving, O Lord, art Thou.

Wg[1]

8 | In Her Own Hand

St. Andrew and the Lad
(John 6:8–11)

St. A.: "Tell me, lad, why you come
With your basket on your elbow—
Climbing here, up the hill,
Far above the shining lake?"

Lad: "Sir, I come, climbing here,
With my basket on my elbow,
Selling fare on the hill,
Just to see what I can make."

St. A.: "Tell me, lad, may I see
In your basket just a minute;
May I see what you'll sell
To the people on the hill?"

Lad: "In it, sir, there are loaves—
Loaves and little fishes in it.
I will sell loaves and fish
To the people on the hill."

St. A.: "Tell me, lad, if He said:
'Give the five loaves in your basket'—
If He said: 'Give them Me.'
Would you spare them for the Lord?"

Lad: "He may have my five loaves—
And the basket, if He ask it!
If He says: 'Give them Me,'
I will give them to the Lord."

St. A.: "Tell me, lad, if He said:
'Give Me now your little fishes'—
If He said: 'Give them Me,'
Would you spare them for the Lord?"

Lad: "Sir, you know, He may have
My two fishes, if He wishes;
If He says: 'Give them Me,'
I will give them to the Lord."

• • • • •

Then were seen, on the green,
People eating, people eating;
And the boy laughed for joy,
And the people praised the Lord.

Unp

Tell the Children

Over the sea there are little brown children,
Fathers and mothers and babies dear.
They do not know of the dear Lord Jesus;
No one has told them He is near.

Swift let the Message go over the ocean
Telling the children God is near.

Sometimes at night as the darkness deepens
Little brown children begin to fear.
They do not know of the dear Lord Jesus;
No one has told them He is near.

Unp

These two unpublished poems were discovered, handwritten, in Amy Carmichael's personal copy of Pans

❖

St. Andrew and the Lad

St. A.: Tell me lad, why you come, with your basket
on your elbow,
Climbing here, up the hill, far above the
shining Lake.

Lad: Sir I come, climbing here, with my basket
on my elbow
Selling here
Climbing here, up the hill, just to see what
I can make

St. A. Tell me lad, may I see, in your basket just
a minute
May I see what you'll sell, to the people
on the hill.

Lad. In it Sir There are loaves loaves and little
fishes in it
I will sell loaves and fish to the people
on the hill.

St A. Tell me lad, if He said: "give the five loaves
in your basket."
If He said: Give them me Would you
spare them for the Lord?

Lad. ~~Sir you know, He m~~
He may have my five loaves, and the
basket, if He ask it,
If He says: Give them me, I will give
them to the Lord.

St A. Tell me lad, if He said "Give me now your little fishes
If He said, "Give them me." would you give them to the Lord.

Lad. Sir, you know, He may have, my two fishes, if He wishes
If He says: "Give them me." I will give them to the Lord."

. . . .

Then were seen, on the green, people eating people eating
And the boy laughed for joy. and the people praised the Lord.

Telling the Children

1. Over the sea there are little brown children
Fathers and mothers and babies dear
They do not know of the dear Lord Jesus
No one has told them He is near
Swift let the Message go over the ocean
Telling the children God is near.

2. Sometimes at night as the darkness deepens
Little brown children begin to fear
They do not know of the dear Lord Jesus
No one has told them He is near

Note

In the production of this volume certain liberties have been taken. Though completeness was our aim, where a poem existed in variant forms, only one was selected. We have provided titles to all poems lacking them. Spelling has been Americanized, and where helpful, punctuation has been modified. On the rare occasion where a minor word change improved the poem's meter, we chose to do so, provided the change did not alter the meaning intended.

Most of the out-of-print works of Amy Carmichael can be accessed via the interlibrary loan system at your public library. You will not find any poetry in them, however, outside of the 29 books we have drawn upon to produce this anthology. With one exception: The book *Pools and the Valley of Vision* consists of two very lengthy poems which—because they would have expanded the present volume beyond reason—have not been included in it. However, a dozen choice segments of those two poems do exist as separate poems and are included, as noted in the references.

The Editors

Amy Carmichael's Published Works and Other Sources of Her Poetry

Title	Date of Publication	Out of Print
From Sunrise Land	1895	OP
From the Fight	About 1901	OP
Raisins	About 1901	OP
Things as They Are	1903	OP
Overweights of Joy	1906	OP
Beginning of a Story	1908	OP
Lotus Buds	1909	OP
Continuation of a Story	1914	OP
Walker of Tinnevelly	1916	OP
Pans	Prior to 1917	OP
Made in the Pans	1917	OP
Ponnammal	1918	OP
From the Forest	1920	OP
Dohnavur Songs	1921	OP
Nor Scrip	1922	OP
Ragland, Spiritual Pioneer	1922	OP
Tables in the Wilderness	1923	OP
The Valley of Vision	1924	OP
Mimosa	1924	OP
Raj	1926	OP
The Widow of the Jewels	1928	OP
Meal in a Barrel	1929	OP
Gold Cord	1932	
Rose From Brier	1933	
Ploughed Under	1934	OP
Gold by Moonlight	1935	
Buds and Teddies (compiled by Barbara C. Osman)	1936	OP
Toward Jerusalem	1936	
Windows	1937	OP
If	1938	
Figures of the True	1938	
Pools and the Valley of Vision	1938	OP
God's Missionary	1939	
Kohila	1939	OP
His Thoughts Said . . . His Father Said . . .	1941	
Though the Mountains Shake	1943	OP
Before the Door Shuts	1948	OP
This One Thing	1950	OP
Amy Carmichael of Dohnavur (by Frank L. Houghton)	1953	
Edges of His Ways	1955	
Thou Givest . . . They Gather	1958	
Wings (with music)	1960	OP
Candles in the Dark	1981	
Whispers of His Power (compiled by Bee Trehane)	1982	
Learning of God (compiled by Stuart & Brenda Blanch)	1985	
Fragments That Remain (compiled by Bee Trehane)	1987	OP

Index of First Lines and Titles